CRIMINAL JUSTICE AND FORENSIC SCIENCE

CRIMINAL JUSTICE AND FORENSIC SCIENCE

A MULTIDISCIPLINARY INTRODUCTION

LISA SMITH & JOHN BOND

BLOOMSBURY
NEW DELHI • LONDON • OXFORD • NEW YORK • SYDNEY

BLOOMSBURY INDIA
Bloomsbury Publishing India Pvt. Ltd
Second Floor, LSC Building No. 4, DDA Complex, Pocket C–6&7,
Vasant Kunj, New Delhi 110070

BLOOMSBURY, BLOOMSBURY ACADEMIC INDIA and the Diana logo are
trademarks of Bloomsbury Publishing Plc

First published in India 2025
First published 2015

This edition published with permission from Bloomsbury Publishing Plc,
50 Bedford Square, London, WC1B3DP, UK

A catalogue record for this book is available from the British Library.
A catalog record for this book is available from the Library of Congress.

Exclusively distributed in the Indian subcontinent by
Satyam Books Pvt. Ltd.
2/13, Ansari Road, Darya Ganj
New Delhi-110002 (India)

ISBN: 978-93-69520-81-7

Printed and bound in India by Replika Press Pvt. Ltd

To find out more about our authors and books
visit www.bloomsbury.com and sign up for our newsletters

CONTENTS

LIST OF FIGURES

FOREWORD

Andrew Rennison, former UK Forensic Science Regulator

Forensic science has the unique ability to attract public, legal and academic curiosity and interest that is not diminished over time or subject by fashionable ebbs and flows. Having spent the last six years working across all aspects of forensic science I can see, and fully understand, how and why people across the board cannot help but be fascinated by the use of science in the hunt for clues.

This book provides an effective platform for students and other interested readers who may not have a background in science or forensic science, and will give them an informed and illustrated insight into the modern world of science used in the investigation of crimes. It demystifies some of the mysteries of forensic science, from the early stages during the search for evidence at a crime scene, through to the presentation of opinions by experts in the courtroom. The authors quite properly point out some of the imperfections and steer readers away from the glamorised fictional world that sometimes portrays science as operating without any flaws or misconceptions.

The use of case studies throughout the chapters provides valuable insights into the real world of forensic science, underpinned by some straightforward and easy-to-grasp text. Readers will quickly understand that the term 'forensic science' is commonly used nowadays as a noun encompassing a wide range of scientific methods, many of which cannot be covered in a book of this nature. However, those aspects of forensic science that are included are highly relevant and form the bulk of everyday work by forensic practitioners, who have to operate within the context of a criminal justice system that sets justifiably high expectations. Every chapter in this book is relevant to the work I do in regulating the quality standards that should apply to all aspects of forensic science. The authors are able to provide considerable practical, research and teaching experience to provide fresh insights into this captivating subject.

1

A MULTIDISCIPLINARY APPROACH TO FORENSIC STUDIES

A recent history of forensic science

Although there are early examples of using some form of physical evidence found at a crime scene to provide a link to a possible offender (Kind and Overman, 1972), it was in the nineteenth century that the use of scientific techniques to assist the police in solving crime became well established. Invariably, this early use of science was to assist in the police investigation of violent crime and it was from a bloodstained fingerprint that Juan Vucetich, an Argentinean police official, provided the first positive identification to an offender in 1892 (Beavan, 2002). Vucetich also founded the first Fingerprint Identification Bureau (also in Argentina), building on the work of Sir Francis Galton, Henry Faulds and others in the UK who had, some years earlier, suggested the use of fingerprints as a means of identifying offenders and solving crime (Beavan, 2002).

As we will see in Chapter 2, the first conviction for murder in the UK based on fingerprint evidence was obtained in 1904. Thereafter, throughout the first half of the twentieth century, the use of a wide range of scientific disciplines to assist in the identification of offenders became more widespread across many countries. These disciplines covered diverse areas including the examination of particulates (such as glass, hair, fibres or soil), impressions (such as might be left at a crime scene by footwear or vehicle tyres) and ballistics (based on the marks etched into both bullets and cartridge casings). The establishment of some of these disciplines was the result of years of research and development, such as the work of Colonel Calvin Goddard in forensic ballistics, while others arose from individuals' realisation that their own field of expertise could be applied to forensic science and solving crime. A representative of this latter category is the wood anatomist Arthur Koehler. The examples of Calvin Goddard, Arthur Koehler and others will be considered in Chapter 3 when we examine different comparison evidence types in detail.

By the second half of the twentieth century, the term *forensics* (from the latin *forensis*, relating to Roman legal proceedings) or *forensic science* became synonymous with the use of science in a legal or courtroom context to assist in solving crime, with dedicated staff employed by police forces to search for and recover evidence of forensic interest from crime scenes. Coupled with this was the establishment of dedicated laboratories to process forensic material and to make comparisons between the material recovered from a crime scene and that from a suspect, across a range of disciplines. Possibly the first dedicated forensic laboratory was that set up in 1910 in Lyon, France by Edmond Locard. In the UK, forensic examinations were increasingly being performed in small, locally run laboratories and, by the 1930s, some of these laboratories were transferred to government control to form what eventually became the UK Forensic Science Service (FSS). By the 1960s there were nine specialist forensic laboratories in England and Wales.

In the USA, the Director of the Federal Bureau of Investigation (J. Edgar Hoover) and experts such as Calvin Goddard were instrumental in setting up the Bureau's Scientific Crime Detection Laboratory in 1932. However, the vast majority of forensic evidence was (and still is) processed in government (public) laboratories organised at city, county or state level. By the end of the twentieth century, there were approximately 400 laboratories operating in the USA (Johns and Kahn, 2004). The first laboratory to be established in North America was, however, in Montreal, Canada by Wilfred Dérôme in 1914, with the Royal Canadian Mounted Police opening their own forensic laboratory in Regina, Saskatchewan in 1937. Current issues related to the organisation and finance of forensic science laboratories are considered in Chapter 8.

In the 1980s, a major advance in forensic science was made with the discovery by Alec Jeffreys (at the University of Leicester, UK) that the make-up of the DNA (deoxyribonucleic acid) molecule could be used to distinguish between individuals. Jeffreys realised that human DNA could produce consistent, unique patterns and that these could be used not only to identify individuals, but also to indicate familial relationships. The first legal case to use this new technique was an immigration case, which hinged on proving whether a woman and a young boy were mother/son or aunt/nephew. A paternity case followed shortly thereafter and for two years Jeffreys' university laboratory in Leicester was the only place in the world offering this kind of service. The attention of the police was drawn to this new technology and a double murder case from the mid-1980s was solved by Jeffreys showing that DNA recovered from both murder scenes was consistent with the DNA of an individual who was not otherwise obviously associated with the murders. This discovery has ultimately led to the biggest advance in identification forensic evidence since the work of Vucetich and others with fingerprints in the late nineteenth century.

Today, both DNA and fingerprint evidence types are known as identification evidence, as they offer not only the ability to give police investigators evidence that can be used during the interview with a suspect, but also the ability to identify individuals. From the advent of fingerprint identification up until the late 1980s, linking a suspect to a crime scene was made by manual searching of a crime scene fingerprint against the fingerprints of known offenders, which were held by individual police forces or countries. Clearly, this method of searching was only as good as the skill of the fingerprint examiner or the quality of police intelligence to suggest names of suspects who may have committed the crime. This all changed with computer technology, which enabled collections of fingerprints of known offenders to be stored and searched on computer databases. Not only did this make the searching process quicker, it also enabled many more offenders' fingerprints to be checked against a fingerprint from a crime scene than ever was possible with manual searching methods.

Also, for the first time, fingerprints from a crime scene could be searched easily against the fingerprints of known offenders from neighbouring police forces or even other countries. This opened up the possibility of using fingerprint evidence to solve many more crimes, including what are termed *volume crimes* such as burglaries and vehicle offences. We will see in Chapter 2 how the introduction of computer technology in this way forever changed the manner in which fingerprint examiners undertake their work. DNA identifications have also, since 1995, been made using computerised databases to store and search the profiles of DNA recovered from crime scenes and that taken from offenders. In

Chapter 8 we will explore some of the controversies associated with the use of biometric databases, which have arisen as a result of the proliferation of DNA databases worldwide.

How forensic science is evolving and is changing policing

The development of computerised databases for DNA and fingerprints enabled the police to undertake more speculative comparisons of offender records against evidence recovered from the crime scene. To capitalise on this ability, governments quickly recognised the benefits of increasing the size of the database so that more people could be checked against crime scene evidence. However, once all convicted offender records were being acquired, it became necessary to include suspected criminals as well. In the UK, legislation enabling police to acquire and retain DNA and fingerprint data from arrested individuals was introduced in 2001 and 2004, and this led to a significant increase in the size of the UK DNA and fingerprint databases. However, as we will see in Chapter 8, there have been recent successful challenges to this legislation in the European Court of Human Rights, which prompted the UK to introduce new legislation in 2012 to address these concerns. In the USA, legislation is more complicated as a result of both state and federal law systems and, until recently, US jurisdictions were not permitted to obtain DNA samples from arrestees.

A positive aspect for law enforcement arising from computerised databases, and one that is used to argue for the acquisition and retention of records from non-offenders, is the increase in the number of crimes now solved with DNA and fingerprint evidence. The ability to search a person's DNA or fingerprints speculatively against evidence recovered from a crime scene has contributed to the increasing reliance by police investigators on these two evidence types to solve volume crime. Today, since crimes such as burglary or stealing a motor vehicle rarely have witnesses, the police have become ever more reliant on a forensic evidence system that delivers both the evidence and the name of a suspect. Despite the recent trend in countries like the UK and USA to improve community policing, it is likely that reliance on forensic identification evidence (particularly DNA and fingerprints) will only increase in the future.

By the 1980s, increasing reliance on all forensic evidence types (*comparison* as well as *identification*) had led, in the UK, to the demands placed on the FSS by police forces for forensic exhibit examination exceeding what the FSS could deliver. The government decided therefore that the best way to address this imbalance between supply and demand was to change arrangements for funding the FSS. In 1991, it devolved the budget for forensic science examinations to individual police forces. The rationale for this was that if forces had to pay for forensic science examinations, then they would be more selective about the amount of evidence being submitted. This situation led to the emergence in the UK of a forensic marketplace, with private laboratories competing with the national FSS to supply forensic science services to police forces. Initially this was felt to be a positive move, as the competitive marketplace led to improvements in turnaround times and decreases in the cost of examinations. However, private laboratories tended to focus on analysis methods that did not require huge capital investment, with the result that the FSS was continuing to provide an all-encompassing service in a shrinking marketplace.

Coupled with this, more recently there has been a contraction of police budgets and a concentration of expenditure on identification evidence types (DNA and fingerprints). This has been at the expense of more traditional comparison evidence types, which, as we have seen above, require the police to provide a suspect in order that a comparison with evidence recovered from the crime scene can be made. In the UK, this led in 2012 to the closing of the FSS, with forensic science provision to the police henceforth being undertaken by private laboratories, which bid for contracts with individual or groups of police forces. In an effort to cut costs further, some police forces started to undertake basic evidence examination themselves, rather than having this work carried out by the contracted private laboratory. An example of this might be searching an item of clothing for blood and then recovering and submitting the blood, rather than sending the clothing itself to the laboratory. Ensuring quality standards in the police's own laboratories has led to the UK Forensic Regulator producing quality standards for all forensic processes (Forensic Science Regulator, 2012). In the USA, the American Society of Crime Laboratory Directors (ASCLD) oversees laboratory accreditation and, like the UK Regulator, has introduced quality standards. As we will see in Chapter 8, these standards are to ISO 17025, which is an international standard for laboratory competence. The implications of public versus private laboratories, and police forces undertaking forensic examinations, are considered further in that chapter.

In the USA, the overwhelming majority of forensic evidence continues to be processed by government-funded local or state laboratories rather than by private laboratories. In 2004, the ASCLD reported on the backlog of work in these US government laboratories (Johns and Kahn, 2004). The report noted that for the 50 largest forensic laboratories in the USA, 80% of the backlog was accounted for by identification evidence (DNA and fingerprints) and by the analysis of controlled substances. For the purposes of the report, 'backlog' was taken to mean a processing time greater than 30 days between the submission of an item and a report on its examination being produced. The increased reliance on identification evidence types discussed earlier in relation to the UK is also clearly affecting the volume of work submitted by law enforcement agencies to forensic laboratories in the USA, with a consequent impact on turnaround times and the effectiveness of the evidence in solving crime.

While the current UK forensic science provision by private laboratories may have positively affected turnaround times, it has had a negative impact on innovation. Traditionally in the UK, forensic science innovation was primarily undertaken by the FSS as part of its remit (as a government-funded laboratory) to seek to enhance the quality of forensic science provided to police forces. However, since the demise of the FSS, innovation has been largely neglected in favour of the private laboratories cutting costs to provide police forces with a competitively priced service. In the USA, 20% of government forensic laboratories undertake applied research, although this work has historically been performed by universities. In the UK, the gap in innovation left by the FSS is only now being addressed through government-funded initiatives to get universities and the private laboratories working together, something that has also been suggested as a longer-term strategy for ensuring the continuance of forensic science innovation in the USA (Edwards and Gastonis, 2009). Other countries, such as the Netherlands, are now also considering the future governance and structure of forensic science provision (Tjin-A-Tsoi, 2013).

The need for a multidisciplinary approach to forensic studies

Due to the extremely broad nature of forensic science, as we have seen in previous sections, the term can be used to refer to the use of any scientific discipline towards the resolution of legal matters. These legal matters need not be solely criminal, and may instead relate to a wide range of issues including (but not limited to) civil proceedings, breaches of environmental laws and treaties, paternity matters or the determination of insurance fraud. It is clear that the scope for forensic science is far-reaching, and that it therefore involves many different disciplines often coming together to resolve legal issues.

It is useful to conceptualise forensic science as not existing as a single, scientific discipline. Although many well-established scientific approaches comprise the forensic sciences, such as biology, chemistry and medicine, none of these disciplines in isolation can be referred to as 'forensic' science. Any particular scientific discipline is only considered to be 'forensic' when it is functioning within a criminal justice setting. So forensic science requires consideration of law and criminal justice and, as we will see in Chapter 7, this sometimes causes conflict or discomfort for practitioners in the criminal justice system.

The traditional approach to teaching and writing about forensic science tends to be focused on the scientific aspects of forensic analyses, aimed primarily at students who wish to pursue a career in a forensic laboratory. Far less common are approaches emphasising other important aspects of forensic science, such as the legal context and social implications of forensic practice. Without an appreciation of these wider issues, however, students do not obtain a holistic understanding of forensic science and criminal justice. It is crucial that practitioners, such as police and the legal profession, have an understanding of how forensic science operates in the wider criminal justice context, in order to maximise the effective use of science to solve crime. This book therefore aims to provide the reader with a general understanding of some commonly used forensic science techniques, so as to provide a basis for exploring contemporary, multidisciplinary issues relating to the use of forensic science in the criminal justice system. These issues will draw on academic literature and research in the natural sciences, law, criminology, sociology and psychology throughout the chapters that follow.

How to use this book

This book is not simply another forensic science or criminal justice undergraduate text intended for students majoring in either of those disciplines. Rather, it contributes to the current library of criminal justice–related texts, in that it bridges the gap between forensic science and criminal justice in order to enable the reader to appreciate more fully the related methods, current issues and future challenges. In this regard, this text will be of interest to those wishing to gain an appreciation of how forensic science is used by law enforcement agencies to provide evidence to put before a court of law. What form this evidence might take, and how it is recovered and processed, are included here, as are how both defence and prosecution attorneys might then present that evidence to a jury and the associated pitfalls that can arise. The book also considers the effect that popular culture has on how forensic evidence is perceived, as well as current issues and challenges in both forensic science and criminal justice.

Those studying criminal justice as part of a degree programme will find that this text provides sufficient insight into forensic science without the reader becoming bogged down by detail on scientific methods that, if required, can readily be found in many existing texts. Throughout this book, case studies are provided from many countries that demonstrate real-life examples of how a particular scientific method was used or how a criminal justice issue was encountered and resolved. Natural science students will be able to use this text to understand the application of scientific method in the criminal justice system, while those studying social sciences will learn how forensic science evidence is obtained in a manner that is appropriate for presentation as evidence in court. A key feature of this book is the inclusion of the reasons for particular technologies, evidence types or methods being useful for law enforcement, as well as discussion of why police agencies are able to rely more and more on forensic science as a reliable means of solving a wide range of offence types, from violent crime to burglaries and vehicle offences.

Thus the aim of the book is to provide both natural and social science students with a comprehensive introduction to the range of issues associated with the use of science in the criminal justice system. Throughout the book you will find a selection of references, which can be used to develop further the concepts introduced within the chapter, as well as some questions that we hope will encourage reflection or discussion around the important issues raised. Throughout the chapters a critical perspective is encouraged, which will equip the reader with a well-balanced view of the key issues and result in a deeper understanding of the fascinating world of forensic science.

2

IDENTIFICATION EVIDENCE

Traditional forensic identification has relied on the comparison of material recovered from a crime scene with material recovered from, or being associated with, an individual. From the results of the comparison, the scientist would interpret the likelihood that the material from the crime scene and the individual originated from the same source. Clearly, for this comparison to happen, the police must identify a suspect or material to make the comparison against. As we will see in Chapter 3, we will refer to this type of forensic analysis as comparison evidence. With the advent of computer databases that can store and search identifying features both from crime scenes and from individuals, the need for the police first to identify a suspect can be removed. We refer to this type of forensic comparison, which does not require the prior identification of a suspect, as identification evidence. Thus, forensic identification evidence has the ability to determine the identity of an individual based on material recovered from the crime scene. For the police investigator, being given not only evidence to present to a suspect during interview, such as a fingerprint from inside a burglary scene or a blood stain on a carpet, but also the name of the donor and, therefore, potentially the name of the suspect enables crimes to be investigated and successfully prosecuted that might otherwise go undetected. The use of *biometric databases* will be explored further in Chapter 8, a topic that highlights the importance of considering the use of scientific evidence together with social policy.

Consider a typical domestic burglary, committed during the day when the householder was at work. On returning home in the evening, the householder finds their home burgled and reports this to the police. Imagine, for a moment, that we do not have forensic science at our disposal. The police investigator relies on traditional policing methods, such as witness evidence (did a neighbour see anyone acting suspiciously?) and detective skills to try to deduce the identity of the offender from the *modus operandi* (*MO*; perhaps the method of entry to the premises or the way the offender's search was conducted) and where stolen property might be sold. In previous times, these skills were well honed by the local detective working a local area who knew the MO of local offenders. For example, if the MO at the scene of a domestic burglary was that the offender had gained entry to the premises by forcing the lock on the rear door, then as the starting point for their enquiries the investigating officer would be thinking of any burglars who employed that method of entry. Today, the high volume of crimes such as domestic burglary means that police investigators find it much more difficult to identify an offender based solely on their behaviour at the crime scene, although community-based policing seeks to address this issue (Bossler and Holt, 2013; Bullock, 2013). In recent years this has led to more and more reliance on forensic identification evidence, not only to provide the evidence to put to the suspect but also to prove the identity of the offender. This has led to an increased use by the police of forensic identification evidence at volume crimes, such as burglary and vehicle crime, as well as serious and major crime (Wu and Chrichton, 2010; Raymond et al., 2004).

What makes identification evidence so useful for forensic science?

First, the characteristics of identification evidence (such as DNA or fingerprints) do not change throughout a person's lifetime, so a sample provided to the police when a person is a teenager will still be valid when they are drawing a pension. Contrast this with, say, footwear evidence: a person will not only get through many pairs of shoes during their lifetime, the imperfections in the sole pattern of one pair of shoes will also change constantly as the shoes are worn. Thus, for identification evidence such as fingerprints and DNA, the police have reference samples that remain constant. As well as this consistency, both fingerprint and DNA characteristics are very specific to an individual (with the exception of identical twins sharing the same DNA). Therefore, the police not only have an unchanging reference to a person's identity, this reference is also very specific to that individual; just how specific we will see later. Fingerprint evidence is often referred to as 'unique' in forensic science texts, for example: 'Human friction ridge skin arrangements are unique and permanent' (Girard, 2013, p. 142) or '[Fingerprints are] unique, immutable, universal, easy to classify' (Lennard, 2007, p. 55). This terminology is also used by the legal profession, as in this example from a UK judge: 'I should think there are not more than 27 million males in the United Kingdom, which means that it is unique' (Saks and Koehler, 2008, p. 203). Increasingly, though, this view is being challenged (Saks and Koehler, 2008; Meuwly, 2006; Biedermann and Taroni, 2013; Cole, 2010), as it is recognised that there is no scientific basis for saying that fingerprint evidence is unique. This issues of the scientific basis for fingerprint (and other) evidence and how it is presented to a jury in court are considered in more detail in this and later chapters. Nevertheless, DNA and fingerprints do present the best sort of forensic evidence a forensic scientist could hope to obtain: an association to a named individual with evidence that is very specific to that individual. However, as we will see in Chapter 5, both fingerprint and DNA characteristics require interpretation for the courts by a forensic scientist, based on the limits of technology and the evidence itself.

Another positive feature is that these identifying characteristics can be readily stored and searched on computer databases. National and regional databases of both fingerprint and DNA characteristics are now held by many countries and are used not only to confirm identity, but also speculatively to search a person's characteristics against those that have been recovered from crime scenes. Particularly for volume crimes, which have a high rate of recidivism (Langan and Levin, 2002), there is an increased likelihood that a speculative search will reveal an identification and potential offender. For fingerprint identification, the introduction of a computer database (known generically as an Automated Fingerprint Identification System, or AFIS) enabled crime scene fingerprints to be searched against many more offenders than was ever possible with manual searching techniques.

While such databases changed fingerprint identification techniques forever, for DNA the introduction of computerised storage and searching of profiles coincided with its widespread use as a means of identifying offenders and detecting crime, particularly volume crime. This ability to store and search huge amounts of biometric information has great potential as a crime-fighting tool, although it also requires careful consideration of the use of such science alongside legal and social policy debates. In Chapter 8 the proliferation of biometric databases, particularly DNA databases, will be discussed along with the law enforcement uses of such databases and the inherent privacy and ethical concerns associated with the retention of personal information.

We will now look in some detail at how both DNA and fingerprint evidence has developed to its current use in the forensic investigation of many offence types, how it is employed today, and some of the difficulties that can be encountered with these evidence types.

Deoxyribonucleic acid (DNA)

DNA for criminal investigation

Although the use of DNA in criminal investigation first occurred in 1985, the story of DNA can be traced back to 1953 and a model for the double helical structure of the deoxyribonucleic acid molecule proposed by James Watson and Francis Crick (for which they shared the 1962 Nobel prize). This double helix DNA molecule is in fact a polymer of much simpler molecules known as *nucleotides,* which are themselves composed of a base, a sugar and a phosphate. Within the DNA molecule there are only four nucleotides and they differ in the base they contain. The four bases available are *adenine, cytosine, guanine* and *thymine,* which are abbreviated to A, C, G and T respectively. The double helix of DNA comprises two strands, linked together by many *base pairs,* with each base pair comprising two of the four bases. However, the bases do not pair in a random fashion: A can pair only with T, and G can pair only with C, as shown in Figure 2.1. Sequences of base pairs along the DNA strand make up a *gene* that can run from a few base pairs to many hundreds of millions of base pairs. These genes help to determine human characteristics such as gender and blood type and a child inherits half of its genes from its father and half from its mother. Different versions of individual genes, known as *alleles,* give rise to variations such as blood type, in which different alleles of the gene lead to blood types A, B, AB or O. The position of a gene (sequence of base pairs) within the DNA molecule is known as its *locus* (plural loci).

The discovery of DNA profiling for criminal justice, by Sir Alec Jeffreys at the University of Leicester in 1984, used sequences of base pairs that repeated over 6 and 100 base pairs and that are known as *variable number tandem repeats* (*VNTR*). As the number of base pair repeats differs between individuals, Jeffreys was able to use this to discriminate between

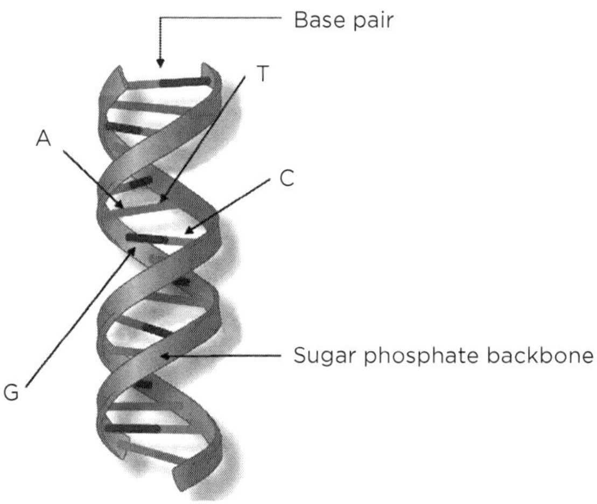

Figure 2.1 The double helix nature of DNA comprising two strands, linked together by many base pairs, with each base pair comprising two of the four bases (A with T and G with C).

individuals. However, modern DNA profiling is based on amplification of the area of DNA of interest, a process known as *polymerase chain reaction (PCR)*, developed in 1983 by Kari Mullis. This process effectively makes copies of the parts of the DNA molecule of interest. The invention of PCR represents one of the technological prerequisites to enable the widespread use of DNA in crime investigation; that is, the ability to replicate DNA and therefore to be able to take a sample of DNA recovered from the crime scene (such as might be found on a discarded cigarette) and amplify it to a level that enables it to be profiled. Without PCR, the range of specimen types that today are routinely recovered for DNA analysis from the crime scene would be severely limited.

As well as DNA amplification, a second prerequisite necessary to enable DNA profiling to provide strong evidential value is good discriminating power. That is, the probability of a DNA profile from a crime scene that 'matches' the suspect but belongs to another individual, or a coincidental 'match', must be extremely small. As we will see in Chapter 5, the use of the word 'match' has caused much controversy in recent years, as it conveys an extremely high level of confidence. Unfortunately, on its own without qualification, 'match' does not convey the level of confidence in the association being made by DNA for material obtained from, for example, a crime scene and a suspect. Despite this, 'match' is used throughout the criminal justice system, not only for DNA but also for other evidence types, such as fingerprints. Here we will use the term 'association' rather than match and, unless otherwise stated, 'association' should be taken to mean a likelihood that two objects have originated from the same source. We will learn more in Chapter 5 about likelihood calculation and how the term is used in many forensic science disciplines to express the degree of confidence that two objects have originated from the same source. However, the reader should be aware of the possibility of encountering frequent use of the word 'match' in the criminal justice system to represent varying degrees of confidence in the association between two objects.

The required discriminating power in DNA comes from tandem repeats. This is not the VNTR used by Jeffreys, but *short tandem repeats* (*STR*), in which the repeating sequence is, by definition, short and between 1 and 14 base pairs. By careful selection of a number of loci within the DNA molecule, the discriminating power can be built up to a level sufficient to provide strong evidential value for a DNA association between a sample from the crime scene and a sample from an individual. In the UK in 1995, *second-generation multiplex* (*SGM*) was introduced, which sampled seven areas of DNA (six STR loci plus a sex indicator area) and had a discriminating power of 1 in 50 000 000. Subjecting the extracted DNA to PCR and then sampling seven areas provided sufficient DNA and discrimination for routine profiling of material recovered from crime scenes (Jobling and Gill, 2004; Kashyap et al., 2004). The discriminating power of modern DNA techniques is communicated during trials using a statistic known as random match probability (RMP); in Chapter 7 we will explore how this is presented by DNA expert witnesses and how the figure is understood and interpreted by jurors.

In England and Wales, the third and final requirement to enable DNA profiling to be used as a means of speculatively searching crime scene DNA against known offenders required changes in legislation. The Police and Criminal Evidence Act (PACE) 1984 controls police powers in England and Wales and the PACE codes of practice control the way in which those powers are exercised. In 1995, the PACE codes of practice were amended to reclassify samples taken from the mouth (buccal swabs taken from the cheek) and plucked hair (from anywhere on the body, except pubic hair) as *non-intimate*. Prior to this change, such samples were classed as *intimate* and could not be taken without the consent of the donor. The amendments to PACE also allowed for the profiled non-intimate samples to be subject to a speculative search (such as on a computer database). At the same time, speculative searching of fingerprints was also included in the amendments to PACE. From 2004 onwards, samples for speculative searching could be taken from anyone arrested for any *recordable offence* (any offence punishable by imprisonment), by force if necessary. These changes to the legislation paved the way for the advances in technology (the ability to amplify and discriminate DNA samples) to be used to associate crime scene profiles against those of known offenders, and thus the UK *National DNA Database (NDNAD)* was launched in April 1995. The NDNAD is managed on behalf of the Association of Chief Police Officers (ACPO) by a custodian who is responsible for ensuring that the database is populated by profiles supplied by private companies who profile DNA material for the UK police service.

Box 2.1 The first crime to be solved with DNA

Within the space of three years in the early 1980s, two teenage girls were murdered in Leicestershire, UK. Semen samples recovered from both victims were blood type A. A local youth, Richard Buckland, confessed to the second murder but denied the first. In an effort to prove that Buckland murdered both girls, the local police engaged Dr Alec Jeffreys from the University of Leicester to use a new technique that could profile DNA from body fluids. Jeffreys concluded that both girls were murdered by the same man, but that the crime scene DNA did not belong to Buckland. In 1987, the police conducted the first ever mass DNA elimination in order to find the murderer. Over 4000 local men were screened, but a DNA association to the crime scene samples did not emerge. Then, Ian Kelly was overheard bragging that he had been paid to give a sample for his friend, Colin Pitchfork. The police arrested Pitchfork and his DNA profile 'matched' the crime scene samples. In 1998, Pitchfork was convicted of both murders.

Analysis: After carrying out the DNA profiling of the semen samples, Jeffreys stated, 'I have no doubt whatsoever that he [Buckland] would have been found guilty had it not been for DNA evidence.' It is likely that, had DNA evidence not been available, Buckland would have been charged with both murders on the basis of evidence of similar fact between the two offences. Would a jury have convicted Buckland? Jeffreys certainly felt that it would. Today, the police are still acutely aware of what is termed the *Pitchfork syndrome* and the need to ensure that when a DNA elimination screen is being undertaken, precautions are in place to verify the identity of the donors. How the police address this issue will be considered in Box 2.2.

Is DNA evidence as useful as fingerprint evidence?

Although a discrimination of 1 in 50 000 000 is high, the Forensic Science Service in England and Wales worked towards improving this and in 1999 introduced *second-generation multiplex* + (*SGM*+), which sampled 11 areas of DNA (10 STR loci plus a sex indicator area). This gave an improved discrimination of 1 in 1 000 000 000, which is much greater than the population of the UK. Although the improved discrimination significantly lowered the possibility of a coincidental association between a crime scene sample and an individual's DNA profile on the NDNAD, in a UK court of law DNA evidence is still presented by the forensic scientist quoting these odds. This is different to the way in which fingerprint evidence is presented where, traditionally, a fingerprint examiner will state that the fingerprint impression recovered from the crime scene is identical with a particular fingerprint impression from an individual and that, in their experience, no two fingerprint impressions have ever been found to be the same from two different people (the same applies to palm impressions). Clearly, this is a logical fallacy. A statement that no two fingerprint impressions have ever been found to be the same from two different people does not address the question of the probability of finding consistent impressions, if they did not originate from the same source. The use of DNA in criminal investigations has always been presented with this probabilistic approach. However, fingerprint evidence has developed over the years without the benefit of such an approach. We have already seen that there is a common perception that fingerprints are 'unique' and we will consider later in this chapter recent studies that have sought to bring a more scientific and probabilistic approach to fingerprint evidence; that is, to bring it more in line with DNA evidence. In addition, in Chapter 5 the interpretation of fingerprints and other evidence types to a jury will be considered. For DNA, it is debatable how well a jury can make a distinction between odds of 1 in 50 000 000 (SGM) and 1 in 1 000 000 000 (SGM+), and this will be discussed further in Chapters 5 and 7.

Box 2.2 Operation Quicksilver – Solving an old case with DNA

Between 1984 and 1990, seven offences of rape were committed in three different police force areas in the UK. The MO of the offender was similar in each case: he gained entry via the rear of the premises and then locked or bolted the front door before attacking the lone female occupant. Despite a massive police investigation, the offences stopped in 1990 and the case remained unsolved for a number of years. In 1999, through advances in DNA profiling and the introduction of SGM+, a small trace of semen recovered from a single pubic hair found on the bed linen of the first victim produced a full DNA profile. Northamptonshire Police led an enquiry on behalf of all three police forces and set about producing a list of individuals to be eliminated by providing a DNA sample. This was no easy task, as the first of these offences was now 15 years old. To avoid the Pitchfork syndrome (see Box 2.1), Northamptonshire Police's Head of Forensics, Dr John Bond, devised a protocol for taking a DNA sample from those of interest. This protocol required the fingerprints and an instant camera image of the donor to be taken as well as a DNA sample. Further, a witness statement was required from someone who was not a relative of the donor, who was able to confirm the donor's identity. Days before the mass elimination screen commenced, Keith Samuels was arrested for attempting to cash a stolen cheque. As was routine at the time, a DNA sample was taken from Samuels and this 'matched' the DNA from the semen to the current UK standard. Samuels confessed to the seven rapes and had nearly 90 other offences taken into consideration. He stated at the time that he knew that one day his past would catch up with him.

Analysis: On the list of those to be eliminated in the DNA screening was Keith Samuels, so he would still have been identified as the offender had he not been arrested for the stolen cheque. He was known to the police at the time the offences were being committed as a burglar, but did not feature prominently enough in the enquiry to be arrested then. Today, with computer technology, police intelligence is much more easily researched than it was in the 1980s with paper-based systems. Therefore, such a series of offences being committed today would result in a very different approach by the police both in terms of intelligence analysis and the use of DNA technology.

Where is DNA found at the crime scene?

DNA recovery presents a potentially difficult scenario for the *crime scene investigator* (*CSI*), as the DNA may be located on surfaces that present no visible stain. Therefore, the CSI has to speculatively attempt to recover DNA that is not visible, or may not be there at all. As well as this invisible DNA being left at a crime scene through contact (by touching objects or picking them up), it may also be left by coughing or sneezing over an item (Daly et al., 2012; Aditya et al., 2011; Pang and Cheung, 2007; Thomasma and Foran, 2013). This not only makes the problem of what to examine for DNA more problematic for the CSI, but also increases the possibility of innocent contamination, as we will see in more detail later. Visible stains (such as blood or semen) can provide not only the identity of the donor, but also evidence to incriminate them in the offence (such as semen on a victim's underwear or a blood spot on a carpet). The different sources of DNA are often referred to as *specimen types* and are shown in Figure 2.2. In Chapter 5 we will explore how decision-making theory and research contribute to understanding the crime scene examination process.

Decreasing visibility ↓

- Blood
- Semen (excellent, aspermic or sperm-depleted semen (e.g. infertile or vasectomised male) possible profile from cells shed during ejaculation)
- Nasal secretions
- Vaginal fluid (may be present in a semen stain)
- Hair (root)
- Saliva
  - Cigarette butts
  - Chewing gum
  - Drinks can/bottle etc.
- Cellular

Figure 2.2 Examples of common sources of crime scene DNA, in order of decreasing visibility.

Blood, semen, nasal secretions and vaginal fluid provide visible stains, while hair might be shed following a violent attack or inside a mask. As well as items that may have saliva on them, such as cigarette butts or chewing gum (Hochmeister et al., 1991), saliva may also be found on cans and bottles that have been in contact with the mouth (Sweet and Hildebrand, 1999). The latter, however, represent invisible stains, so the CSI undertakes a speculative examination. Cellular DNA, such as skin cells rubbed off in sweat, is also not visible and is invariably searched for speculatively on items that the offender may have touched, such as a screwdriver, cup, steering wheel and so on. Of the above specimen types, cellular DNA represents the most difficult from which to obtain a full, single SGM+ profile. Often a partial profile (which reduces the discriminating power) or a mixed profile is obtained, which can then be difficult for the forensic scientist to separate out and attribute to different individuals.

Box 2.3 Plant DNA in a criminal investigation

One Sunday morning in 1992 in Arizona's Maricopa County, USA, a woman's body was found under a Palo Verde tree in the desert. A boy riding his bicycle found the nude body of the woman lying face down in the brush. She had been strangled. Near the body was a pager that was traced to its owner, Mark Bogan. Bogan admitted picking up the victim in his father's truck, but claimed that she had robbed him of his wallet and pager and had run off from his vehicle. He stated that he had retrieved his wallet but not the pager. At the crime scene the investigating police found evidence of a 'scuff' to the bark of the Palo Verde tree, possibly made by a vehicle, so Brogan's vehicle was examined forensically. No evidence of the corresponding scuff on the vehicle was found, but the police did find a few seed pods from a Palo Verde tree in the back of the truck. The police engaged the services of Dr T. Helentjaris, a Professor of Molecular Genetics from the University of Arizona, to establish whether the seed pods from the back of the truck could be associated to the Palo Verde tree where the victim had been found. Helentjaris used *randomly amplified polymorphic DNA* (*RAPD*) analysis and found that the Palo Verde trees at the crime scene showed high genetic variability, and could easily be distinguished from one another. From trials that included Palo Verde trees in the vicinity of the crime scene and others chosen at random from around Phoenix, Helentjaris was able to associate the seed pods to the crime scene tree. While the seed pods did not prove that Brogan was at the crime scene, they did prove that his father's truck was there. Helentjaris's evidence in court helped convict Mark Bogan of murder.

Analysis: It is not unusual for a defendant to try to innocently explain the presence at the crime scene of evidence that implicates them, whether this is forensic evidence (such as a fingerprint) or physical evidence (such as the pager). Without the pager providing the link to Bogan and the vehicle, the forensic aspect of this case (the seed pods) would possibly never have been found. The work of Helentjaris illustrates that seemingly innocent material can provide evidence of association, in this case between the vehicle and the Palo Verde tree (the crime scene). While the forensic evidence does not directly put Bogan at the crime scene, a jury would need to evaluate this evidence and consider the likelihood of other possibilities if Bogan was not the offender.

Other types of DNA and DNA searching methods

When a DNA sample from a crime scene is degraded (possibly through exposure to the elements) or a partial or mixed profile is obtained (possibly from cellular DNA), the Forensic Science Service in England and Wales developed a technique to amplify the DNA by applying more than the normal number of cycles for PCR (34 instead of 28). This technique is known as *low copy number* (*LCN*) DNA processing, and enables old or degraded samples to have a better chance of producing an identifiable profile (Pizzamiglio et al., 2004; Graham, 2008). LCN has found favour with old cases (where DNA is likely to be degraded) and for other serious offences where the DNA evidence is likely to be crucial to secure a conviction in court. The increased time taken to process the DNA with LCN means that this technique is more expensive than standard SGM+ profiling and so it is not used routinely on volume crimes. Furthermore, a potential problem with LCN is that, as well as amplifying the DNA of interest, any contaminants (such as another individual's DNA in a mixed profile sample) will also be amplified. The limitations of LCN need to be considered when interpreting results, as we will see in more detail in Chapter 5.

Box 2.4 LCN profiles

In 1998, 29 people were murdered in a car bomb explosion in Omagh, UK. The Real Irish Republican Army claimed responsibility for the attack. In 2005, Sean Hoey was charged with the 29 murders and other offences related to terrorism. The prosecution case relied on DNA evidence gathered from bomb timers used in the bombing and also DNA material from other bomb scenes. The DNA evidence had been obtained using low copy number (LCN) profiling, a technique devised by the FSS that was not universally accepted and, at the time, was only in use in UK courts. At the trial, the judge was critical of the LCN technique and the UK Forensic Institute, retained by Hoey's defence, employed the US Specialist Working Group on DNA Analysis and Methods (SWGDAM) methodology to attempt to discredit the results. Hoey was acquitted of all 29 murders.

Analysis: After the trial, LCN was suspended from use in UK courts until its effectiveness and reliability were further tested. Nevertheless, the UK Forensic Science Regulator has now endorsed its continued use in the UK. It is sometimes a difficult decision for prosecutors whether the forensic evidence (in this case DNA from bomb timers) is sufficiently robust and meaningful to have a realistic chance of securing a conviction. In this case, the difficulty was compounded by the use of a new technique (LCN) and the defence was able to convince a jury that, at the time, the scientific basis of the procedure was not safe.

Often a full SGM+ profile is obtained from the crime scene yet produces no association on the NDNAD, as the donor has not had occasion to provide any DNA in the past. In these cases, and if the seriousness of the offence warrants it, the database can provide details of people who are on the database who share some alleles with the profile from the crime scene. One or more of the profiles with shared alleles may be relatives of the donor of the crime scene profile, which may then lead the police to the donor. Unrelated people may also share some alleles with the profile from the crime scene (as some alleles are common), so it is by no means certain that this process will provide the identity sought by the police. Just how many shared alleles are considered in this process depends on how many respondents the police are able to investigate.

The fewer the number of shared alleles, the more respondents are obtained, but this increases the amount of police work required to investigate relatives of the person whose profile is on the database. There is also an implied assumption that if the donor of the crime scene profile is a criminal, it is likely that someone to whom they are related may be as well, hence the relative's profile would be on the NDNAD. This process of searching for relatives on the NDNAD is known as *familial searching*. In selecting respondents, the police will also be mindful of the feasibility of the relationship between the person sought and the person whose profile is on the NDNAD. For example, if the person sought is known from a witness account to be an elderly person, then there is little point looking on the NDNAD for relatives likely to be their parents.

Box 2.5 The roaming rapist – a case involving familial DNA

Between 1998 and 2003, nine women were sexually assaulted in Sacramento County, California, USA. All of the cases were linked by DNA. The MO of the offender was to engage his victims in conversation before attacking them. He was described as a black male, about 5 feet 9 inches tall, between 150 and 200 lb and 20–35 years old. As the offender's profile was not on the California DNA database, detectives decided to run a familial search of the database. That obtained a familial association to Ladell Sanders, the elder brother of Dereck Jermaine Sanders. Ladell's DNA was on the database for a felony conviction. Following this familial DNA association, detectives followed Dereck Sanders to a restaurant and recovered his DNA from a drinking straw that he had discarded. Sanders was charged with 35 counts of forcible sexual assault involving 10 victims aged 14–42, in 9 separate incidents.

Analysis: In the UK, on the basis of a familial DNA association, police would have the power to arrest a suspect on suspicion if they failed to provide a voluntary DNA sample for elimination purposes. Once they had been arrested, a DNA sample could be taken by force if necessary. It would not be admissible in UK courts to obtain DNA from the suspect covertly, as was done here, as PACE allows the police to demand a DNA sample to prove or disprove that person's involvement with a crime if there are grounds to suspect their involvement. In this case, the familial DNA association would be considered grounds. In Chapter 5 we will discuss the differences between forensic intelligence (such as a criminal justice sample of DNA for speculative searching) and evidence (such as a DNA sample to provide evidence for court).

When *cellular* (or *nuclear*) DNA is degraded, this greatly reduces the potential to obtain a usable SGM+ profile. In such circumstances, the profiling of *mitochondrial DNA* (*mtDNA*) has been developed. MtDNA in humans is a circular molecule found in the cell mitochondria, many thousands of base pairs in circumference, and is much more abundant in each cell than nuclear DNA. This means that if a sample is degraded, the abundance of mtDNA means that this is likely to remain present even if nuclear DNA has degraded to a point where SGM+ is no longer viable. Therefore samples such as unrooted hair shafts or bones may still yield a mtDNA profile.

Fortunately for criminal investigation, part of the circular mtDNA molecule displays sequence variation that differs between individuals. mtDNA is profiled in a similar fashion to nuclear DNA by the use of PCR. However, as a person's mtDNA is inherited solely from their mother, siblings will all have the same mtDNA profile, as will their mother. Nevertheless, mtDNA profiling for criminal investigation is able to discriminate between individuals, although it does not have the discriminating power of SGM+ and is generally employed when SGM+ analysis has failed to produce a usable profile. mtDNA is not compatible with SGM+ and there is no NDNAD or speculative searching for mtDNA. Therefore, its use is limited to comparing profiles from a crime scene with individuals identified by the police as of interest to the investigation. The chance that two random, unrelated individuals in a population would have similar mtDNA profiles is one in a few hundred, very much less than nuclear DNA in the NDNAD (Holland and Parsons, 1999).

Box 2.6 The case of an unknown victim and mtDNA

On 5 November 1930, two cousins returning home to Hardingstone in Northamptonshire, UK after celebrating Bonfire Night (the anniversary of Guy Fawkes' plot to blow up Parliament) noticed a large fire in the distance. Initially they thought that this was yet another Guy Fawkes celebration, but then they noticed a man walking towards them who commented that 'somebody must be lighting a bonfire'. This man walked past the cousins and appeared disorientated. The two cousins made their way to the fire, to discover a burning car, inside which were the incinerated remains of an adult male. The vehicle registration identified the car as belonging to Alfred Arthur Rouse, who was later identified as the man the two cousins had met that night. Rouse was arrested for murder and, after being convicted, confessed that he had picked up a vagrant earlier that day and had driven north from London with the intention of killing his passenger and then setting light to the car in an attempt to stage his own death. His motive was to escape numerous claims for child support from the mothers of a number of children he had fathered. Rouse was hanged in 1931, but the identity of his victim was never determined. Over the years, many relatives of males who went missing around November 1930 came forward claiming that the victim may have been related to them. In 2012, a family who had always thought the victim was their relative approached Northamptonshire Police. Unable to assist directly, the police asked the University of Leicester to see if advances in DNA technology might be able to resolve this question. Remarkably, two of the original post mortem pathology slides of the deceased taken by the pathologist, Dr Bernard Spilsbury, survived in a London hospital archive. One of these slides was examined for mtDNA and a profile was obtained confirming that the mtDNA on the slide originated from a male, but, from an unbroken maternal line in the family, that Rouse's victim was not their missing relative.

Analysis: In this example, mtDNA was used not to solve a crime but to try to solve a mystery related to the crime. While not necessarily of direct interest to police investigators, such work can (as in this case) bring some form of closure to potential relatives of the victim. But we still do not know who the victim was - could this mtDNA profile be used, at long last, to identify him?

DNA databases

As well as profiles of samples recovered from crime scenes, the NDNAD (or, indeed, any database for speculative searching) requires profiles against which to compare those crime scene samples. In the case of criminal investigation databases (such as for DNA and fingerprints), these other profiles relate to offenders. We have seen how, in England

and Wales, PACE was amended in 1995 to facilitate the collection of DNA from offenders on arrest and while in police custody. Leading up to the launch of the NDNAD in 1995, the FSS experimented with different ways of collecting this sample from the arrestee and selected a specially shaped comb with a serrated edge (known as a *buccal scrape*), as in Figure 2.3. Kits were provided to police forces to enable a trained person in the custody suite to take two samples from an arrestee that would then be placed in separate sterile vials for transport to the processing laboratory.

In the event that an arrestee refuses to cooperate in providing a buccal scrape (for example if the donor refuses to open their mouth), the legislation allows for the collection of plucked, rooted hair (by force if necessary). Again, two samples of hair would be taken. In the UK an arrestee

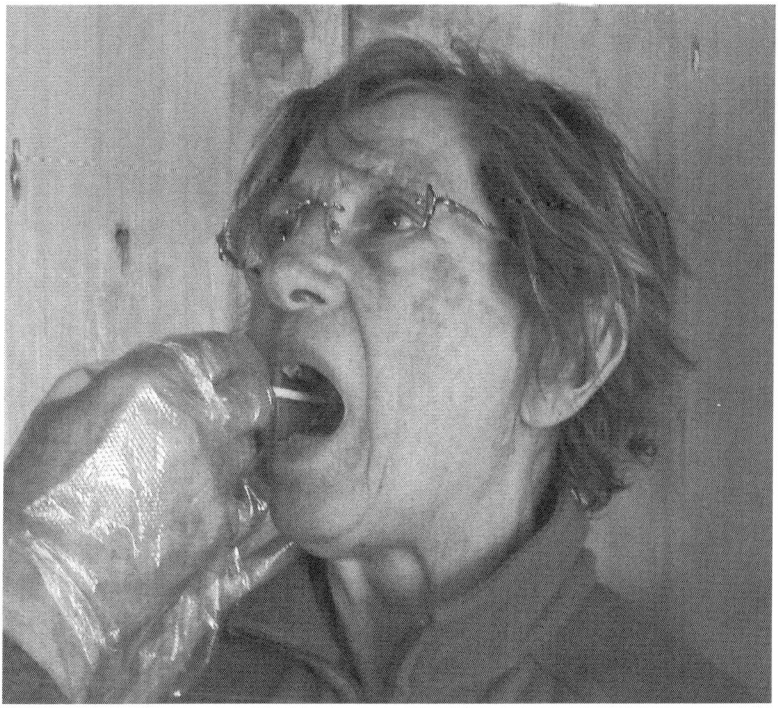

Figure 2.3 The approved method of taking a DNA sample when the UK National DNA Database was established in 1995. Note that the person taking the sample wears disposable gloves to prevent innocent contamination of the sample.

sample is known as a criminal justice sample or CJ sample. Two samples are taken in case the first fails to yield a profile suitable for loading onto the NDNAD. In the event that the first sample produces a profile, the second sample is retained to enable a new profile to be produced in the event of an upgrade in technology. A good example of this is the conversion from SGM to SGM+ in 1999. After that date, the statistical odds of crime scene profiles that could be associated with an SGM profile could be improved by upgrading the SGM sample to SGM+ using the retained second sample from the arrestee.

Following the success of the UK database, many other DNA databases have been set up. The largest is the *Combined DNA Index System* (*CODIS*), set up originally by the US Federal Bureau of Investigation (FBI) in 1990. CODIS allows federal, state and local agencies to compare stored DNA profiles. An Australian database was set up in 2000 and is known as the *National Criminal Investigation DNA Database* (*NCIDD*). In Canada, legislation passed in 2000 allowed the setting up of a *National DNA Data Bank* (*NDDB*), maintained by the Royal Canadian Mounted Police. Further detail and a comparative discussion of these worldwide databases is provided in Chapter 8. Different jurisdictions have approached DNA databases and associated legislation in very different ways, and there are important legal and ethical debates surrounding the retention of individuals' DNA profiles, as we will see in that chapter.

Box 2.7 A killer in the family

UK family man Philip Austin murdered his entire immediate family over the course of one day in July 2000. The mother of Austin's wife Claire became concerned when she had not heard from Philip or Claire for a few days, so she drove to their home to see if all was well. On opening the front door, she was confronted with the sight of her daughter lying dead on the kitchen floor. It was evident that Claire had been attacked about the head and had bleeding injuries. Next to Claire lay one of the family's pet dogs, which also appeared to have been hit on the head. Upstairs, Claire's mother discovered the bodies of her two grandchildren, 8-year-old Keiran and his 7-year-old sister Jade, in separate bedrooms. It was clear to the attending CSIs that the family had been dead for several days. During the examination of the scene, the body of the family's second pet dog was found, with similar injuries to the first. There was considerable blood distribution in the kitchen where Claire's body lay and the services of a blood pattern analyst and DNA biologist were employed to interpret the sequence of events that took place in the kitchen that tragic day. This showed that there had been a frantic struggle between the offender and Claire, during which Claire had tried to escape through the front door, but the offender had dragged her back into the kitchen. DNA profiling of the blood showed that it had all originated from Claire and the two pet dogs. Philip and the family vehicle were missing. Following an appeal to the public for information about Philip or his vehicle, the vehicle was traced to a second-hand car dealer in Northampton. It was ascertained that (most likely on the day of the murders) Philip had part-exchanged the vehicle for a new one. A forensic examination of the family vehicle revealed a mallet in the boot (trunk), on which was found a mixture of human and animal blood. DNA profiling showed the blood to have originated from Claire and the two dogs. During questioning, Philip confessed and explained how he had bought the mallet and planned to kill his wife. Later the same day, he picked his children up from school, gave them some sleeping tablets and, when they were drowsy, put them to bed and then strangled them one after the other. Despite initially pleading not guilty and then changing his plea to one of diminished responsibility, he was found guilty of all three murders.

Analysis: In this case, DNA profiling and blood pattern analysis were used in the early days of the enquiry to show that there was no forensic evidence to suggest the presence of a third party being involved in these murders. This assisted the police investigators in the nature of their appeals for Philip to come forward. In court, the forensic evidence was used to confirm the sequence of events that Philip provided. His claim of diminished responsibility was dismissed by the jury on the basis of his malice aforethought in the murder of his children.

Problems with DNA evidence

The quality of DNA evidence is very much affected by human intervention. It might be thought that DNA evidence would be more robust because, as we have seen, the scientific methods for analysing DNA are well established and there are definitive procedures and protocols for recovering, storing, handling and examining DNA evidence. Unfortunately, it is at the human intervention stage that difficulties arise, partly as a result of not following accepted procedure, but also from the nature of the DNA evidence itself. This is a very different problem to misidentification (stating that two samples are from the same source when they are not), which is possible with DNA as a profile can be wrongly attributed to an individual by human error. However, with DNA we also have the possibility (albeit remote) of an adventitious association, where the SGM+ profiles of the crime scene DNA and the individual appear the same although the individual was in fact not the donor of the DNA. This is possible due to the fact that DNA profiles only represent a portion of the entire DNA code, not an individual's entire genome. Perhaps the most troublesome problem with DNA, though, is contamination, a problem for which there is no parallel with fingerprint evidence. By innocently contaminating samples during the evidential process, it is possible to show an association between a crime scene profile and an individual's profile (Lowe et al., 2002; Goray et al., 2010). An example of this would be semen recovered from the intimate swabs of a rape victim. Clearly, the semen is likely to belong to the offender, but if a suspect's DNA and the semen DNA become contaminated, it might appear that the semen originated (incorrectly) from the suspect.

Box 2.8 A case of DNA misidentification

In October 2011 a female was raped in the area of Blackley in Manchester, UK. A swab from the victim was DNA profiled and produced an association to Adam Scott. Scott was arrested in Devon (a long way from Manchester) three weeks after the offence. He protested his innocence and denied that he had ever been to Manchester, but was nevertheless remanded in custody. Some weeks later, the investigating police officers began to have concerns, as telephone records showed that Scott was in Plymouth, about 300 miles from Manchester, a few hours after the offence. As a result of these concerns, the company that had carried out the DNA analysis discovered that a plastic tray containing a sample of Scott's DNA had been reused to analyse DNA from the victim's swab. As a result of this potential contamination, the charges against Scott were dropped. The UK Forensic Science Regulator said that the errors were compounded by the failure of the company to consider contamination, despite concerns expressed by the investigating police officer about the reliability of the DNA association.

Analysis: This case shows how human intervention and a breakdown of accepted practice can potentially lead to a miscarriage of justice. The diligence of the police in seeking to gather all the evidence (telephone records), rather than simply relying on the DNA evidence, assisted in these mistakes coming to light. The science of DNA profiling is not brought into question by this case, although it is often reported in the popular media as such, which does nothing to reassure the public (and a jury) that the scientific basis of DNA profiling is valid. As we will see in Chapter 5, jury members' belief in the validity of a scientific process is crucial to their correct interpretation of the evidence.

Fingerprints

Sweat and fingerprint deposits

Three glands, *eccrine, sebaceous* and *apocrine,* contribute to sweat secretion (Girod et al., 2012; Croxton et al., 2010; Ramotowski, 2001). Both the hands and soles of the feet contain only eccrine glands, while sebaceous glands are generally localised to regions of the body containing hair follicles, such as the face and scalp. Apocrine glands are restricted to regions of the body such as armpits and genital areas (Ramotowski, 2001). Therefore, eccrine and sebaceous secretions are normally the only contributors to fingerprint sweat deposits. Eccrine sweat comprises mostly water (> 98%) together with inorganic secretions (such as alkali metal salts), amino acids and sugars. Sebaceous sweat comprises mainly fatty acids, waxes and squalene.

What makes fingerprints useful for forensic science?

The use of fingerprints deposited at the scene of a crime as a means of identifying an offender and hence solving the crime was first suggested in the nineteenth century (Faulds, 1880; Herschel, 1880). Subsequent work by Francis Galton, Sir Edward Henry and others well over 100 years ago led to the establishment of fingerprint identification as a recognised means of identifying offenders (Berry and Stoney, 2001).

A fingerprint pattern is made up of a number of ridges and furrows and these evolved to enable us to dissipate heat through eccrine sweat pores on top of the ridges, to provide a tactile facility (so we can feel whether a surface is rough or smooth) and a friction grip. Francis Galton first suggested a means of classifying fingerprint characteristics and, in

1892, calculated the odds against two people having identical fingerprint characteristics on a finger as 64 billion to 1. A few years later, at the turn of the nineteenth century, Sir Edward Henry proposed a fingerprint classification system that was subsequently adopted by many countries worldwide and is still in use today. In fact, it is only in recent years with the advent of computerised storage of fingerprint characteristics that the *Henry classification system* as a means of storing and retrieving a person's fingerprints has fallen into disuse. This was based around the three basic types of fingerprint pattern, referred to as *loops, arches* and *whorls,* which are shown in Figure 2.4. Approximately 60% of all fingerprints are classified as loops, 5% arches and 35% whorls. Within each pattern type a number of sub-types can exist (Girard, 2013).

Figure 2.4 The three basic types of fingerprint pattern.

Box 2.9 Can you change your fingerprint patterns?

Over the years, many criminals have tried to evade capture by attempting to change or obliterate their fingerprint ridge patterns. One infamous person who attempted this was a notorious US bank robber during the Great Depression, John Dillinger. After being named the FBI's first Public Enemy Number One, Dillinger decided to obliterate his fingerprints using acid. Although partially successful, and despite leaving a scar pattern on the fingertips, faint ridge lines were still visible on his hands after death.

Analysis: That criminals would want to undertake this painful process shows that it was well known to the public that fingerprints could link the offender to the crime scene. Although Dillinger's attempts were partially successful, the scar pattern left behind on his fingertips would also have provided a tell-tale 'signature' of his presence at a crime scene.

Clearly, the existence of only a small number of pattern types cannot provide the level of association between a fingerprint recovered from a crime scene and a suspect that forensic science demands. This association derives from the characteristics of the pattern of ridges, rather than the pattern type itself. On a given fingerprint, the pattern of ridges displays certain characteristics or *minutiae*, and it is the spatial position of the minutiae and their features that give a fingerprint its distribution of minutiae that is very specific (64 billion to 1 as calculated by Galton). Typical examples of minutiae commonly encountered on a pattern of ridges are shown in Figure 2.5, although more exist and are used by fingerprint experts to identify a fingerprint (Girard, 2013). Clearly, for two fingerprints to be deemed identical there must be sufficient minutiae that are the same between the fingerprints and no features that differ.

In the UK there was originally no set number of minutiae required to declare two fingerprints identical, although it was generally accepted that a minimum of 12 minutiae would be required to make an identification beyond doubt. In 1953, a national standard of 16 similar minutiae was adopted, with the objective of setting a standard that was so high that no one would seek to challenge the evidence. This 16-point standard had already been in use by London's Metropolitan Police (UK) since 1924. The introduction of a national standard of 16 similar minutiae or points of agreement, along with the previously held view that a minimum of 12 points of agreement would be required to make an identification, led to the situation in the UK where fingerprint identifications with 12 or more points of agreement but fewer than 16 were known as identical but not provable identifications. In other words, the police

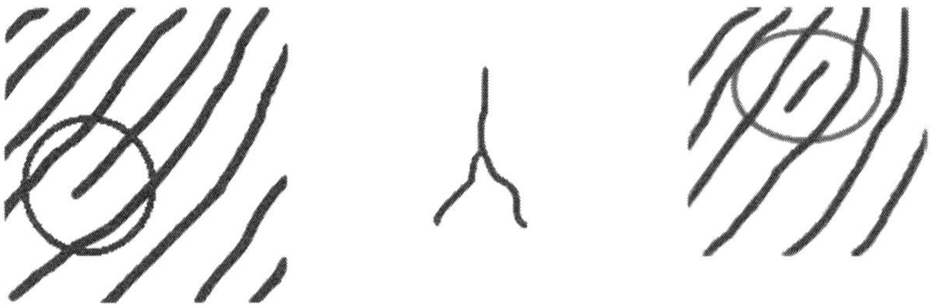

Figure 2.5 Typical examples of minutiae commonly encountered on a pattern of ridges. From left to right: ridge ending, bifurcation and isolated ridge.

investigators could use these identifications as intelligence, but not as evidence in a court of law (the difference between intelligence and evidence will be discussed in detail in Chapter 5). By the 1980s, it was generally accepted that there could be provable fingerprint identifications with fewer than 16 points in agreement and also that, in exceptional circumstances (such as for terrorism), fingerprint evidence could be produced with fewer than 16 points by a fingerprint examiner with many years' experience. This led the UK Home Office and ACPO to commission a study that concluded there was no scientific basis for the 16-point numerical standard. In 2001, England and Wales adopted a non-numerical standard for fingerprint identification and relied on the independent verification of an identification (made by a qualified or unqualified fingerprint examiner) by a further two qualified fingerprint examiners.

Box 2.10 The first murders solved by fingerprints in the UK

In the London area of Deptford in 1904, one day young Willie Jones found the door to his employer's shop locked, which was unusual as the manager, Thomas Farrow, lived above the shop with his wife Annie. Eventually gaining access from the rear of the premises, Willie was confronted with the sight of Thomas lying dead against the hearth of the fireplace with injuries to his head. After the police were summoned, the unconscious body of Mrs Farrow was found upstairs in bed, she also having been attacked about the head. The police surmised that the motive was robbery, as the cash box, found under Mrs Farrow's bed, was empty. At the scene, Assistant Commissioner Melville Macnaghten found a fingerprint on the underside of the cash box. Unfortunately, the fingerprint was different to any of those in the fledgling collection of fingerprints of offenders held at Scotland Yard. However, a witness had seen two men near the shop that morning and recognised one of them as Alfred Stratton. Alfred and his younger brother Albert, who were known to the police, were arrested and their fingerprints taken and compared with the fingerprint from the cash box. An association was found to the right thumb impression of Alfred Stratton. Both men were tried for the murders of Thomas and Annie Farrow (Annie died without regaining consciousness) and were hanged in 1905 by the public executioner, Henry

Pierrepoint, who noted in his diary that both men had 'strong necks'.

Analysis: The MO of this offence is not untypical of what might be encountered today, as is the finding of a fingerprint on the cash box that could well be the offender's print. Taking elimination fingerprints from those present at the crime scene (the police officers) and those with legitimate access to the cash box (Mr and Mrs Farrow and Willie Jones) would still be accepted practice today. Looking for other evidence (witnesses who saw the offenders) would also be undertaken today, although the emphasis would be on identifying the fingerprint. Without the fingerprint on the cash box, would the Stratton brothers have been convicted, as there was no evidence to place them at the crime scene?

Common fingerprint-recovery methods

At a crime scene, items likely to have sweat fingerprint deposits can be divided into two categories that determine both the method and location of an examination. These categories relate to whether or not the item is *porous* (such as paper or cardboard) or *non-porous* (such as polythene, plastic, metal, glass). The examination and treatment of items for fingerprints are different depending on to which of these two categories the item belongs. There is also a third category of semi-porous, which would include items such as glossy paper, but these are generally taken as non-porous for the purposes of determining a suitable treatment to enhance any fingerprints. Sweat fingerprint deposits are generally referred to as *latent* fingerprints, as they are invisible to the naked eye and require some form of enhancement in order to be able to visualise them (Yamashita and French, 2014; Bleay et al., 2012).

Porous surfaces

The most common methods for the treatment and enhancement of sweat fingerprints on porous surfaces are based on solutions of chemicals into which the item of interest is dipped for a few seconds, then it is dried (usually in a warm humid atmosphere) and observed under an appropriate light source. Some of these chemicals react with amino acids present in the sweat to produce a colour change in the chemical, which then renders the fingerprint deposit visible. The most common and widely used of these is a chemical known as *ninhydrin*, which turns a purple colour (known as *Ruhemann's purple*) following contact with amino acids present in the sweat (Crown, 1969). Ninhydrin can continue to develop fingerprints for some weeks after treatment and these prints may not be accounted for if they are not observed over this period (Charlton, 2009). Furthermore, it has been suggested that a number of physical factors, relating to the donor, may affect the efficiency of ninhydrin. For example, unexpected results may be related to the concentration and distribution of amino acids between fingerprints, as opposed to the actual amount of sweat (Ramatowski, 2012). The age of the donor may also be a factor, with older donors potentially having lower positive results then younger donors (Ramatowski, 2012). Another common chemical known as *1,8-diazafluoren-9-one*, or more commonly *DFO*, also reacts with amino acids but has the added property of *fluorescing* (Ramatowski, 2012). DFO has been shown to develop more fingerprints than ninhydrin (Saferstein, 2014); however, when used sequentially, both ninhydrin and DFO can develop more fingerprints than when used separately (Marriott et al., 2014). Ninhydrin and DFO are also both capable of enhancing fingerprints in blood, but only on porous surfaces (Charlton, 2009; Thomas & Farrugia, 2013). Furthermore, it has been suggested that DFO is the least likely of the reagents used on porous surfaces to affect DNA recovery adversely (Ramatowski, 2012).

One of the difficulties in fingerprint enhancement (which is applicable to both porous and non-porous surfaces) is whether or not the item has been exposed to water prior to recovery for fingerprint enhancement (Ramatowski, 2012; Jelly et al., 2009). For example, a piece of paper left outside in the rain will, to some extent, have the water-soluble amino acids washed out. This means not only that amino acid-based chemical treatments are less likely to be successful, but also that the person undertaking the enhancement must know the history of the item (i.e. whether it has been wet) in order to determine the best treatment to apply. This is a dilemma for those undertaking fingerprint enhancement. If the item is known to have been wet, then a common enhancement treatment is immersion in an aqueous solution of chemicals, including silver and iron ions, and a detergent, known as a *physical developer* or *PD*. Silver atoms deposit from the solution more heavily on the fingerprint deposit than the item, with the deposited silver having a grey appearance, thus rendering the fingerprint sweat visible.

Non-porous surfaces

Application of a granular or flake powder to fingerprint deposits is the most common method of enhancing fingerprint deposits on smooth, non-porous surfaces. The powders are applied with a brush and so the technique is known as dusting for fingerprints. Powder size is usually a few microns and the technique works by the powder adhering to tackiness in the sweat deposit or to contaminants, such as oil or grease. The oils secreted by the sebaceous glands produce this tacky sweat, which tends to lose its tackiness over time, so freshly deposited fingerprints enhance easily with powder application. Powders are available in many colours to suit different coloured surfaces, a popular choice in the UK being aluminium powder, which is easy and quick to apply to a large area when speculatively searching for fingerprints (James et al., 1991). An alternative applicator to a conventional brush is a magnetic brush that applies a magnetic powder, which is attracted to the magnetic brush but then, again, adheres to the tackiness in the sweat. This method of application does not require the applicator to touch the surface and has the advantage that powder not adhering to the sweat deposit can easily be removed from the surface by the applicator. Both fluorescent and phosphorescent powders are also available that can enhance the contrast between the developed fingerprint and the background surface.

If the surface is suitable, items will preferably be examined for fingerprints in situ at the crime scene by powdering, rather than removing them for subsequent examination in a laboratory. Dusting for fingerprints presents a quick, cheap and easy means of speculatively searching large areas such as doors and windows for latent fingerprints. Once visualised, dusted fingerprints are recovered from the crime scene by placing the sticky side of low-tack tape onto the enhanced fingerprint. When removed, this tape brings with it the powder, which retains the outline of the fingerprint ridges and minutiae. The tape is placed, sticky side down, onto a clear acetate sheet for safe transport and examination and the complete exhibit is known as a fingerprint lift. Often, the orientation of the recovered fingerprint is of interest and the CSI will indicate the orientation (and possibly height from a known fixed point) on the lift. Marking the orientation in this way is known as a *gravity mark*.

Some non-porous items tend not to lend themselves well to enhancement with powders applied with a brush. These would include non-rigid items such as polythene sheeting, bin liners, polythene shopping bags and cling film. For these items, a common method of enhancement is what is known as *cyanoacrylate fuming* or *superglue fuming*. Here, superglue (ethyl cyanoacrylate) is evaporated in an environment with raised relative humidity (about 85%) and the vapour selectively polymerises onto the fingerprint deposit. Initially, it was thought that water present in the sweat catalysed the polymerisation, but more recent research by Wargacki et al. (2007) has shown polymerisation of ethyl cyanoacrylate vapour in the presence of either lactate or alanine, both components of eccrine sweat.

Cyanoacrylate-fumed fingerprints exhibit a white colouration, so it is common practice either to dust the treated object with a fluorescent dye (such as fluorescein) or to dip the object into a solution of dye (such as *rhodamine* or *basic yellow 40*). After dipping the treated object in the dye solution, excess dye is easily removed by holding the object under running water.

Like porous items, cyanoacrylate fuming is not particularly effective if the surface containing the fingerprint deposit has been wet. In these circumstances, a common technique is to dip or spray the item with an aqueous suspension of an insoluble powder such as molybdenum disulphide containing a detergent. This powder suspension is known as a *small particle regent* (*SPR*). The molybdenum disulphide adheres to sebaceous sweat components present in the sweat, forming a grey deposit. Another powder suspension becoming popular as an alternative to cyanoacrylate fuming for small areas is an aqueous solution of coloured powders of iron oxide or carbon (black) and titanium dioxide (white). These powders are usually applied with a brush and then the item rinsed under a running tap.

In addition to latent fingerprints being deposited in sweat, they may be also be found at the crime scene deposited in a contaminant such as oil, grease or blood. These fingerprints are more easily visible to the naked eye and are known as *visible fingerprints*, although they can be enhanced further with a suitable treatment, such as ninhydrin for fingerprints in blood (as the amino acids in blood will react with ninhydrin). When a finger is placed in, and then withdrawn from, a soft substance (such as wet paint), a negative impression of the fingerprint ridges is made. This is known as a *plastic* fingerprint.

While the above discussion describes the most common forms of fingerprint enhancement likely to be encountered, there are many more techniques available that through either a chemical or a physical interaction with the sweat can render the fingerprint visible. Use of these techniques tends to be limited to more serious crime when time is less of a constraint to using a sequence of treatments to recover fingerprints. New, conventional methods of enhancing fingerprints continue to be investigated (Jelly et al. 2008; Wallace-Kinkell et al., 2007), although any new treatment needs to demonstrate a benefit over existing techniques.

Box 2.11 Solving a crime with the victim's fingerprints

Not all cases are solved by identifying the offender's fingerprints. In 1933 the notorious US robber George 'Machine Gun' Kelly and an accomplice kidnapped a wealthy businessman. After a sizeable ransom demand was paid, the victim was released some days later. However, unfortunately for the kidnappers, the victim had, during his captivity, paid careful attention to the sounds of his surroundings and was able to give the police a detailed description, from which they identified possible locations where he had been held. At one such location, a farm owned by a relative of Kelly, police found the fingerprints of the victim, which he had liberally planted all over the house. Kelly was tried for the kidnap and sentenced to life imprisonment.

Analysis: This case shows that forensic evidence (in this case fingerprints) is used to provide an association between two items without one of the items necessarily belonging to the offender. Here we had the victim's fingerprint and numerous objects from the premises where he was held captive.

Development of fingerprint databases

In the early 1990s, the UK looked to computerising its collection of fingerprint forms and to enabling police forces to search crime scene fingerprints against computer records of known offenders. In 1991, Scotland introduced an *Automated Fingerprint Recognition System* (*AFR*) and, in the following year, some of the police forces in England and Wales introduced AFR. The English and Welsh AFR was a consortium made up of chief police officers from participating forces. However, the AFR Consortium did not represent a national system for England and Wales and in 2001 a national system was introduced, known as the *National Automated Fingerprint Identification System* (*NAFIS*), the English and Welsh equivalent of the Scottish AFR. In 2005, NAFIS was replaced with the next generation of AFIS, known as *IDENT1*. This system amalgamated the databases of England, Wales and Scotland and by the end of 2006 the system included a palm print storage and searching facility for all three countries. By now, police forces had also acquired *Livescan*, an electronic means of capturing an arrestee's finger and palm impressions in a police station custody suite. Livescan removed the need for traditional ink and paper impressions (although a paper copy of the finger and palm impressions can be printed from IDENT1) and greatly improved the quality of fingerprints taken, as the Livescan unit automatically assesses the quality of the image while it is being captured.

In the USA, the FBI introduced an *Integrated Automated Fingerprint Identification System* (*IAFIS*) in 1999 to replace a largely manual searching process. As well as storing fingerprints, IAFIS also stores criminal histories, offender photographs, physical characteristics and so on that in the UK would be stored on the *Police National Computer* (*PNC*) database. Law enforcement agencies at all levels in the USA can submit searches to IAFIS, which is the largest biometric database in the world, holding over 70 million criminal subjects (Komarinski, 2005).

Problems with fingerprint evidence

By its nature, fingerprint evidence requires human interpretation, both in the initial searching and recovery of fingerprints at the crime scene and then in the comparison and identification of a fingerprint. There is the possibility that human error can occur, or that one or more of the examiners may neglect to discharge their responsibilities properly. If this occurs, there is the possibility that a fingerprint from a crime scene will be wrongly attributed to an individual; such misidentification has been borne out by recent cases in both North America and Europe. In Chapter 5 we will discuss a number of possible sources of error in fingerprint identification and other forensic disciplines.

In the USA in 2005, Congress mandated the *National Academy of Sciences* (*NAS*) to conduct a study of the state of forensic science in the country. The NAS published its report in 2009 and included a commentary on the lack of scientific method applied to many disciplines in forensic science, including fingerprints (viewed as expert-based) compared with laboratory-based disciplines such as DNA (Edwards and Gatsonis, 2009). We have seen earlier how the distribution of minutiae on a finger is often referred to as 'unique' and how a fingerprint examiner in the UK will, in their witness statement, often state that in their experience, no two fingerprint impressions have ever been found to be the same from two different people. The NAS report simply picked up on the way in which the validity of fingerprint evidence is generally understood and reported (Lawson, 2003; Cole, 2004; Haber and Haber, 2008). It noted that a way forward for fingerprint evidence is to accumulate data to identify the degree to which the distribution of fingerprint minutiae varies between individuals. With this data, fingerprint examiners could then attach confidence limits to their conclusions about whether a fingerprint from a crime scene could be associated with the finger impression of a particular person (what we have termed in this chapter an 'identification'). Thus, for fingerprint evidence at least, a probabilistic approach could be undertaken along the same lines as is currently employed for DNA evidence (Osterburg et al., 1977). This would at least update the pioneering work of Francis Galton, whose calculations are still referred to by fingerprint examiners well over 100 years after they were made. We will return to the NAS report and the implications for other evidence types in Chapter 8 when we consider some of the current issues facing forensic science.

In Boxes 2.12 and 2.13 we look at two separate instances of misidentification with fingerprint evidence in the UK; that is, when an incorrect association was made between a fingerprint recovered from a crime scene and the impression of a finger from a particular individual.

Box 2.12 Fingerprint misidentification I

In 2011, the conviction of Peter Smith for the murder of 71-year-old Hilda Owen was quashed by the Court of Appeal for England and Wales on the grounds that the fingerprint evidence in the original trial was unsafe. At that trial, Nottinghamshire Police fingerprint experts had agreed that a mark found in a blood-like substance on a door handle belonged to Smith's left forefinger impression. However, at the appeal, two former police fingerprint experts testified that the Nottinghamshire experts had confused ridges with furrows and had completely ignored a part of the image that excluded Smith as the donor of the fingerprint. The Court of Appeal commented that these fingerprint practices appeared to be at odds with modern forensic science and that 'there is plainly a need for the points that have arisen in this case to be the subject of wider examination'.

Analysis: This case highlights errors that arose by those making the identification (Nottinghamshire fingerprint experts) misinterpreting the image of the fingerprint from the door handle. How could this happen when, as we have seen in the UK, a fingerprint identification is judged to be reliable evidence based on independent checking by three separate examiners? In Chapter 5 we will examine error and bias in reasoning, and discuss some operational issues that may contribute to potential bias in the interpretation of forensic results.

Box 2.13 Fingerprint misidentification II

In January 1997, Marion Ross was stabbed to death at her home in Kilmarnock, Scotland. During the police investigation, the Scottish Criminal Records Office (SCRO) identified a thumb impression found on the bathroom door frame of the deceased's premises to a serving police officer, Shirley McKie. Subsequently, a fingerprint with the same minutiae as the deceased was found on a box in the home of David Asbury, who was tried for the murder of Marion Ross. At the trial, in which Asbury was convicted, McKie denied that the thumb impression was hers. However, in March 1998, McKie was arrested by the police force in which she was serving and charged with perjury. At her trial, the court rejected the SCRO evidence based on testimony from US experts and McKie was acquitted. The fingerprint evidence used to convict Asbury was also considered unsafe and his conviction was quashed. The ramifications of this led to a Parliamentary Inquiry and, in 2006, the SCRO and other Scottish Fingerprint Bureaux were reformed into a new Scottish Fingerprint Service. In 2008, a Public Inquiry commenced, which reported in 2011 that McKie did not leave the thumb impression on the door frame. Further, the inquiry found that fingerprint examiners are presently ill-equipped to reason through their conclusions, as they are accustomed to regarding those conclusions as a matter of certainty and are seldom challenged. The inquiry recommended that, in future, fingerprint examiners should discontinue reporting conclusions on identification or exclusion with a claim to 100% certainty; that is, they should give evidence of opinion, not fact.

Analysis: This case had far-reaching implications, not only for the Scottish Fingerprint Service but also for how a court should view fingerprint evidence. The implications of this and the need to place fingerprint evidence on a sound scientific basis were discussed earlier, particularly in respect to the NAS report of 2009. The 2008 Public Inquiry recommended that fingerprint examiners should 'discontinue reporting conclusions on identification or exclusion with a claim to 100% certainty', which means, essentially, that fingerprint evidence should be evidence of opinion rather than fact. This means that fingerprint evidence would become akin to how expert witnesses present other forms of forensic evidence; that is, their professional interpretation of how likely it is that an association can be made between two or more items that they have examined. This will be considered in more detail in Chapter 7 when we look at how forensic evidence is presented in court.

Other forms of identification evidence

For evidence to provide an overwhelming association to an individual, it must be long-lasting and, ideally, constant throughout a person's lifetime (such as DNA and fingerprints). There are, however, other forms of identification evidence that, from time to time, can be used to try to identify an individual. This might be to confirm their identity (such as to identify buried remains) or to link them to a crime scene (such as from CCTV images). In the former case, dental records are often used. While there is no UK national database of dental records, locating a possible dentist of the deceased and comparing their records with the dentition of a recovered body can lead to a positive identification. The alignment of teeth, extractions and repairs (such as fillings) can all enable a forensic *odontologist* to make this identification. This method is of great use when remains are badly decomposed, as the teeth set in the jaws provide a long-lasting means of identification. In a similar fashion to teeth, identification may also be made from the anatomical structure of the deceased. Old injuries to bones, surgical implants (such as a replacement hip) or amputations can be used, along with medical records, to aid in identification. Facial reconstruction may also be used to build up in layers the appearance of facial features from a bare skull for comparison with a photograph of the deceased (although this technique is not considered sufficient for an identification on its own).

Identification of an individual at a crime scene with witness evidence or CCTV images can be assisted by distinguishing features on the suspect such as tattoos and scars and also by facial features, which have been used to map CCTV images to a photograph of the suspect.

Summary

In this chapter we have examined identification evidence that provides the police not only with evidence to put to a suspect, but also the ability to identify the perpetrator. This identification evidence is primarily derived from fingerprints or DNA, as both of these evidence types provide good discrimination between individuals and remain unchanged throughout a person's life. Today, both of these evidence types benefit from computer databases containing fingerprint and DNA records of known offenders, which enable the police to conduct a speculative search of evidence recovered from a crime scene to try to identify the donor. The setting up of these databases has, in some jurisdictions, required changes to the law to enable samples to be taken and retained from offenders, which highlights the importance of multidisciplinary discussions of these evidence types and the uses of this information. We have also considered where, and in what form, DNA evidence is likely to be found at the crime scene and also the standard methods of enhancing and visualising a fingerprint on a variety of surfaces. Other forms of identification evidence, such as dental records, may also be used to provide evidence of a person's identity to the police. In the next chapter we will consider an alternative to identification evidence, comparison evidence.

Study questions

1 We have looked at some of the problems with both DNA and fingerprints as identification evidence and have considered how DNA evidence can provide an adventitious or contaminated 'match' and how fingerprints can be incorrectly matched through human error. Consider what other factors associated with DNA or fingerprint evidence might require interpretation for the courts by a forensic scientist.

2 We have looked at DNA specimen types and seen how items such as cigarette ends and drink cans or bottles provide a good source of DNA of the person smoking the cigarette or drinking from the can or bottle. Items such as these provide what has been termed mobile DNA, as the items themselves are easily moved between locations. Consider how DNA from mobile items might be used by an offender to implicate an innocent person.

3

COMPARISON EVIDENCE

Forensic comparison evidence provides what many people think of as traditional forensic science – the comparison of two items to establish a connection or association between them, such as comparing two hairs or fibres, or a footwear impression with the underside of a shoe. When one of these items was recovered from a suspect and the other from a crime scene, then the association has the ability to link the suspect to the crime scene. This can be expressed in a basic principle of forensic science formulated by Dr Edmond Locard, a pioneering French forensic scientist. In essence, *Locard's Exchange Principle* states that the offender will bring something into the crime scene and leave with something from the crime scene (Saferstein, 2014). Therefore, in theory at least, every contact between an offender and the crime scene should result in something being left behind by the offender at the scene and something being taken away from the scene by the offender. This principle is often seen expressed as 'every contact leaves a trace' (Kind and Overman, 1972, p. 23), which is more of an aphorism, or aspiration, rather than a validated scientific statement or fact. Of course, this principle also holds true for identification evidence, discussed in Chapter 2 (such as fingerprints or DNA). However, as we saw in Chapter 1, the difference between identification and comparison evidence as defined in this book is that the latter requires the police to find a suspect in order to conduct comparisons. Furthermore, this suspect must yield some form of evidence (such as hair, fibres, glass and so on) in order for a comparison to be made with similar evidence types recovered from the crime scene. Identification evidence provides the police not only with the evidence (such as a fingerprint) but also the identity of the person of interest.

Therefore, while the collection of evidence for comparison starts at the crime scene, it also requires more traditional police work to identify a potential offender.

Comparison evidence differs in another way from identification evidence in that it is more transient. We have seen how both DNA and fingerprints (and other forms of identification evidence such as surgical implants or tattoos) are either long-lasting or constant throughout a person's life, whereas typical comparison evidence is subject to change. Consider a footwear impression recovered from a crime scene being compared with the footwear of the suspect. Not only will the suspect have many pairs of shoes during their lifetime, the features of the suspect's footwear that enable identification to crime scene impressions will also change. Other forms of comparison evidence (such as glass or fibres) are liable to be lost or shed quickly from a suspect's clothing (lack of retention), so timely apprehension of the suspect is required in order for comparison evidence to be meaningful.

Is comparison evidence useful to forensic science?

Despite these difficulties that lead to comparison evidence relying more on traditional police methods to produce a suspect and hence a forensic comparison, this kind of evidence is very useful in assisting with the detection of crime. The nature of the evidence (such as glass fragments or soil samples) means that the items being compared often do not have a very specific association and may be very common (such as modern float glass). This means that comparison evidence is generally interpreted by the forensic scientist in terms of the strength of evidence to support the proposition of the prosecution, taking into account the context under which the evidence was recovered (for example, fragments of glass recovered from a suspect's clothing). We will see in Chapter 5 how Bayes' theorem and conditional probabilities are used by scientists to interpret findings and then how conclusions from these findings are communicated to a jury during court testimony. In forensic terms, the proposition of the prosecution might be that the suspect was present at the crime scene when the window glass was being broken. Finding glass on the suspect's clothing consistent with glass recovered from the crime scene would not necessarily provide strong evidence, if the glass was a commonly encountered kind. However, the location of the glass on the suspect may add to the significance of the evidence and produce moderate evidence to support the prosecution's proposition. In a circumstance such as this, glass fragments found on the suspect's upper clothing or head hair would have more evidential value than glass found (say) embedded in the sole of their footwear. Thus, the frequency of occurrence and location of evidence both contribute to the strength of any comparison reported by the forensic scientist. The relevance of terms such as 'moderate' or 'strong' evidence will be discussed in more detail in Chapter 5. If a comparison shows that a sample recovered from the suspect is different to that recovered from the crime scene, then this would be seen as not supporting the prosecution's proposition. Furthermore, with some comparison evidence types such as hair, the suspect's hair being different to that recovered from (say) a mask worn during a bank robbery would be seen as a positive exclusion.

Comparison evidence recovered from the crime scene can assist the police in establishing the identity of the offender in order that a comparison can then be made. For example, if the make and model of footwear can be identified from the sole pattern impression left at the crime scene, then the police can be advised of the appearance of the footwear the offender would have been wearing. Similarly, ginger hair found in a bank robber's mask will inform the police of the hair colour of their suspect.

Comparison evidence may also be used to link crimes to the same offender or to the same instrument or weapon used during the crime without knowing the identity of the offender. For example, the same footwear impression (with sufficient detail) found at different crime scenes can be used to link these crimes to the same offender. Similarly, spent ammunition casings found at different crime scenes but fired from the same weapon can link these crimes. Many comparison evidence types (such as those described in this chapter) are commonly encountered, whereas others, such as pollen (studied through what is known as palynology; Morgan et al., 2014) would be employed less frequently. Typically, pollen samples recovered from a body would be compared with pollen samples of known species to seek to identify a location (and hence potential crime scene) that the deceased had visited.

This chapter describes commonly encountered types of comparison evidence. However, this is not an exhaustive list and, in principle, any scientific discipline can have a forensic context, for example forensic geoscience (Morgan et al., 2010) or forensic botany (Hall and Byrd, 2012).

Ballistics and firearms

Types of firearm and ammunition

Firearms are generally classified by how they are used (Di Maio, 1999). For example, handguns such as revolvers and pistols are designed to be used with one hand. Long guns, such as rifles and shotguns, are used with two hands and are stabilised when being fired, often against the shoulder. Both of these categories of firearms come in many different sizes that are referred to as the *calibre* of the weapon, with calibre referring to the approximate internal diameter of the barrel of the firearm (such as a 0.22 inch or 9 mm calibre). For shotguns, it is more common to refer to the *bore* or *gauge* of the shotgun (such as 12-gauge), the bore being determined by the weight of a solid sphere of lead that will just pass along the inside of the barrel, expressed as a fraction of a pound (approximately 0.5 kg) in weight. The barrels of many hand guns and rifles (but not shotguns) are *rifled*. This is a process in which a series of helical grooves are cut into the inside wall of the barrel and is intended to impart spin to the bullet projectile as it makes its way down the barrel. This spinning continues once the bullet has left the barrel and, through the conservation of angular momentum, improves the accuracy of the bullet in reaching its intended target. With the absence of rifling, shotguns are known as *smooth-bore* weapons.

Before firing, the bullet forms part of the *cartridge*, which is the ammunition that is used in a firearm to produce a bullet projectile. The cartridge includes the cartridge case, which contains the main *propellant* that undergoes a chemical reaction during the firing process, resulting in the rapid production of gaseous products that force the bullet out of the cartridge case and along the barrel of the firearm. The propellant is ignited by a *primer*, which itself is ignited when the *firing pin* of the weapon strikes the *primer cup* containing the primer (see Figure 3.1). Usually the bullet will be recovered from the crime scene, either embedded in a solid object (such as a door or wall) or inside the victim's body. In addition, as most firearms are *self-loading*, spent cartridge cases are also recovered at the crime scene (see Box 3.1). Self-loading means that the firearm automatically uses some of the energy of the firing process to eject the cartridge case that has just been fired and to reload a live cartridge ready for the next discharge. Shotguns, which are not rifled and are designed to fire a quantity of small metal pellets or shot (known as *birdshot* or *buckshot* depending on the size of the pellets), also eject

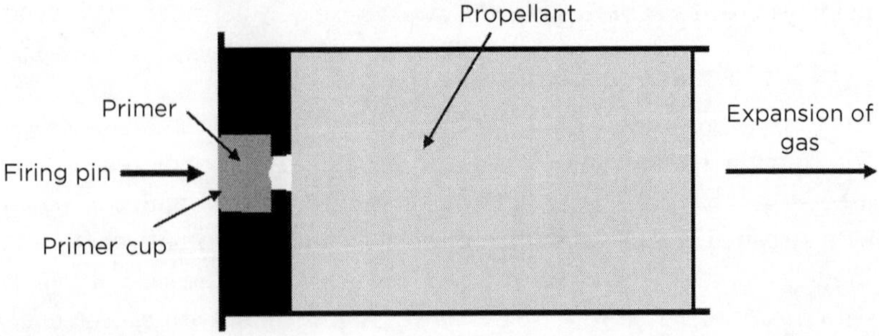

Figure 3.1 Ignition of a centre-fire cartridge. The propellant is ignited by a primer, which itself is ignited when the firing pin of the weapon strikes the primer cup containing the primer.

wadding, which in the cartridge forms a physical barrier between the propellant and the shot. The wadding is normally made of plastic, but other materials (such as felt) are also used.

Ballistic examination at the crime scene

An examination of the crime scene at which a firearm has been discharged can reveal important information about the circumstances of the offence. From the behaviour and trajectory of the bullet after it leaves the firearm, a forensic scientist can endeavour to reconstruct the scene at the time the firearm was discharged. For example, from the angle at which one or more bullets have entered a solid object (such as a wall), the trajectories can be traced back to locate a common area of origin; that is, the approximate position of the shooter. The scientist would need to take into account the effects of gravity and air resistance on the bullet after leaving the barrel and a number of models exist to assist in the accurate calculation of the trajectory (Heard, 2008). In addition, a bullet may have ricocheted off one surface before coming to rest on another. The examination of evidence from the crime scene in this way is known as *external ballistics*; that is, the examination of the bullet in flight.

On impact, a bullet is likely to deform, especially if the impact is on a solid target. An examination of the deformation can yield information about the nature of the surface struck by the bullet. In addition, an examination of the entry (and exit) holes made by the bullet can provide information about which hole is which and thus assist in determining the trajectory of the bullet and position of the shooter. If the target is living, then this behaviour of the bullet is sometimes referred to as its *stopping power* and an examination of these entry and exit wounds will also provide information about the trajectory of the bullet. If the firearm was a shotgun, then the spread of pellets can be used to estimate the *range*; that is, the distance from the end of the barrel (known as the *muzzle*) to the target. The forensic scientist can conduct a series of experiments with a similar shotgun to establish the spread of pellets as the range increases. When the range is small, there may also be evidence of bruising from the wadding and blackening from unburned propellant. For a small range there may also be charring from the flash emanating from the muzzle. This examination of the behaviour of the bullet or shot after impact on a target is known as *terminal ballistics*.

Linking a firearm to the crime scene

While the above techniques can provide the police with useful information and intelligence about the circumstances of the offence and the type of firearm used, an examination of a recovered firearm or recovered bullets and cartridge casings can associate a weapon to a particular offence and also can associate offences together. This examination relies on the specific pattern of markings imparted to a bullet and cartridge case by the firearm during the firing process and is known as *internal ballistics*. As the bullet travels down the barrel of a rifled weapon, the action of the rifling causes *striation marks* along the side of the bullet. These striation marks can give an indication of the handedness of the rifling grooves in the barrel (left or right) and it is often possible to associate a fired bullet to the firearm that fired it based on these striation marks. To achieve this, the weapon needs to be recovered soon after the suspected firing was made, as striation marks imparted to a bullet change as the barrel of the firearm wears (remember that earlier we mentioned that comparison evidence is subject to change). Obviously, an easier test to perform first is to check that the firearm is capable of firing a cartridge of the same calibre as that recovered from the crime scene.

If it is necessary to fire the suspect weapon, then it is important that the process to slow down and capture the bullet discharged during the test firing does not affect the pattern of striation marks on it. To achieve this, bullets from test firings are made into a tank of water. To compare striation marks on a bullet recovered from the crime scene with one from a test-firing of the suspect weapon, a *comparison microscope* is used. This is an instrument that has two identical stages under which both bullets can be placed (one bullet per stage). Both bullets can be viewed at the same time, side by side, and the relative orientation of the bullets adjusted to see if an association can be made between the patterns of striation marks on both. Such marks can provide a very specific association between the bullets and determine whether a suspect weapon fired a particular bullet recovered from the crime scene. We will see later in this chapter how a comparison microscope can have application to other evidence types.

In addition to bullets, cartridge casings also have a specific pattern of marks, known as *impressed action* marks. These occur during the loading, firing and ejection process of the cartridge casing. Loading a live cartridge into the chamber of the firearm causes *chambering marks* on the side of the cartridge case, while the firing action (pulling the trigger) causes the weapon's firing pin to strike the primer cup of the cartridge, igniting the primer but also leaving an impression of its tip on the primer cup. Depending on the firearm, the firing pin may strike either the centre (*centre fire*) or rim (*rim fire*) of the cartridge case. As the propellant expands in the cartridge case, the latter is forced backwards towards the end of the chamber furthest from the muzzle (known as the *breech*), resulting in *breech marks*, which are negative impressions of any marks present on the face of the breech. After firing and depending on whether the weapon is self-loading, there may be marks on the cartridge casing from the extraction and ejection of the spent casing. *Extraction marks* are formed by the pulling from the chamber of the casing by an *extractor claw*, which engages with the *extractor groove* of the cartridge (Figure 3.2).

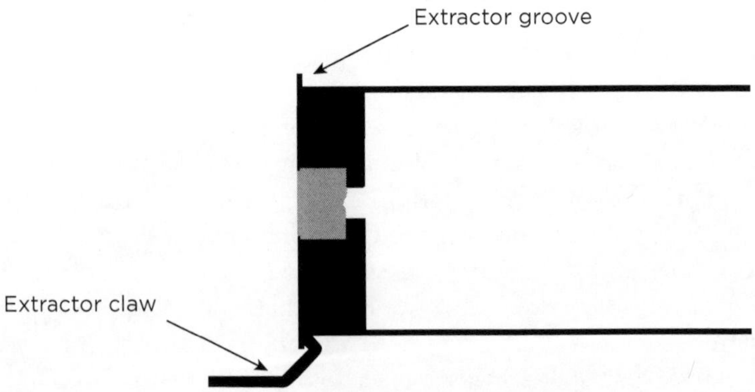

Figure 3.2 Extraction marks are formed by an extractor claw engaging with the extractor groove of the cartridge and pulling the casing from the chamber.

The ejection of the casing can produce further chambering marks. All of these features can be examined under a comparison microscope, comparing a test-fired cartridge casing with one recovered from a crime scene. Like bullet striation marks, they have the potential to provide a very specific association between two casings and hence identify the firearm used at a crime scene.

Box 3.1 The St Valentine's Day massacre

On 14 February 1929, members of Al Capone's gang murdered seven members of the gang of his rival, George 'Bugs' Moran, in Chicago, USA. The bullets and shell casings recovered from the crime scene were examined by Calvin Goddard, widely regarded as a pioneer in establishing ballistics as a forensic discipline. Goddard was able to say what weapons the offenders had used. Importantly, he was able to demonstrate that two submachine guns recovered from the home of a suspect had been used in the murders by finding an association between recovered casings and those test-fired from the weapons.

Analysis: This famous case illustrates that spent casings recovered from a scene where a weapon has been discharged are important physical evidence. Not only, as in this case, can those casings be associated with a weapon, the casings may also provide fingerprint or DNA evidence from those who have handled the casings prior to their being loaded into the weapon. Such physical evidence may sometimes be the only physical evidence to be recovered from a crime scene where no physical contact has taken place between the offender and the victim. Recent research has shown how technology can be developed to improve the recovery of both DNA and fingerprints from metals subject to environmental extremes, such as spent shell casings or fragments of improvised explosive devices (Bille et al., 2009; Bond, 2013; Bond and Brady, 2013).

Firearms databases

In view of the ability for comparisons to be made between bullets or cartridge casings recovered from crime scenes with those fired from known weapons, the storage, retrieval and searching of marks produced during the loading, firing and ejection process are now undertaken on computer systems using an *Integrated Ballistics Identification System* (*IBIS*). In the UK, the *National Ballistics Intelligence Service* (*NABIS*) was set up in 2008 and uses IBIS to acquire and search markings of spent bullets and cartridge casings. In the USA, the equivalent system is known as the *National Integrated Ballistic Information Network* (*NIBIN*). Clearly, as we have already seen with fingerprint and DNA databases, computer storage enables more rapid searching of a greater quantity of data (in this case ballistic marks) than would be possible with manual systems.

Gunshot residue

When a weapon is fired, not only does the expanding gas from the propellant force the bullet from the barrel, secondary emissions occur of small particles of combusted and unburned primer and propellant, as well as material from the firearm itself. These secondary emissions are known as *gunshot residue* (*GSR*) and they occur in weapons that fire either shot or bullets (Schwoeble and Exline, 2000; Dalby et al., 2010). The combustion of both the primer and the propellant produces an extremely high temperature and pressure within the barrel of the weapon, vapourising a mix of unburned and partially burned propellant, the combustion products of the propellant and primer, stray particles from the grease and lubricant used in the firearm, and metals from the projectile, cartridge and weapon itself. This vapour then escapes from the barrel behind the fired projectile and any areas of the firearm that are not airtight.

The organic compounds released mainly originate from the propellant and lubricants used in the weapon, and are often found as unburned or partially burned particles. Inorganic compounds, which are of particular importance in identifying GSR, are generally particulate matter stemming from the primer, propellant, projectile, cartridge case and weapon barrel. The most common examples of organic GSR are nitrocellulose, nitroglycerine and nitroguanidine. Common inorganic GSR are the elements antimony, barium and lead. If found at high enough levels, using a *scanning electron microscope* to identify and quantify them (Reid et al., 2010), identification of GSR can be used to show that an individual has been in close proximity to a weapon when it was being discharged. As well as quantity, the persistence of GSR, for example on skin and clothing, is a consideration for the scientist when interpreting the evidential value of recovered GSR (Rosenburg and Dockery, 2008; Elspeth & McVicar, 2011; see Boxes 3.2 and 6.3). GSR and other particulate evidence types, which are described in the following sections, are often referred to as *trace evidence* (Gallop and Stockdale, 1998; Houck, 2013).

Box 3.2 A death involving GSR and terminal ballistics

In February 1998, the Sheriff's Office in Montgomery, Ohio, USA received a call from Stephen James Hawn, who reported that his girlfriend, Sue Jack, had just committed suicide by shooting herself at the home they shared. When police arrived, they found Hawn with blood on his clothes and hands. The deceased had a single gunshot wound to the chest. A revolver was found on the floor close by. Hawn stated that he was in bed when he heard the single shot and found the deceased lying on the floor. The post-mortem examination showed that Jack died of a single gunshot wound to the chest. There was no evidence of GSR on Jack's clothing, on her skin around the wound or inside the wound itself, which would have been consistent with the weapon being fired at close range. There was also no evidence of burning, singeing or blackening on Jack's clothing or skin around the wound. Based on test-firing of the weapon and an examination of the deceased's clothing, a firearms expert concluded that the gun was likely to have been nearly 2 metres away when it was fired into Jack's chest. Hawn was convicted of Jack's murder.

Analysis: This is an example of how the absence of GSR can be used in evidence by the prosecution to attempt to refute the version of events given by a suspect. Clearly, factors such as elapsed time since the incident and whether any attempt has been made to wash or clean clothing need to be taken into account by the scientist when interpreting their findings to a jury. In this case, the source of recovered GSR would be the body and clothing of the deceased victim, so these factors are less likely than, for example, looking for GSR on the clothing of a suspect or other live person who is moving around and potentially shedding GSR from their skin and clothing (see also Box 6.3).

Marks and impressions

Footwear impressions

While wearing protective clothing such as gloves or a mask will inhibit the leaving of fingerprints and DNA at a crime scene, it is much more difficult not to leave impressions of footwear. Despite Locard's Exchange Principle, sometimes the trace evidence is difficult for the CSI to find and recover. Footwear impressions are found at many crime scenes and, as such, are used extensively in forensic science to link crime scenes or to link a suspect to a crime scene (Bodziak, 2000). An impression can be defined as the retention of the characteristics of an item by another object. In the case of footwear, a distinction is made between two-dimensional and three-dimensional impressions, which are then further categorised depending on whether material is deposited or removed from the surface on which the impression is made.

Two-dimensional footwear impressions occur when the underside of a shoe comes into contact with a hard, flat surface and deposits material (such as blood, dust or mud) that was adhering to the underside of the shoe. These are known as *positive* impressions. Conversely, *negative* impressions result from the sole of the shoe removing material from the surface, and often occur on dust-covered surfaces (Naples and Miller, 2004). We have already seen analogous categories for fingerprints, which could be found as plastic (negative), visible (positive or negative) or latent impressions. For footwear impressions, latent would refer to impressions that are invisible to the naked eye, such as in dust.

For two-dimensional footwear impressions, visible light can be shone obliquely onto the surface of interest, causing a shadow produced by the deposits left behind and hence giving improved contrast and visibility. Impressions left in blood can be enhanced by the application of chemical techniques that react with chemicals in the blood (such as ninhydrin with amino acids, as we have already seen for fingerprints in Chapter 2). In addition to photographing the enhanced contrast between the footwear impression and the background, two-dimensional impressions in a substance (such as dust) that is not strongly adhering to the floor may be recovered from the crime scene by the use of a *gelatine lifter*. This is a colourless, black or white tacky gelatine layer that is applied over the impression, which, after rolling flat to remove any air pockets, is carefully lifted so that deposits (retaining an impression of the underside of the footwear) stick to the gelatine layer. Two-dimensional footwear impressions may be searched for speculatively by the use of an *electrostatic lifting apparatus* (*ESLA*). This can be used on a variety of surfaces such as linoleum, carpet and car body panels. Dust particles on the floor are attracted by an electrostatic charge onto a stretched polyester film, commonly known as *Mylar*, of varying length to suit the area being examined. With all footwear impression photography or recovery, the orientation of the impression (that is, the direction in which the person was walking) is also recorded.

Three-dimensional footwear impressions differ in that they are formed by the footwear being impressed into a soft material, such as snow, soil or sand. Depending on the nature of the surface material, these impressions can either be temporary (in snow) or permanent (in wet cement). To record and enhance three-dimensional impressions, casts are made using a casting material that is suitable for the material in which the impression was made. Plaster of Paris, silicon and wax are commonly used, and once set they provide an accurate representation of the original three-dimensional impression (Naples and Miller, 2004). Recently, the less invasive method of recording three-dimensional impressions using three-dimensional scanning techniques is showing increasing potential, in which an impression is scanned to give a series of data points, which can be digitally recreated into a three-dimensional image (Andalo et al., 2011).

Increasing complexity in the patterns of training shoes, which account for the largest section of the footwear market, means that a significant amount of information can be gathered from footwear impressions recovered from a crime scene. In the UK, there is now a *National Footwear Reference Collection* (*NFRC*), which provides a nationally agreed method of classifying footwear underside pattern types and also a reference collection of patterns. Patterns recovered from the crime scene can be encoded and searched against the reference collection and, if identified, can provide investigators with an image of the make and model (and sometimes size) of footwear that is being sought. This information can give an indication of how rare the footwear is in the population. For example, the average male shoe size in the UK is 9, meaning that shoe sizes far outside this range are likely to be less common. Small changes of the sole pattern over time are also characteristic of different walking patterns, and have been shown to be predictive of the stature of the individual (Krishan, 2008). Further information can be gained from three-dimensional impressions by analysing the material adhering to the surface of the cast, which represents the preservation of the moment the impression was made. Analysis of the interface between the cast and the soil in three-dimensional earth impressions has been shown to allow reconstruction of different locations to which a suspect had been prior to the crime scene. This has been achieved through studying pollen count, carbon-to-nitrogen ratios of water residue and fibre analysis (Bull et al., 2006).

However, more significant comparisons are achieved through recovering footwear from a suspect, possibly as a result of identifying the make and model of footwear from the crime scene impression. By comparing small details of wear and damage, the degree of individuality of the underside of the footwear can be inferred, as these minute changes occur randomly and hence are unlikely to be repeated exactly in more than one shoe. As wear is continuous, this limits the time after a crime has been committed that a useful comparison between a crime scene impression and a recovered item of footwear can be made (Napier, 2009).

Box 3.3 Fingerprints and footwear impressions left by the offender

In November 2005, the body of Catherine Woods was found in her New York apartment by her roommate David Haughn. Catherine had wounds to her throat. Police investigators found a bloody footwear impression near to the body, and two further bloody footwear impressions (similar to the impression near the body) on Catherine's bed and on the back of the shirt she was wearing. They also found a bloody fingerprint on a wall inside the apartment. There was no sign of forced entry to the apartment. This led police to suspect that the offender was someone known to Catherine whom she had willingly let in. Their attention focused on Paul Cortez, who had been having a relationship with Catherine for some time. The police found that the size of the footwear impressions recovered was the same as the size of shoe worn by Cortez. Following press reports of the murder, a woman came forward and told police that she had been assaulted by Cortez some time earlier. This enabled police to arrest Cortez and thereby obtain a set of his fingerprints for comparison with the one found in the apartment. The crime scene fingerprint was deemed to be identical with one of Cortez's fingerprints.

Analysis: Had this offence occurred in the UK, legislation (PACE) would have enabled the police to arrest Cortez on suspicion of murder if he had not voluntarily given his fingerprints for elimination against the fingerprint found at the crime scene (see Chapter 1). A court order would also have allowed UK police to search Cortez's home and seize any footwear for comparison against the footwear impressions found at the crime scene. If Cortez's other victim had not come forward, would he ever have been charged with this offence? Compare this variation in UK and US law with that described in Box 2.5. Another important issue in this case is that Cortez did not contest that the fingerprint impression was his. Rather, the issue was when the fingerprint had been deposited in the apartment (i.e. some time before the murder) and whether this could be determined by any chemical or visual analysis (Midkiff, 1993; De Alcaraz-Fossoul et al., 2013). Ultimately, in this and all cases, the jury must decide the most likely explanation for the occurrence of the evidence. Clearly, the jury will give weight to the scientific interpretation of the evidential value (see Chapter 5 for a more detailed explanation of how this is given to a jury). In this case, the jury found Cortez guilty of second-degree murder.

Tyre impressions

Vehicles involved in crime may leave impressions from their tyres at the crime scene in a similar fashion to the criminal leaving footwear impressions. Tyre marks found at the crime scene may be categorised in the same way as footwear impressions; that is, as plastic, visible and latent. For tyre impressions, plastic impressions are generally three dimensional given the weight of the vehicle pressing on a soft material (e.g. soil, snow etc.). Tyre impressions may be recorded and recovered in the same way as footwear impressions. Like footwear, tyre tread patterns come in many shapes and sizes and a tyre impression recovered from the crime scene, if identified, can give investigators information about the makes and models of vehicle that could have that type of tyre fitted. Furthermore, like footwear impressions, tyre impressions can provide time-limited individual wear and damage features that can be used to link a particular tyre (and hence a particular vehicle) to the crime scene (McDonald, 1993).

Tool impressions

During the commission of a crime in which force is required to gain entry to premises or a vehicle, it is common for the offender to use a tool to assist them. The tools that might be used are many and varied, but generally can be classified into two broad categories: those used as cutting instruments (such as bolt cutters, drills, knives, axes) and those used as levering instruments (such as jemmies, screwdrivers, chisels, crowbars).

Levering instruments might typically be used to lever open a window or to force a lock. After photography, any impressions may be recovered by casting with a silicone rubber or dental putty material, in a similar fashion to casting three-dimensional footwear impressions, albeit the area of the cast is much smaller. This technique is particularly effective when the tool has been used to force a softwood window frame, which easily 'gives' when force from the tool is applied to it. Such cast impressions can give the general size and shape of the tool and, in the absence of a suspect tool, can be used to link offences from the wear and damage features apparent in the cast. Clearly, if a suspect tool is available, then a comparison can be made using a comparison microscope and a cast from the suspect tool, in a similar fashion to that described for ballistics (Chumbley et al., 2010). Also similarly to other types of impression discussed above, continuous wear of a tool will limit the time after a crime has been committed that a useful comparison between a crime scene impression and a recovered tool can be made. Clearly, the less use a tool has, the longer can be the elapsed time between the crime being committed and the recovery of the tool.

Box 3.4 Tool impressions from a murder

In August 1981, Leah Rosenthal was reported to the police as missing. She had last been seen visiting her son Danny, in London, UK, where she went to ask him about his father Milton (her ex-husband) who had been reported missing in France. A police search of Danny Rosenthal's home revealed a hacksaw with a missing blade, which had traces of human blood and fragments of bone on the handle. In France, police found the dismembered body of Milton Rosenthal buried in a wooded area not far from his home. A search of Milton's home in France revealed, among other evidence, a hacksaw blade. A forensic tool mark examiner was able to show that tool impressions on Milton's bones were consistent with the teeth of the hacksaw blade found in his home in France. It was suspected that Leah Rosenthal was probably killed in a similar manner; however, her body has never been found despite a sea, air and land search at the time of her disappearance. Danny Rosenthal was convicted of double murder.

Analysis: Despite the fact that Leah's body has never been recovered, Danny Rosenthal was convicted of her murder as well as Milton's. In reaching this decision, no doubt the jury took note of the forensic evidence related to the association between the tool impressions on Milton's bones and the teeth of the hacksaw blade, as well as the evidence of similar fact; that is, that both Milton and Leah just disappeared. To convince a jury that someone is dead even without a body, the police will demonstrate that there is no evidence of that person's continued existence. This is done through an examination of the lack of use of their bank account, credit cards and so on.

Cutting instruments can be used to cut through material such as a chain-link fence or a padlock. In these cases, the CSI would recover the cut ends of the material from the crime scene. If a suspect tool is available, then a series of *test cuts* would be made on similar wire or material and the crime scene and test cuts compared under a comparison microscope. If the cutting tool is subjected to normal use, the cutting edge undergoes wear and damage, producing specific features on the cutting edge that are then transferred to the cut end of the wire (Chumbley et al., 2010).

Box 3.5 Bite marks used as evidence

One of the most famous cases involving bite mark evidence concerns the murder of two females in Florida, USA in 1978. Some weeks later an escaped fugitive, Ted Bundy, was re-arrested in Florida. As a result of other evidence, Bundy was charged with the murders. At the trial, evidence related to a bite mark on one of the victims was presented. It was demonstrated to the court that the bite mark impression on the victim was consistent with the outline of Bundy's front teeth.

Analysis: The bite mark evidence assisted in Bundy's conviction and he was eventually executed in 1989. Before his execution, Bundy indicated that he had murdered 30–40 women in several states during the decade prior to the Florida murders. Although described here under comparison evidence, bite mark evidence might also arguably be included under identification evidence in Chapter 2; that is, an evidence type where the characteristics of identification are less subject to change over time (Mohan et al., 2012; Kaur et al., 2012).

Mechanical fit

A final category in marks and impressions is what is generally referred to as *mechanical fit* or *physical fit*. This means proving an association between two items by showing that at one time they were joined together as one item and have subsequently been separated (Klein et al., 2000). A common example of the use of mechanical fit by a forensic scientist is with drugs wraps. These are small pieces of paper or Cling-film™ used to wrap individual 'deals' of a solid drug. By examining the torn or cut edge of a wrap with a larger piece of paper or a roll of Cling-film, the forensic scientist may be able to show that the pattern of cuts or tears is very similar between the two pieces. Another example would be a piece of broken wing mirror from a vehicle, found at the side of the road next to the victim of a hit and run where the driver of the vehicle did not stop. After identifying a suspect vehicle, the forensic scientist may be able to fit the broken piece of wing mirror back to that remaining on the vehicle. Because the break line is generated randomly or along a weak point of the wing mirror, the scientist may be able to say that there is extremely strong evidence to suggest that the two items were joined together at one time. In Chapter 5 we will consider how a statement such as 'extremely strong evidence' by the scientist can be related quantitatively to the likelihood of (in this example) the two items having originally been joined together.

Box 3.6 A mechanical fit from wood

In March 1932, the 20-month-old son of the famous US aviator Charles Lindbergh was snatched from his second-floor room in the family home. A homemade ladder used to gain access to the premises was found at the scene. Arthur Koehler, a wood anatomist from Wisconsin, was asked by the FBI to examine the ladder. Koehler was able to determine the different woods used to make the ladder as well as physical marks left by tools during its construction. In May, the baby's body was found near to the Lindberghs' home. He had been killed on the night of the kidnapping. In 1934, police arrested Bruno Hauptmann as a suspect for the kidnapping/murder when he was apprehended spending some of the ransom money that the Lindberghs had paid. A search of his premises yielded two tools that 'matched' the marks identified by Koehler, as well as nails similar to those used in the ladder's construction. Police also discovered a floorboard in Hauptmann's attic that had been partially sawn off. Koehler demonstrated that the ladder rail and the remaining part of the floorboard had once been one piece of wood. Hauptmann was convicted of, and executed for, the kidnapping.

Analysis: In court, the defence argued against Koehler being admitted as an expert witness, stating that wood anatomy was not a science 'in a class with handwriting experts, with fingerprint experts or with ballistic experts'. These arguments were overruled by the judge and the wood evidence was one of the most incriminating parts of the prosecution's case against Hauptmann. This case demonstrates that the first time a scientific method is introduced in court, there needs to be a sound basis for the underlying science and interpretation of evidence, to avoid, as in this case, the defence being able to argue that the work of Koehler and wood anatomy was not a science. This issue of the scientific basis and admissibility of forensic evidence will be discussed in more detail in Chapter 7.

Fibres, glass and other trace evidence

Fibres

Fibres originate from a variety of natural and man-made sources, are ever present in the world around us and often readily shed from clothing, upholstery and so on. This means that fibres can be very easily transferred between objects simply by contact (Locard's Exchange Principle). As a consequence, fibres may be recovered at the crime scene on many objects such as weapons, clothing, footwear and furniture. The ease with which fibres are both shed and transferred can make their evidential value problematic to interpret and the forensic scientist will be looking for unusual characteristics (such as composition or colour) as well as ease of shedding to aid in the interpretation of the significance of fibre evidence (Roberts et al., 2012). At the crime scene or in the laboratory, fibres may be recovered for analysis by repeatedly placing the sticky side of low-tack adhesive tape onto the item of interest (such as clothing or an upholstered chair). On items with their own population of fibres (such as clothing), a reference sample will also be required so that fibres originating from the item can be eliminated (De Wael et al., 2008). Large items (such as bedding) can be recovered from the crime scene by folding them before packaging.

Fibres can be categorised as either natural or man-made. Natural fibres comprise material that exists naturally and is then processed for use in fabrics, while man-made fibres can be entirely synthetic (such as polyester and nylon) or derived from plant cellulose (such as Rayon™) and produced by extrusion. Natural fibres can be derived from animals (such as wool or silk) or from plants (such as cotton, flax and jute).

Consider the scenario in which a victim has been attacked in the street by an unknown offender. A struggle ensued and the victim's outer clothing was seized by the police for forensic analysis. The victim's sweater was examined for fibres and a sample recovered by taping. The scientist also obtained a reference sample of fibres originating from the garment and examined these fibres to see whether they were different from any fibres recovered from the garment (Cook and Wilson, 1986). Several fibres were identified as being different to those originating from the garment and, among them, a group appeared similar to each other. Using a range of analysis techniques that we will now consider, the scientist would be trying to identify the type of fibre, the sorts of garment in which it might be used and how easily it would be shed and then retained. Even if a suspect has not been identified, this information can provide valuable intelligence to the police to assist in identifying a suspect. Depending on the frequency of occurrence of this group of fibres in garment manufacture, this intelligence might include, for example, the colour and design of the garment, retail outlets where it could be purchased, how long the garment has been manufactured and so on. Once a suspect has been identified, the scientist may be able to produce comparison evidence between the fibres recovered from the victim's sweater and clothing from the suspect.

A range of techniques can be employed both to identify a type of fibre (such as polyester or acrylic) and to link fibres together from a crime scene and suspect. For the former, it is common to commence with visible or ultraviolet light microscopy, which enables the morphology (form and structure) of the fibre (such as its thickness) and optical properties to be determined. These may both be considered in order to determine the type of fibre. The optical properties of fibres are usually examined using *polarised light microscopy*, in which the orientation of the light waves striking the fibre is restricted.

To link fibres together, a comparison microscope can be employed together with a further examination of the optical properties of both the crime scene and suspect fibres. These further optical properties relate to subjecting both fibres to varying wavelengths of radiation, principally ultraviolet. Different materials will absorb radiation from different parts of the electromagnetic spectrum, with the result that by quantifying the absorption at a particular wavelength, the type of fibre can be determined, a procedure known as *spectrophotometry*. Although these are destructive, information about dye used to colour a fibre may be obtained from *chromatographic techniques* (Carey et al., 2013) such as *thin layer chromatography*, in which liquid samples of the dye separate into different colours when placed on a sheet (such as glass) that has been coated with an adsorbent material that enables dye molecules to adhere to it (such as silica gel).

Box 3.7 The disappearance of Leanne Tiernan

In 2001 the body of 16-year-old Leanne Tiernan was discovered in a shallow grave in woods in West Yorkshire, UK. There was a plastic bag over her head, held in place with a dog's collar, also a scarf and cable tie around her neck and more cables ties around her wrists, which were bound together. The body was wrapped in a plastic bin liner and tied with twine. The investigating police officers were able to trace suppliers of the dog's collar, one of which had sold such a collar to John Taylor, who lived a few miles from the murder scene. A search of Taylor's home revealed twine, cable ties and bin liners similar to those found at the deposition site. The police also searched Taylor's home for carpet containing distinctive red nylon fibres, as these had been found on the deceased's clothing. The police found that Taylor had recently removed all the carpeting from his house, but similar small traces of fibres were found caught to nails in the floorboards. In 2003, Taylor was sentenced to a minimum of 25 years in custody before being considered for release under licence.

Analysis: This case illustrates how a number of pieces of seemingly innocent, everyday evidence (twine, cable ties and bin liners) can together be used to improve the likelihood of the suspect's being involved in the murder. Added together, the individual pieces of evidence provide a more compelling argument for the prosecution's proposition than they do on their own. Similarly, the jury would also be asked to consider the significance of the recent removal of the carpets. In 2003, Taylor was also convicted of two rapes, based on DNA evidence, and given two additional life sentences.

Hair

In terms of its forensic opportunities, hair may be considered similar to fibres, in that the basic size and shape are similar. This means that the method of recovery from the crime scene and subsequent forensic analysis are also similar. However, as hair originates from those involved in crime (victims and offenders), it also offers the possibility of providing intelligence on the appearance of an unknown offender and of linking an offender to a crime scene.

Hair is made up of two parts, the *follicle* and the *shaft* (Buffoli et al., 2014). The follicle is that part of the skin that grows hair and, as it is supplied with blood vessels, records in the shaft as it grows a history of that person's habits (such as drug abuse; Chatterton and Kintz, 2014; Vinceti et al., 2013). The shaft is composed of three layers, *cuticle, cortex* and *medulla*. The cuticle is the outside covering of the hair and contained within this is the cortex, which gives hair its strength, elasticity and curl. The medulla occurs in the centre of the hair shaft and is not present in all hair. Hair has three stages of growth. The first, when the hair is actively growing, is known as the *anagen phase* and hair removed from the body at this stage may contain a DNA-rich follicle. In the second (*catagen*) phase, the growth of the hair slows down; in the final (*telogen*) phase, the hair is eventually naturally shed.

Hair from the crime scene and suspect may be compared using a comparison microscope. In general, examination of hair morphology can provide enough information for the forensic scientist to say that the two samples of hair were likely to originate from the same person or could not have originated from the same person. Like fibres, how long after an offence an item is recovered and how well hair is retained on it (for example, a mask worn by a bank robber) will influence its evidential value.

Glass

Glass is a hard, brittle material that when cooled forms a rigid structure without crystallising. The atomic structure of glass is unordered and lacks the symmetrical and ordered nature of crystalline solids. The materials used in the production of glass consist mainly of silica and a combination of oxides. Although the modern process of making glass is highly automated, each of these materials contains impurities that vary both in and between each batch of glass produced. Additional impurities are often added intentionally for decorative purposes or to give the glass specific optical properties. As a result of these impurities, glass can be very specific, with pieces from the same or closely related batches sharing similar optical, physical and chemical properties (Zadora, 2007).

Differences in the *tempering* (heat-treatment) process can also result in glass that is easily distinguishable based on breaking patterns formed when it is struck. Non-tempered glass is easily breakable, splintering into large, sharp fragments (Locke and Unikowski, 1991); however, tempered glass, such as that used in the rear and side windows of vehicles, is much stronger. Tempering introduces internal stresses in the glass, making it more resistant to breakage. Heat-sealing thin plastic sheets between pieces of tempered glass, forming what is known as laminated glass, can further strengthen the final product. Laminated glass is commonly used for front windshields and 'bulletproof' windows, as it is much less likely to shatter completely due to the added integrity provided by the plastic. As a result of the heat treatment used on tempered glass, the glass forms a large number of small, cuboid fragments when broken. These fragments will be spread in distinct patterns indicative of the direction and magnitude of the force that caused the break. The physical properties of both non-tempered and tempered glass provide key information that determines the evidential value of glass fragments in forensic investigations. However, these tests are typically not able to confirm whether two samples originated from the same source and more sophisticated techniques are required to analyse the optical and chemical properties of glass.

As the optical properties of glass differ both within and between production runs, the behaviour of light when it enters glass will vary from sample to sample. The behaviour of light in glass is determined by the *refractive index* (*RI*) of the glass. This is a ratio that expresses the amount that light bends when it passes from one medium (such as air) to another (such as glass). The most commonly used forensic technique for determining the RI of glass is an automated immersion method that involves submerging the sample of glass in a thermally stable, transparent liquid with a high boiling point (such as oil). As the liquid's RI varies with temperature, by slowly heating the oil the RI will change to a point at which it is the same as that of the glass sample and, at that point, the boundary between the oil and the glass disappears. As the RI of the liquid at a given temperature is known, the RI of the glass can therefore be deduced.

If the RI measurements suggest that two samples of glass (one from a crime scene and one from a suspect's clothing) could have originated from the same source, then further analysis is carried out to ascertain the elemental composition of the samples using a *scanning electron microscope* (Curran et al., 1997). Clearly, as we have already seen with fibre and other evidence types, how easily glass samples can be transferred or shed is of interest to the scientist in evaluating the evidential value of glass (Hicks et al., 1996; McQuillan and Edgar, 1992), as is the ability to discriminate between samples (Koons and Buscagalia, 2002). In addition to recovering glass from doors and windows, glass from other sources (such as vehicle headlights) may also be of interest to the scientist (Suzuki et al., 2003).

Box 3.8 The Williams brothers - Part I

In 1999, brothers Matthew and Tyler Williams were arrested following the attempted use of stolen credit cards belonging to one of the victims of a double murder that had occurred some days earlier in Redding, California, USA. Police had linked this double murder to earlier arson attacks on synagogues and an abortion clinic. A search of the brothers' premises and vehicle revealed glass fragments on several items, including metal bars and clothing, and also in the trunk (boot) of the vehicle. These glass fragments were consistent with a broken window at the abortion clinic.

Analysis: As we saw in Box 3.7, evidence from different items combined can produce more compelling evidence than that found in isolation. In this case glass fragments were recovered from multiple items, which may have made the prosecution's proposition that the brothers were responsible for these offences more believable for a jury. We will see more about likelihood and how it is used to convey the evidential value of forensic evidence to a jury in Chapter 5. (See Box 3.9 for the second part of this story.)

Paint

Many objects are finished with a surface layer of paint for either protective (to prevent corrosion) or decorative purposes (Muehlethaler et al., 2013). The colour of paint is determined by the inclusion of various inorganic and organic compounds, known as pigments. It follows, therefore, that a sample of paint recovered from a crime scene may be examined in order to establish its composition as well as to link it to a paint sample recovered from a suspect. Dried paint may present itself at the crime scene as either a smear (such as from colliding vehicles) or a flake (from a tool used to force open a window in a painted window frame). Loose flakes can be recovered with low-tack tape, a scalpel or a pair of tweezers (Moore et al., 2012). Reference samples (for instance, from a vehicle) may be scraped from an undamaged area using a scalpel. As most painted objects have multiple layers of paint (Alwi and Kuppuswamy, 2004; He et al., 2013), an association between two paint samples may be made from an analysis of the colour, thickness and composition of each of the layers.

As we have already seen for other trace evidence types, an initial analysis of a paint sample can be made with visible light. Under a microscope, the colour, layering and wear of paint can be examined. Where both reference and crime scene samples exist, this examination can be carried out using a comparison microscope.

However, paint also lends itself to analysis to determine its composition and for this a range of techniques such as infrared and Raman spectroscopy can be used (Zieba-Palus et al., 2011; Zieba-Palus and Trzcinska, 2013; Trzcinska et al., 2013; Harroun et al., 2011). These are known as *vibrational spectroscopy* techniques, as they depend on energy exchange between molecules in the paint and incident radiation through vibration of the paint molecules. In addition, crystalline components present in paint may be examined using a technique known as *x-ray powder diffraction* (*XRD*). Here, specific combinations of x-ray wavelengths are reflected by the regular array of atoms, which enables the composition of the paint to be determined. In the absence of a reference sample from a suspect, these techniques can be used to provide intelligence for police investigators.

Box 3.9 The Williams brothers - Part II

Further examination of the metal bars recovered from the Williams brothers' vehicle showed the presence of fragments of paint. Some of this paint could have originated from one of the synagogues, while paint found on broken glass at the abortion clinic could have originated from another of the metal bars. All of these crimes formed part of a series of hate crimes for which the brothers were convicted.

Analysis: Again (like Boxes 3.7 and 3.8), evidence was found on more than one item, in this example paint fragments on metal bars. Transference of paint could have occurred from both crime scenes to the items found in the possession of the brothers and vice versa. When evidence is found on multiple items, the combined effect of this can influence a jury even if, when taken individually, the association made between an item and the crime scene relates to a commonly occurring material such as glass or paint. This is discussed in more depth in Chapter 5.

Soil

Soil encountered at a crime scene is likely to be made up not only of naturally occurring minerals, but also a host of contaminants such as organic matter and micro-organisms as well as man-made minerals such as brick or cement (Reidy et al., 2013). Therefore, as well as linking a suspect to a crime scene, soil evidence may also be used to identify a location. A challenge for the forensic scientist, however, is assessing the degree of variation of soils between locations, either to link a suspect to a scene or to identify a scene's specific location. Soil is very easily picked up and transferred and so may be found not only on the footwear of those involved in a crime, but also on clothing, inside vehicles, on carpets and so on. Recovery of soil from clothing may also be used to identify the circumstances of an offence. For example, soil in the seat area of a pair of trousers worn by a victim who alleges they were pulled along the ground would support the victim's account. Soil may also be used to establish that the deposition site of a body is different to the site where a violent attack took place and where soil was deposited on the victim's outer clothing. Soil composition also varies with depth, variation that may be used by a forensic archaeologist to identify a freshly dug grave (Ruwanpura et al., 2006; Haglund, 2001).

When analysing soil samples either to establish composition or to compare two samples to each other, they must be analysed under identical conditions. To do this, it is usual to dry samples before examination. In addition to the spectroscopic techniques discussed earlier (Edwards et al., 2012; Baron et al., 2011), soil samples may also be sieved to obtain particle soil. Furthermore, soil samples may be compared by *thermal analysis*, in which the energy required to maintain a zero-temperature difference between two samples as they are heated is monitored. The amount of energy varies as the water and organic components of the soil evaporate and this variation may be used to differentiate samples (Lee et al., 2012).

Box 3.10 Particulate evidence

In 1977, widow Rosa Simper was murdered in her home in Adelaide, Australia. The police investigators identified Edward Splatt as a suspect. An examination of Splatt's clothing revealed particles that could have originated from welding as well as paint particles. Both of these particulates were consistent with those found on the outside of the victim's premises. As these premises were located close to a factory that carried out both welding and spray painting, the particulates could easily have been carried on the air from the factory to the victim's premises. Splatt was convicted in 1978. However, he maintained his innocence and a local reporter campaigned against the conviction. This led to a Royal Commission and Splatt was pardoned in 1984 (a pardon meaning that he was excused further punishment, rather than being acquitted).

Analysis: The Commissioner was critical of the evidence presented at the trial, particularly the fact that Splatt worked at the factory and could easily have picked up the particulates by innocent contamination. The Commissioner noted that a forensic system that did not differentiate between scientific observations (the presence of particulates) and deductions (how they could have originated on Splatt's clothing or the victim's premises) was defective and unacceptable. The Commissioner adopted the recommendations from UK scientists about how such evidence should be interpreted and presented in Australia in the future. This example shows the need to interpret the results from scientific analysis correctly and for that interpretation to be conveyed to a jury. Taken in isolation, the evidence may appear convincing, but when placed in the context of the business of the factory, Splatt's employment there and its vicinity to the victim's premises, other, innocent explanations become valid and reduce the evidential value of the forensic evidence, as we will see in Chapter 5.

Other evidence types

Along with the identification evidence types discussed in Chapter 2, the comparison evidence types already described are those that are most often encountered. There are, however, many other types of evidence, too numerous to consider here. Some of these are generally well known to law enforcement agencies, such as handwriting analysis and comparison (Found and Ganas, 2013) and, to a lesser extent, voice analysis and comparison (Neuhauser, 2013; Zhang et al., 2013). Others are less well known, such as palynology (the study of pollen), mentioned at the beginning of this chapter.

Other areas of forensic analysis and interpretation include disciplines that provide a qualitative or quantitative measurement, which is not necessarily then compared with some other reference measurement. Examples of these would include blood pattern analysis at the crime scene (Attinger et al., 2013) and toxicology (Negrusz and Cooper, 2013). Toxicology can include determination of the presence of a substance (such as alcohol or drugs of abuse) followed by quantification; that is, the likely effect on the donor of the amount of substance consumed. As described earlier for hair samples, toxicology can provide a recent history of drug abuse. It can also be used to provide comparison evidence between, for example, different batches of recovered drugs. Such intelligence is of value to the police in making an association between drug seizures that could have originated from the same source.

The police may also, from time to time, require an unusual forensic analysis and interpretation, such as an examination of a meter to determine the theft of electricity (Erol-Kantarci and Mouftah, 2013). Furthermore, a growing area of forensic examination relates to digital technology. This means the retrieval, analysis and interpretation of evidence that exists in a digital format and includes cell phones, cellular networks, the internet and encryption or hiding data (Sammons, 2012). Digital media can provide evidence when it has been used to plan a crime, such as a murder (see Box 3.11), or to execute a crime such as cyber fraud (Graham, 2009).

Box 3.11 Digital forensics

In 2009 in the US city of Boston, Massachusetts, Julissa Brisman, a masseuse, was waiting in a hotel for her next appointment when she was attacked and murdered. Shocked hotel guests saw Julissa's body through the open bedroom door and summoned the police. Julissa's skull had been caved in and there were three bullet holes in her upper body. At the crime scene, police found three spent shell casings and a plastic zip tie (used for binding wrists). There was no fingerprint or DNA evidence to identify the offender and no sign of sexual assault. Surveillance CCTV footage at the hotel showed a male leaving at the material time. Julissa had arranged her appointment online through craigslist, a classified advertisement website. Police linked the murder to a separate attack some days earlier in another hotel in Boston in which the victim had her wrists tied and was robbed. CCTV footage of this attack showed a similar figure to the murderer. To find out who had responded to Julissa's online advertisement and made the appointment with her, the agency employing Julissa provided police with the email address from which the appointment was made. From the corresponding ten-digit IP address for the email, police performed an IP trace-back to locate the street address of the sender. They determined that the IP address was in the suburb of Quincy, Massachusetts. To narrow the search further, the police requested a court order to force the internet service provider to disclose the street address. From this, the police were able to pinpoint the specific street address to the apartment of a medical student, Philip Markoff. However, Markoff's wi-fi router was not password protected, meaning that someone else could have accessed it without his knowledge. The surviving victim identified Markoff as her attacker from his image. This provided police with enough suspicion to search his apartment, where they found plastic ties and the firearm used to murder Julissa. Markoff was charged with murder and, while in custody awaiting trial, he committed suicide.

Analysis: This case illustrates how the relatively new discipline of digital forensics can be used to locate a potential offender by their digital signature and their use of the internet and email. However, the evidential value of this new evidence type needs to be as robust as other, more traditional evidence types and here the possibility that someone else could have accessed Markoff's router meant that other evidence was required. In this case, that other evidence was identification from a witness and the recovery of plastic ties.

Summary

In this chapter we have considered a range of evidence types that constitute comparison evidence. These embody Locard's Exchange Principle (that the offender will bring something into the crime scene and leave with something from the crime scene) and require the police to deliver a suspect or other form of evidence in order that a comparison can be made with an item recovered from the crime scene. This need for police work to deliver one half of the data for analysis and comparison separates comparison evidence from identification evidence. Another difference is that the relevant features of some comparison evidence types, such as footwear, are transient. Furthermore, other comparison evidence types, such as glass or fibres, rarely provide strong evidence, as their occurrence is common and therefore they can be present through innocent cross-contamination. Nevertheless, comparison evidence is still widely used as a means of linking an offender to a crime scene. Many comparison evidence types require specialised methods of analysis, often including a range of optical or spectroscopic techniques to determine the constituent elements or compounds in an item. In the next chapter we will consider how both comparison and identification evidence types might be identified at, and recovered from, the crime scene.

Study questions

1 We have seen how, as part of a forensic examination, a weapon might be required to be test-fired. If this weapon also needed to be

examined for fingerprints, consider in what order the examinations would be carried out and why. As we saw in Chapter 2, processing an exhibit for multiple evidence types in this way is known as sequential treatment.

2 We have seen how comparison evidence differs from identification evidence, the latter being able to provide the name of a suspect as well as evidence to show their possible involvement with a crime. Particularly with DNA evidence, quantifiable statistics are provided to help a jury understand the likelihood of the DNA match being adventitious. Consider how feasible it would be to better quantify the evidential value of comparison evidence. For example, what could be done to provide quantifiable statistics for particulate evidence such as glass or fibres? Would this also be applicable, for example, to footwear impressions?

4

CRIME SCENE EXAMINATION

The successful involvement of forensic science as a means of solving a crime must always start with the effective examination of the crime scene (Harrison, 2006; Jamieson, 2004). This examination should be carried out by police personnel who have been specially trained in how to examine a scene for forensic evidence, a task that is different to, for example, searching a crime scene for drugs, weapons or carrying out an intelligence search. Crime scene examination can be undertaken by police officers or police staff, the essential consideration being not who it is doing the examination but their level of training. In the UK, this examination is now almost exclusively carried out by civilian police staff with varying job titles, such as scenes of crimes officer (SOCO), crime scene examiner (CSE) and crime scene investigator (CSI). The latter title tends to be favoured by some other countries (such as the USA) where a mixture of both police officers and staff undertake CSI work.

At the crime scene, the CSI will principally be looking for forensic evidence that has the potential to link an individual (e.g. the perpetrator of the crime) to the crime scene. As we have seen in previous chapters, this can be by a range of evidence types, such as fingerprints, DNA, footwear and so on, the type of evidence being searched for depending on the circumstances and nature of the offence. For example, if premises were burgled by an offender entering through an open door, there would be little point in searching for broken glass at the *point of entry* (the door). However, if entry had been gained by breaking a window in a secure door, then recording and recovering some broken glass fragments would be reasonable in order to enable a forensic scientist to undertake a comparison with any fragments of glass that may be recovered from a suspect's clothing.

In the case of, for example, a domestic burglary where the victim is present during the CSI's examination, much information about the route of the offender (their *point of entry* and *point of exit*) and what they may have touched or moved can be gleaned from a careful questioning of the victim. This opportunity to gather intelligence about the offender's modus operandi (MO) can be usefully supplemented by information passed on to the CSI by the police control room that requested the CSI to attend. If the victim is not present during the CSI's examination, then this supplementary information, and the CSI's own initiative, will be all that the CSI has to work with. In Chapter 5 we will discuss decision making during crime scene examination in further detail.

Clearly, at some scenes, such as a sudden death, initial information about the circumstances will be sketchy and the CSI will need to bring their skill and experience to bear to identify clues to what has happened. In this situation, time is likely to be of the essence, as investigating police officers will want to know whether the death is suspicious and whether an offender is at large. This all adds to the pressure on the CSI to deliver, in a timely fashion, both intelligence and evidence related to the offence so that the enquiry and forensic analysis can be undertaken expeditiously (Ribaux et al., 2010a, b; Baber and Butler, 2012). To add to the pressure, the CSI needs to be satisfied that their examination is as complete as is required as, in most cases, it is not possible to return to the crime scene at a later date and have a second opportunity to examine the scene.

Getting the examination process right

The CSI must ensure that their examination is as thorough as it can be, given the nature and circumstances of the offence. At the scene of a major incident such as a homicide, the CSI will have many additional resources to assist them with their examination, which is likely to be carried out over several days. However, at the scene of a *volume crime* such as domestic burglary, the CSI examination is, to some extent, limited by time and resources. This domestic burglary is likely to be only one of several volume crimes that the CSI will have to attend that day, so it is essential for the CSI to plan their workload to enable each scene to be examined and any forensic exhibits recovered. It is now accepted that timeliness is a key consideration in the successful conversion of forensic evidence recovered from the crime scene into crime detection (Her Majesty's Inspectorate of Constabulary, 2000, 2002; Morgan et al., 2004; Prime and Hennelly, 2003; Webb et al., 2005; Bond, 2007b).

At a volume crime, another consideration for the CSI is the need to recover the forensic evidence that is most likely to detect the crime (Bond, 2007a, 2009). A significant factor for the investigating officer that influences the successful conversion of evidence recovery into crime detection is the greatly varying evidential value of different exhibits. For example, at the scene of a domestic burglary, the CSI recovers a spot of blood from just inside the window that was broken to gain access to the premises and also recovers a cigarette end found discarded on the pavement outside the premises. Both can yield a DNA profile, but the blood spot has much greater evidential value, is more incriminating and is stronger evidence for the investigator to use during an interview with a suspect. In earlier chapters we have already looked at evidential value; the difficult task of determining the probative value of evidence will be explored in detail in Chapter 5.

Box 4.1 A case of arson?

In February 2007 in Glassboro, New Jersey, USA, Stephen Edwards and Michelle Henry awoke to find their home ablaze. They escaped the fire, but with burns covering over 80% of their bodies, and they did not survive. Their 16-year-old son, Jason Henry, did survive. Jason told police that he tried to rescue his parents and sustained a burn to his arm in the process. Detective Dan Williams questioned the boy's story, and his limited injuries, and asked fire investigators to try to find the cause of the fire. Investigators found several seats of fire (the locations in which the fire started) on several floors in the house. They also found a plastic gasoline container in a cupboard on the first floor. This evidence was presented to Jason who, after questioning, said that he had set the fire for his parents as part of an insurance fraud. He also said that he never intended his parents to become trapped. Jason was charged with the murder of both his parents. Investigators from the Alcohol, Tobacco and Firearms (ATF) Fire Research Laboratory examined the crime scene and took samples to test for the presence of accelerants. ATF found traces of gasoline on the remains of Stephen and Michelle's bedroom carpet. They staged a full reconstruction of the fire at their laboratory to try to ascertain the size of the fire and, as part of this, recreated the parents' home using similar furniture. The temperatures recorded during the test were used to suggest to the jury that Jason could not have entered the fire multiple times, as he had alleged, nor could the parents have set the fire without meaning to take their own lives. Within 20 seconds after ignition of the test fire, ATF determined that anyone trying to exit the fire after that time would have sustained severe burns. Investigators stated that they believed it was more likely that Jason burnt his hand while lighting the gasoline.

Analysis: This case illustrates the lengths to which it is sometimes necessary to go in order to try to establish the facts of what occurred at a crime scene. Careful reconstruction of the family home demonstrated to the court the magnitude of the temperature reached during the fire and the time it took for the fire to establish. Fire Investigators will often seek to show that a fire was started deliberately, but in this case Jason admitted starting the fire, so it was necessary to try to establish whether his version of events was consistent with the way the fire had developed. This was only possible by recreating the fire using furniture similar to that in the family home. However, no fire science provides definite proof as to how a fire started and, similarly to some of the other cases we have considered, it is ultimately for the jury to decide whether the prosecution or defence version of events is more likely. Fire science, like other disciplines in forensic science when employed by the prosecution, seeks to provide a plausible version of events at the crime scene for the jury to consider along with the defence version of events. Jason pleaded guilty and received a 20-year sentence.

The forensic value of crime scenes

Unfortunately, not all crime scenes offer the same potential to yield forensic evidence. From Locard's Exchange Principle we know that there has to be contact for an exchange of evidence to take place. Most violent crime has this contact by the very nature of the offence, such as a physical assault or struggle, which means that crimes such as homicide, rape or assault often rely heavily on forensic science to identify an unknown offender or to corroborate the victim's statement of the circumstances of the offence. Property-related crime such as burglary and vehicle crime also have a high degree of contact, as in order to carry out the crime the offender must enter and search premises or vehicles.

However, there remains the majority of reported crime where forensic science has little opportunity to contribute to its detection. This may be because the evidence does not exist in the first place or, if it does exist and can be recovered by the CSI, it has low evidential value. In the former case, consider a reported offence of personal robbery in the street when the offender demands that the victim hand over their wallet with the threat of violence. There is no physical contact between the offender and the victim and therefore, according to Locard's Exchange Principle, the opportunities to recover forensic evidence from the victim or the scene (the street) are negligible. In the latter case, consider an offence of criminal damage in which a vehicle wing mirror has been deliberately pulled off the vehicle and left at the side of the road. The mirror is examined by a CSI and there is found to be a fingerprint on the mirror that is subsequently identified. At first sight, this might seem like good forensic evidence not only to identify the offender but also to provide the evidence to secure a prosecution.

Unfortunately, the evidential value of the fingerprint is low, as the suspect can offer a defence that they found the wing mirror, already removed from the vehicle, and placed it at the side of the road so as not to cause a danger to other road users. The jury may well believe that this is a plausible explanation for how the defendant's fingerprint came to be on the wing mirror. In these circumstances, the identification of the fingerprint on the mirror could provide useful intelligence to the police and the fingerprint would then be deemed to have *intelligence* value, rather than *evidential* value (this distinction will be explored in further detail in Chapter 5). It can be seen, therefore, that whether a CSI is deployed might also be influenced by the ability to recover forensic material of intelligence value from the crime scene. This adds to the dilemma for the police over when to deploy a CSI to a crime scene. Obviously, for serious and major incidents the decision is straightforward, but for volume crime or crimes with low social or economic impact, how do the police arrive at this decision?

To assist the decision-making process about what is likely to be a crime scene that is able to yield forensic evidence likely to detect the crime, most police forces in the UK have *attendance criteria*, which define not only which crime types should be attended by a CSI but also a decision-making process to follow in order to decide whether such evidence is likely to be present at the scene (Bond and Sheridan, 2007). An example for one police force is shown in Figure 4.1.

Forensic Investigation Attendance Criteria

Please refer to the Forensic Investigation Attendance Criteria document as published on the S.S.D website for further details relating to our current scene attendance priorities

In all cases consider:

Preservation: Have relevant areas been preserved for forensic examination?

YES	Go to DNA
NO	Forensic investigation attendance may not be useful.

DNA: Has the offender left any signs of blood, cigarette ends, clothing, drinks cans, foodstuffs or property?

YES	Request Forensic Investigation attendance
NO	Go to fingerprints

Fingerprints: Have any dry clean smooth surfaces been touched or moved?

YES	Request Forensic Investigation attendance
NO	Go to footprints

Footprints: Can you see shoe marks in or around the crime scene?

YES	Request Forensic Investigation attendance
NO	Do not request Forensic Investigation attendance

If in doubt consult Forensic Investigation

Ensure that the scene is correctly preserved and protected from the weather. Always wear gloves when handling items. Inform Forensic Investigation if suspects are in custody and provide any other relevant information.

Direct Line:
Intranet: Force forms - Form 1056

Figure 4.1 Example of attendance criteria for determining CSI attendance at a crime scene.

CSI deployment

Most offences come to the attention of the police through a member of the public contacting them about a crime that is in progress, one that has occurred or a report of something suspicious. All three of these may warrant the deployment of a CSI, although deployment to a crime in progress would normally be delayed until the scene had been made safe by attending police officers. This is not always the case, however. Consider an anonymous telephone call to the police that a bomb has been placed on one of the shelves in a supermarket. CSI would be required during the police search of the supermarket to provide a photographic record of the scene and the search and also to record and advise on the recovery of any suspect device that is found. Usually, a report of a volume crime that has already occurred (such as a householder returning home to find that their home has been burgled) will invoke the attendance criteria to determine whether or not a CSI should be deployed to the scene. A report of a serious or major crime will generally automatically require the deployment of a CSI, not least to provide an assessment of the forensic opportunities (or difficulties) at the scene and what additional resources might be required (such as supervisory or specialist forensic officers).

Perhaps the most difficult scene for a CSI to assess is a report to the police of something suspicious. If the report is of suspicious activity, such as two men seen behaving suspiciously outside a factory, then (at that stage) no CSI deployment is likely. However, if the report is of a sudden death that may or may not be suspicious, then a CSI (and supervisor) will be required to assess and interpret the scene and, crucially, to provide advice and guidance to the investigating police officers about whether the death is likely to be suspicious. If a body is found in the street with a knife sticking in the back then, clearly, the involvement of someone else is indicated and the decision to consider the death as a major incident is reasonably straightforward. If, however, the body of an elderly female is found at home with no obvious injuries, then a much more thorough examination of the scene by a CSI is required to seek to establish whether or not there are any suspicious circumstances related to the death and whether or not a major incident should be declared.

As well as the obvious requirement not to allow a suspicious death to be treated by the police as non-suspicious and thereby allow an offender to escape prosecution, today another important consideration is not simply to assume that all sudden deaths are suspicious. This is because declaring a death suspicious triggers a course of action by the police that is costly in both resources and finance and is not always easy to step back from once started. This highlights the importance of complex decision making at the crime scene, and the severe consequences that an incorrect decision can have (see Box 4.2 for an example).

Box 4.2 Is the death suspicious?

In 1980, the Chamberlain family were on vacation, camping near Ayers Rock, in the Northern Territory in central Australia. With the parents were their two sons and 10-week-old baby daughter. During the night, the mother (Lindy) cried out that a dingo (a wild Australian dog) had taken the baby from the tent. The parents were charged with the murder of their daughter, with the prosecution alleging that they had cut the baby's throat and removed her from the campsite in their vehicle. To support this proposition, the prosecution produced evidence that there was a spray pattern of foetal haemoglobin inside the vehicle. The parents were convicted of the murder of their daughter. In 1986, however, while investigating the disappearance of a climber, police found a piece of clothing in a dingo lair that was identified as belonging to the Chamberlains' daughter. The parents were released from prison and, in 1988, their convictions were quashed.

Analysis: This case illustrates how the jury must reach a decision based on the available evidence and determine the likelihood of the prosecution and defence propositions given that evidence. Clearly, at the trial, the jury did not believe the mother's version of events. After their release, an Australian Government inquiry found that the spray pattern inside the vehicle was, in fact, paint acquired during the manufacture of the vehicle. As we have already seen (see Box 3.10), there is a need to interpret the results from scientific analysis correctly (in this case the spray inside the vehicle). In 2012, the Northern Territory coroner officially amended the baby's death certificate to show that the cause of death was 'as the result of being attacked and taken by a dingo'. If all the evidence had been available at the original trial, would the Chamberlains have been convicted?

Forensic examination of a suspected major incident

What is a major incident?

A major incident will involve CSIs whether or not a crime has been committed simply on the basis of the requirement to record and recover evidence from the scene. Crimes that would be classified as major incidents include murder and manslaughter, serious sexual offences and assaults, armed robbery, aggravated offences (those involving the use of violence), kidnapping and extortion (such as contamination of food products). As well as being of concern to the public, these offences are likely to be particularly demanding of police resources and often result in protracted and lengthy enquiries before an offender is apprehended. Any prosecutions that follow are likely to be lengthy and complicated, which highlights the importance of building a strong case against a defendant. By their nature, such crimes are also likely to require lengthy and meticulous forensic examination of the several scenes that might make up the major incident enquiry. Offences where the offender is unknown, such as a stranger rape or apparently motiveless homicide, are invariably the most difficult to solve and will require all possible forensic opportunities to be recorded and recovered to assist the investigation.

Different types of major crime will offer different forensic opportunities. For instance, an allegation of rape will not only provide the scene of the offence but also the victim for forensic examination. In this sense, the victim may be considered an additional 'scene' of the investigation and often the evidence to identify the offender will be recovered from the victim (such as semen from intimate swabs/samples). Offences of aggravated burglary will offer forensic opportunities over and above what might normally be encountered at a burglary scene. For example, if the victim has had their hands and feet tied, then DNA from the offender might be recovered from the ties.

Perhaps most demanding for CSIs are major incidents that may also be major crimes, such as homicide. We saw earlier how a sudden death often relies on the forensic aspects of the scene to determine whether or not a crime has been committed, and how it is imperative that suspicious deaths are not incorrectly attributed to, for example, death by natural causes. Although such incorrect assessments may ultimately be corrected at the post-mortem examination, by then it is often too late to return to the original scene and seek to recover evidence that may assist in the apprehension of the offender. Therefore, the CSI must get it right first time.

Major incidents that are not crimes but still require the services of a CSI would include civil emergencies. These can range from natural disasters such as flooding or earthquake to an aircraft crash. At these scenes, the skill and knowledge of the CSI in being able to record and recover evidence provide a vital service to the police operation to contain and deal with the emergency. In addition, the recovery and identification of human remains at these scenes require processes similar to forensic examinations.

The role of the first officer attending the scene

We have already seen that most crimes come to the attention of the police following contact from a member of the public who has witnessed or is reporting a crime or has become suspicious of a set of circumstances or the behaviour of individuals. In the case of a report of a sudden death, possibly in the home or in the street, a police officer will be despatched to attend the scene and make an assessment of the circumstances. In the UK, this officer is known as the *first officer attending* (*FOA*) and has certain responsibilities to fulfil at the scene. The FOA's primary responsibilities are to preserve life (both human and animal) and property. Coupled with this, the FOA should maintain order and seek to apprehend any offenders. After this, the FOA should make an assessment of the scene they are presented with and, if necessary, call for assistance.

That assistance could be additional police officers as well as CSI support. The FOA should seek to preserve the scene of interest by means of barrier tape erected to form an *outer cordon*. The size and shape of this outer cordon will be dictated by the circumstances of the incident. For example, for a sudden death inside secure premises, an outer cordon erected at the property boundary with the street may be appropriate, whereas a sudden death in a field requires a much larger outer cordon, as a potential offender's entry and exit points to the scene of the death may be less obvious. It is essential that, once erected, the outer cordon is adequately protected by police officers to prohibit unauthorised entry. Any forensic material later recovered from outside the outer cordon is likely to have diminished evidential value, as its continuity between the offence being committed and its recovery cannot definitively be established. It is safe policy initially to erect a large outer cordon that can then, in time, be reduced as the circumstances of the scene become clearer. The FOA should commence a scene log that will record details of all those entering the outer cordon (senior police officers, CSIs etc.) and also any significant witnesses in the vicinity of the cordon who may have witnessed the incident or have information related to the offence.

Consider a report from a member of the public who, while walking their dog, comes across what appear to be partially buried remains in a wooded area (Figure 4.2). On arrival, the FOA makes contact with the member of the public and ascertains the location of the buried remains. The FOA will request CSI attendance to make an assessment of the scene and then erects an outer cordon. In this scenario, the shape of the outer cordon is likely to be irregular and determined by the availability of trees or other objects around which to wind the barrier tape. The FOA commences a scene log and notes particulars of the person who reported the incident to the police (Figure 4.3).

The role of the CSI at the scene

On arrival at the scene, the CSI will make contact with the FOA and receive a briefing on the circumstances. At this stage, a supervisory police officer may or may not be present and the priority with which

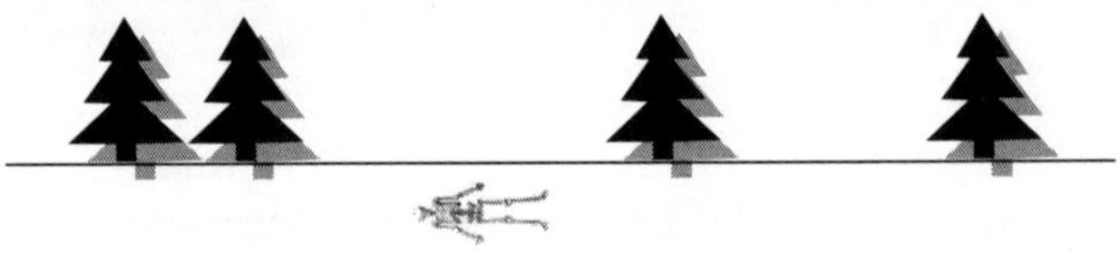

Figure 4.2 A member of the public thinks they have found buried remains in a wooded area.

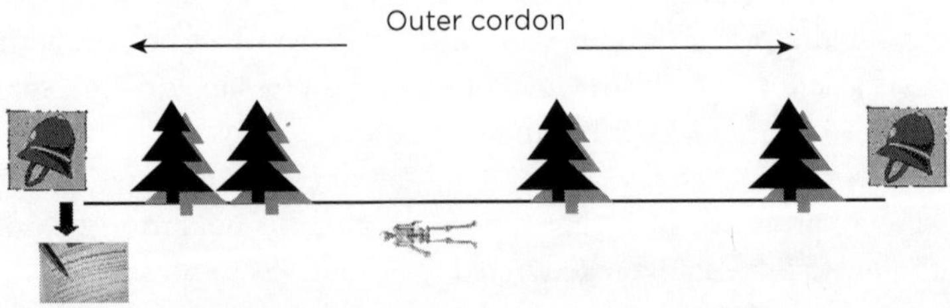

Figure 4.3 First officer attending establishes a secure outer cordon and commences a scene log.

the incident will be dealt with will, in part, be determined by the CSI's assessment. Once briefed, the CSI will need to make their way to the buried remains, having first put on protective clothing to ensure that they do not contaminate any evidence within the outer cordon. This protective clothing comprises an all-in-one body suit with a hood, a face mask, gloves and overshoes, all of which are disposable. On entering the outer cordon, the CSI will be looking to approach the buried remains by a path that is not obviously one that might have been taken either by the victim or an offender. In order not to destroy any physical evidence that might be present, this approach path is first photographed and searched for forensic evidence. Additionally, depending on the scene, the CSI may place metal tread plates along the approach path so that the ground is not directly walked on. This approach path is then used by all those entering the outer cordon and is referred to as a *common approach path* (*CAP*). The CSI will establish an *inner cordon* directly in the vicinity of the buried remains and this will be the initial focus for the forensic examination (Figure 4.4). As this is possibly a major incident and crime, a *crime scene manager* (*CSM*) and additional CSIs will attend to assist in the scene examination (Crispino, 2008). Prior to the recovery of evidence, the CSM will, in conjunction with the senior police officer present, decide what specialist resources might be required in order to examine the scene forensically (Mohandie and Meloy, 2013).

Forensic resources

There are many specialisms that might be required to assist the police and CSI personnel in the forensic examination of the scene to ensure that all forensic opportunities are properly recorded and recovered,

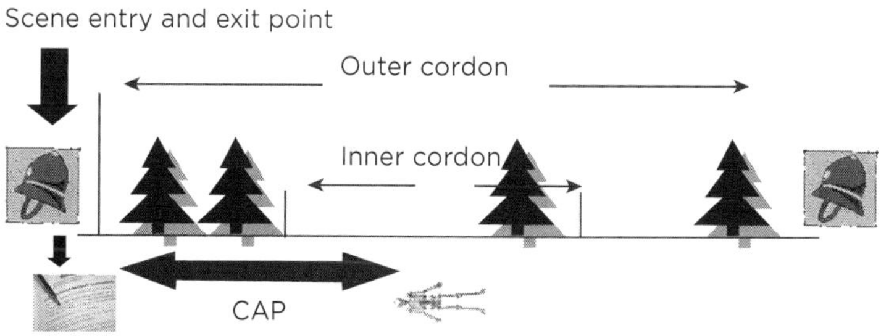

Figure 4.4 An inner cordon and common approach path are established.

and also to advise on future analysis of the material recovered. Clearly, the specialisms required will differ from scene to scene and will be dictated by the circumstances of the incident. For instance, incidents involving the discharge of a firearm may require the services of a ballistics examiner to comment on bullet trajectory, proximity of the shooter and so on, whereas incidents involving the spillage of blood (from the victim, offender or both) may require the services of a blood pattern analyst to make an assessment of the sequence of events in a blood-stained room. In the UK, many common specialisms such as these are available to the police from several private forensic providers. Less common services such as entomology or an examination of knotted material (as might be encountered in cases of hanging or bondage) are usually provided by self-employed practitioners or by academics. When a deceased person remains in situ at the scene, it is common to request the attendance of the pathologist who will be conducting the post-mortem examination.

Recording the scene

Prior to evidence recovery, it is necessary to record the appearance of any crime scene being forensically examined. This would include not only the scene containing the deceased, but also the subsequent post-mortem and other scenes identified during the enquiry. At each scene one CSI will usually be dedicated to making a video record of the scene, while another will make a photographic record, the latter then usually being produced as an album of images for use in court. This record will be taken prior to the removal of any exhibits from the scene. The CSM may also prepare a hand-drawn sketch of the scene and other relevant objects with dimensions marked (Figure 4.5).

After a record has been made of the scene, items of interest can be photographed in detail prior to recovery. In the earlier example of buried remains, it is likely that a forensic archaeologist and anthropologist may attend the scene to assist with the excavation and possibly a forensic entomologist or botanist, depending on how long the body has been buried.

Assessing the scene

If there are no obvious marks on or injuries to the body, the scene needs to be examined for clues as to what has happened, prior to undertaking a post-mortem and establishing cause of death. The decision-making

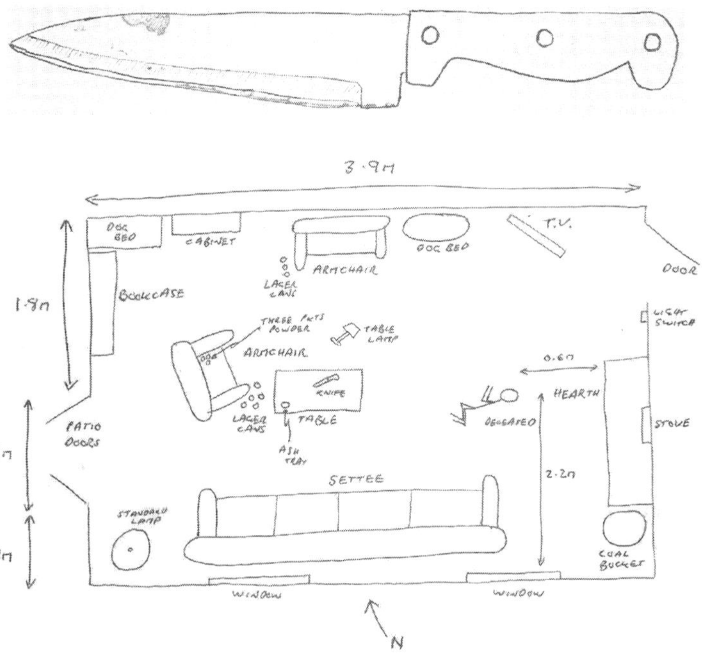

Figure 4.5 Example of a sketch by a CSM of a knife with apparent blood staining (top) and relevant information at the crime scene (bottom).

process that must be undertaken in order to establish whether the death is likely to be suspicious will be along these lines:

- *Is the scene consistent with the circumstances described in the FOA briefing?* Is there anything in the scene that is contrary to the briefing, such as evidence of blood spillage?
- *Are the premises secure?* If it is an indoor scene, are the doors secure and locked? If not, this may be an exit route for the offender. If a door is locked, is it on a drop latch (which means it could have been secured on exit) or is it locked with a mortise lock? If the latter, is there any sign of a key for the lock inside the premises (perhaps in a coat pocket or on the kitchen table)? Are the windows secure and fastened?
- *Are there any signs of a disturbance or an untidy search?* Occasionally an individual's lifestyle may have the appearance of an untidy search, so the general tidiness of the premises should be considered when evaluating this point.

- *Is there any evidence of robbery?* Are there valuables on display in the premises such as jewellery or a wallet, which could easily have been removed by an offender if the motive was robbery?
- *Are there signs of anyone else being present in the recent past?* Is there more than one used cup or glass on a table suggesting that two people may have been drinking together? Are there multiple brands of cigarette butts in an ashtray?
- *Are there any injuries to the deceased?* (Sildo, et al., 2011.) Injuries may arise during a fall, so is there any object in the vicinity of the deceased that might account for their injuries?

While not exhaustive, this list represents the sort of questions the CSIs must ask themselves as they conduct a visual examination of the scene. Unless there is clear evidence of the involvement of someone else, then the decision of whether or not the death is suspicious should be based on the strength of the available evidence.

Box 4.3 The need to perform a competent scene examination

In June 1994, Nicole Brown Simpson and Ronald Goldman were found murdered outside Brown Simpson's house in Los Angeles, California, USA. Brown Simpson had been stabbed multiple times in the head and neck and had defence wounds on her hands. The police suspected retired American football player O.J. Simpson, Brown Simpson's former husband, who had a history of threats and domestic violence. At the trial, the prosecution argued that Simpson had driven to Brown Simpson's home, stabbed her, and then stabbed Goldman when he arrived at the house. A trail of bloody footwear impressions was found leading away from the bodies. The prosecution also argued that Simpson left three drops of blood on the driveway near the gate to his own home. A pair of gloves, one found at the crime scene and the other near to Simpson's home, contained DNA, the source of which could not be definitively said not to come from one or more of Simpson, Brown Simpson and Goldman, with the glove at Simpson's home also containing a long strand of blonde hair, consistent with Brown Simpson's. A federal agent examined the bloody footwear impressions and determined that they appeared to be the same size as Simpson's footwear and that they were an exclusive make, with only a few pairs sold at one store in New

York where Simpson shopped. Although Simpson claimed that he did not own such a pair of shoes, the prosecution was able to produce a photograph of him wearing shoes of similar appearance.

Analysis: Despite what, at first sight, might appear to be significant forensic evidence to implicate O.J. Simpson in these offences, in court the defence argued that previous errors in DNA testing at the laboratory that carried out the DNA analysis, a breakdown in procedures for handling exhibits for this case and poor practice at the crime scene made the evidence unreliable. The defence attacked the credibility of the Los Angeles Police Department (LAPD) after an LAPD criminalist admitted missing some blood spots at the crime scene and returning later to recover them. The same criminalist admitted to not wearing gloves during the collection of the evidence. An LAPD detective who attended the scene was also shown by the defence to have lied about previous use of racially abusive language, leading to an allegation by the defence that the detective had planted the glove at the crime scene. Despite the LAPD criminalist being excluded as a contributor to the DNA profiles of the blood recovered from the scene, this all helped to raise doubts in the minds of the jurors. The defence was successfully able to undermine the evidential value of the forensic evidence. Simpson was acquitted, although in post-trial interviews some of the jury said that they thought Simpson was probably guilty, but that the prosecution had failed to make its case adequately. After the trial, the relatives of the deceased successfully brought a civil suit against Simpson for wrongful death.

Forensic examination of volume crime

What is volume crime?

As indicated earlier, volume crime is generally acknowledged to be one that is not classed as serious (such as rape or grievous bodily harm), but that nevertheless occurs frequently and has a significant impact on many victims and communities. These types of offences include street robbery, burglary, most types of theft, vehicle crime, criminal damage and drugs offences.

From the perspective of the CSI, volume crime differs from major crime in that the CSI will often be the first (and sometimes only) police presence at the crime scene (Ludwig et al., 2012). As we have discussed earlier, the CSI at the scene of a major incident will receive a briefing from the FOA or supervisory police officer present. If a police officer has not attended the volume crime scene, then the briefing and task allocation for the CSI are most likely to come from the police control room. In this case, details of the offence and forensic opportunities passed to the CSI will be based on a telephone conversation between the person reporting the crime (usually the victim) and the police controller. We have also seen how most police forces in the UK use attendance criteria to make an informed decision about the forensic opportunities at a crime scene, the need to request a CSI to attend and the varying opportunities from differing volume crime types. In the next chapter, the effectiveness of various screening approaches will be considered in more detail.

Restricted examination of the scene

As the time at any given volume crime scene is likely to be limited, the CSI must focus their attention on certain areas of the crime scene. The most obvious points to consider are the offender's entry and exit points. For a burglary, the CSI must decide which one(s) of the many windows and doors present were used. Sometimes this will be obvious from the presence of broken window glass or a window that has been forced to gain access. At the other extreme, entry may simply have been by walking through an open door. Both scenarios offer the potential for forensic evidence recovery, as the offender has definitely been at these locations in the scene and therefore may have moved items or left behind items (such as a tool to gain entry) or impressions (such as fingerprints or footwear). It should not be assumed that the point of entry is also the point of exit, as often a burglar, for instance, laden with the spoils of their crime, will find it easier to exist via a door than via the partially open window through which they gained access.

Away from the entry and exit points, and without a briefing from the victim about what has been disturbed, the CSI needs to put themselves in the position of the offender to try to determine where in the burgled premises the offender has been. Signs to look for include areas of an untidy search and items knocked over or out of position (such as a table lamp on the floor). In the case of vehicle crime, the CSI has a much more restricted scene to examine. If the vehicle has been driven by the offender, the CSI would examine the steering wheel, gear lever, hand brake and rear-view mirror. Unfortunately, many of these surfaces are unlikely to be suitable for fingerprint recovery (due to their uneven nature) and, as we have seen in Chapter 2, cellular DNA is very problematic for obtaining a single full profile of the offender. More recently, tapings from the head rest of a seat thought to have been occupied by the offender have also been recovered for cellular DNA analysis. Items likely to have been moved by the offender can more easily be determined in a vehicle than in premises, such as the contents of the glove box or a box of CDs strewn over the passenger seat. Items foreign to the scene (that is, brought to the scene by the offender) can also be identified following consultation with the victim. Such items might include discarded drinks cans or bottles, chewing gum or cigarette butts, all of which may well yield the fingerprints or DNA of the offender.

The evidential value of different volume crime scenes

In the case of a stolen vehicle, placing individuals inside the vehicle after it was stolen (such as by a fingerprint on a drinks can or DNA on a cigarette butt) does not necessarily prove that that person broke into and then drove the vehicle. We considered earlier the forensic value of crime scenes and, in particular, a wing mirror broken off a vehicle. With a stolen vehicle, the best evidence to show that an individual was the driver of the stolen vehicle (as opposed to simply being a passenger in it) will be related to the driving of the vehicle, such as on the rear-view mirror, where the offender may have left a fingerprint while adjusting it. For the police investigators, this can represent the difference between obtaining forensic *intelligence* (that an individual was present inside the stolen vehicle) and forensic *evidence* (that an individual drove the stolen vehicle).

At the scene of a domestic burglary, the CSI will focus their assessment of the interior of the premises on evidence on non-mobile items (such as a fingerprint on an interior door), which offers greater evidential value than that on mobile items (such as DNA on a cigarette end). The CSI will also be mindful that with regard to DNA, material that can be attributed to a stain (such as a blood spot on a carpet) offers better evidential value than cellular DNA (such as a swab from a door handle). In Chapter 5 we will discuss the probative value of various evidence types, and the role of the CSI's decision making.

Preserving exhibits

Different types of packaging

Different evidence types require different methods of recovery. In general, the CSI will look to use packaging that is fit for purpose and enables easy removal of the exhibit for subsequent forensic analysis. Particulate evidence types, such as glass, fibres, hair, soil and paint, are often stored in sterile rigid polythene pots following recovery at the scene. This recovery is often most conveniently performed with a pair of sterile disposable tweezers. The sterile and disposable nature of these items removes any suggestion that the material recovered may have become contaminated, as long as a new item is used during the packaging of each new piece of evidence. The pots are sealed with screw-on lids and then adhesive tape wound round the lid to ensure that it does not become loose. Generally, special *evidence tape* is used that is marked with the name of the police force. The polythene pot would then be placed inside an *evidence bag*. This is either a polythene or a paper bag that can easily be sealed and, as we will see, is specially designed to store all evidence, both forensic and non-forensic. In common use today is the *tamper-evident bag*, which is self-seal and undergoes a colour change on the seal if an attempt is made to open it.

Recovery of trace evidence has already been discussed in Chapter 3. Paint may be scraped, for instance, from the side of a vehicle that has been in collision with another vehicle, with a disposable scalpel directly into the polythene pot. The scalpel is then packaged with the sample of paint. Similarly, soil may be scraped from the inside of a vehicle's wheel arch. Hairs and fibres can also be recovered from, say, a carpet or item of furniture by repeatedly placing the adhesive side of plastic tape onto the item of interest. The tape is then mounted onto acetate sheet and stored in an evidence bag. We have already seen how fingerprints may be recovered from smooth, non-porous surfaces at the crime scene in a similar fashion, following the application of a dry powder to the latent fingerprint, and these would also then be stored in an evidence bag.

Impressions (such as footwear, tyre or instrument marks) would, following recovery, be stored in a purpose-designed *evidence box* (looking similar to a pizza box) that enables the storage of bulky items like casts of footwear impressions. Such items would be secured inside the box (often with the same evidence tape as used to seal the polythene pots) in order that the item does not move around inside the box during transit.

Preventing movement is crucial for exhibits such as these, where the size and shape of the impression taken are required to be associated back to a shoe or tool and so on.

Items suspected of having DNA material of interest (such as a blood, saliva or semen stain) may be packaged in a paper evidence bag if recovered dry. If recovered wet (perhaps having been taken from a washing machine), then the item must be stored in a polythene evidence bag to prevent it wetting the paper bag and thereby reducing the bag's mechanical strength. Dry items should not be placed inside a polythene bag as this will retain any moisture present, thereby encouraging microbial degradation of any DNA. Cigarette butts should be recovered individually and placed in a polythene pot and then inside an evidence bag. DNA should be kept cold and dry to prevent degradation and so most exhibits for DNA analysis should be frozen as soon as possible after being taken. Items like swabs should certainly be frozen; dry clothing may be stored at room temperature and wet clothing dried in air, although freezing is the more usual option. Items that may also contain fingerprints would, wherever possible, not be frozen, as the thermal cycling caused by freezing and thawing can damage the ridge detail present in a fingerprint.

Items thought to contain petrol or other volatile hydrocarbons (such as fire debris from an arson or petrol-soaked clothing) should be stored in a nylon bag, securely sealed, as nylon prevents the permeation of volatile hydrocarbons.

An example of a guide to packaging for a UK police force is shown in Figure 4.6.

Exhibit labels

We have seen that the outermost packaging for an exhibit is an evidence bag, which is generally made of polythene or paper. An evidence bag differs from an ordinary bag in that it has printed on it what is called a *continuity label*. This label is required for all police exhibits and contains not only the details of the exhibit, where and when it was seized and by whom, but also, crucially, details of all other people who have subsequently had possession of that exhibit. These details also include the date and time that an exhibit was handed from one individual to another. This audit trail of possession is known as the continuity of the exhibit. For other types of bag (not specifically manufactured as evidence bags), a card label providing the same information is securely fixed to the outermost layer of an exhibit's packaging.

Contemporaneous notes

As well as ensuring that the continuity of exhibits is maintained, the CSI will meticulously record their activities at the crime scene in writing. This written record is made during the crime scene examination and is referred to as making *contemporaneous notes*. To aid the CSI, many police forces have pro-forma *scene examination reports* for the CSI to complete during their examination (Johnson and Reynolds, 2006). A typical example is shown in Figure 4.7.

SAMPLE	PACKAGING	STORAGE	COMMENTS
Accelerants	Use nylon bag, tied in a knot and swan necked then double bagged. Secure exhibit label to outer bag with seal. A control nylon bag (air sample) must be taken first using the same procedure.	Cool, dry environment.	If liquid accelerant is within container, decant it into a metal tin, follow packaging instructions. Secure a "flammable" label to the exterior
Bodily fluids	Package within a plastic container and place in tamper evident bag.	Freeze. (Toxicology samples fridge)	Ensure BIOHAZARD tape is clearly displayed on front of bag.
Clothing (DRY)	Package in suitable sized paper bag. Fold corners in, fold over twice and secure with forensic tape. Shoes MUST be packaged in separate bags.	Cool, dry environment.	If contaminated with bodily fluids ensure BIOHAZARD tape is clearly displayed on front of bag.
Clothing (WET)	Consider air drying in sterile dedicated drying room (paper bag) or freezing (plastic bag). Shoes MUST be packaged separately.	Cool, dry environment after air drying or store within freezer. If damp or wet items are not dried or frozen they will rot or go mouldy.	Ensure Health and Safety precautions are taken when drying items and if contaminated with bodily fluids ensure BIOHAZARD tape is clearly displayed on front of bag
Documents	Package within tamper evident bag.	Cool, dry environment.	Items to be analysed for impressed marks such as handwriting must be protected in a box or similar rigid container/ envelope.
Drug and related items.	Package within tamper evident bag.	Cool, dry environment.	
Explosive Devices (ie: detonators)	Do not attempt to handle suspect explosive devices untill they have been cleared by E.O.D (Bomb Disposal). Then consult Forensic Investigation or Bomb Scene Manager for advice.		

Continued

Firearms	Must first be made safe by an AFO. Package in suitable paper/ plastic bag or preferably cardboard box, to preserve for fingerprints, etc.	Cool, dry environment.	Ensure "Safe" label and exhibit label are attached to outside of packaging.
Glass	Secure in a cardboard box or other rigid container, seal all edges. Secure exhibit label to box or place in tamper evident bag.	Cool, dry environment.	
Large items (mattress, carpet, etc.)	Package in sheets of brown paper. Seal all edges with tape. Attach exhibit label to outer packaging.	Cool, dry environment.	If contaminated with bodily fluids ensure BIOHAZARD tape is clearly displayed on front of packaging.
Leaves (cannabis, etc.)	Package in suitable sized paper bag.	Cool, dry environment.	Perforate bag with holes to reduce degradation.
Mobile phones and scanners	Package in tamper evident bag. Use a rigid container if preserving for fingerprints, DNA or electronic analysis.	Cool, dry environment.	Package in suitable container to prevent damage of settings, buttons, etc, if item requires analysis
Paint	Packaged in suitable container (plastic, folded paper, etc) and place in tamper evident bag.	Cool, dry environment.	
Particulates (dry building materials and other items)	Package in suitable container (plastic, folded paper, etc) and place in tamper evident bag.	Cool, dry environment.	
Sharps (needles, etc.)	MUST be packaged within a sharps container and packaged in a tamper evident bag. CLEARLY MARK CONTENTS ON BAG FOR HEALTH AND SAFETY.	Cool, dry environment or freeze dependant on contents.	If contaminated with bodily fluids ensure BIOHAZARD tape is clearly displayed on front of bag.
Sharps (screwdrivers, knives, etc.)	Package in screw top knife tube seal outer and inner tube with tape then package in tamper evident bag.	Cool, dry environment.	
Vegetation (cannabis plants, etc.)	Package in suitable sized paper bag.	Cool, dry environment.	Do not water after seizure, one plant per bag.

NOTE: Ensure exhibit label is fully completed and continuity is maintained at all times. If any item is contaminated with bodily fluids ensure BIOHAZARD tape is clearly visible on outer packaging.
If in doubt consult Forensic Investigation for further advice.

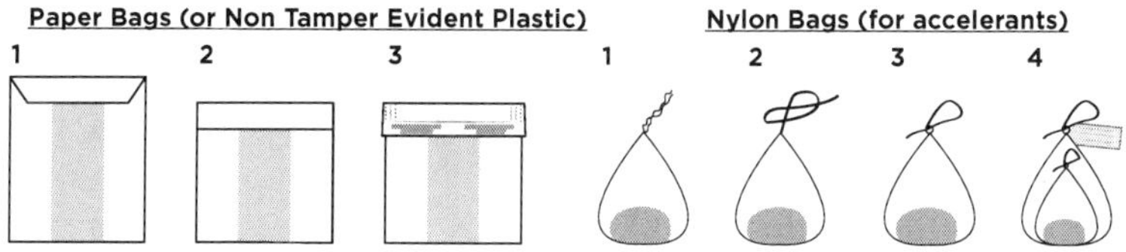

Figure 4.6 Example of a guide to packing forensic exhibits.

CRIME SCENE INVESTIGATION REPORT FORM	
Offence Type:	Crime Scene Investigator:
Division:	Investigating Officer:
Date examined:	Crime Ref No:
Time Start:	Finish:
Location of Offence:	Weather:
Name of Injured Party (if known)	
L/O:	
Details of Examination	Photographs: Y/N Number taken:
	Footwear marks Found: Y/N
	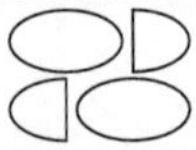
	Tool mark: Y/N Type:
	DNA found: Y/N
	Finger/Palm mark found: Y/N
	Glove Marks: Y/N Type:
	Eliminations: Fingerprints: Y/N Number of sets: DNA: Y/N Number of samples:
Signed:	Date:

Figure 4.7 Example of a CSI scene examination report.

These contemporaneous notes are used by the CSI at a later stage to prepare their witness statement for court. As this may be done many months after the crime scene was examined, it is clear that detailed and accurate contemporaneous notes will enable easier and more accurate production of a witness statement. If called to give evidence in court, the CSI, with the permission of the judge, may refer to their contemporaneous notes in order to refresh their memory. Again, detailed contemporaneous notes will enable the CSI to have a more accurate recall of their actions at the crime scene, possibly many months or even years earlier. We have seen in Box 4.3 how the defence may use inaccuracies in scene recording or examination to attempt to discredit a prosecution witness and to draw attention away from the significance of evidence. Simple inaccuracies in the CSI's contemporaneous notes (such as recording the wrong date or time of attendance) may be seized on by a defence attorney as evidence to a jury that poor record keeping by the CSI reflects poor scene examination technique.

How evidence can become contaminated

Evidence can be contaminated at the crime scene by incorrect methods of recovery (such as repeatedly using the same pair of tweezers to recover multiple exhibits). Innocent contamination can arise through the CSI not wearing appropriate protective clothing and then, for example, contaminating a DNA swab by sneezing (or even speaking) over it. Contamination can also arise through incorrect packaging. If glass recovered from a broken window at the crime scene were packaged together with the clothing of the suspect, then transference of glass onto the clothing would be likely to occur, rendering an examination of the clothing for glass fragments of no evidential value.

Secondary transfer of material may also lead to contamination. Consider an armed police officer who arrests a suspect on suspicion of being in possession of a firearm. That police officer would be likely to be contaminated with GSR, which could be transferred to the suspect's clothing, making any subsequent examination of that clothing for gunshot residue problematic. Secondary transfer may also occur between victim and suspect.

Now consider a suspect transported to a police station in the rear of the same police vehicle used to transport the victim. The defence may well argue at trial that any trace evidence recovered from the suspect was picked up while in the vehicle, having been deposited earlier by the victim. For similar reasons, the CSM should ensure that the same CSI does not visit scenes associated with both the victim and any suspect. In a long-drawn-out enquiry, this can be difficult to manage with limited resources and with a large number of scenes to examine forensically, and assistance from neighbouring police forces may be required. While the likelihood is small that a CSI will (say) transfer fibre evidence from one scene to another if the time between visiting them was several weeks and appropriate protective clothing was worn at each scene, it is generally viewed as bad practice to have a CSI visit multiple scenes, as this offers the defence an opportunity to suggest that contamination of evidence has occurred, particularly if that evidence becomes crucial to the prosecution case (see Box 4.3).

Summary

In this chapter we have considered how specialised police personnel, generically known as crime scene investigators, undertake a forensic examination of the crime scene to identify, recover and preserve items of forensic interest. The actions of the CSI vary depending on the scene being examined and a distinction has been made between volume and major crime. In the former case, the CSI is likely to have time and resource limitations and therefore concentrates the examination in the areas most likely to yield evidence that will assist in identifying an offender and solving the crime. It is common for police forces to employ attendance criteria for volume crime to help in determining whether a particular scene warrants the attendance of a CSI. For major crime, more resources will be deployed to the crime scene and, in some cases, the CSI and crime scene manager will be required to assess the scene and determine whether or not a crime has been committed. We have also examined how evidence is preserved, continuity maintained and contamination of evidence avoided. In the next chapter we will consider how this forensic evidence, once analysed, is interpreted to provide the police and courts with a measure of its evidential value.

Study questions

1 Taking the example of the buried remains in Figures 4.2–4.4, if the remains appeared to have been recently buried, consider what evidence types the CSI might be looking for in and around the outer cordon. Would the forensic strategy differ between the inner and outer cordons?
2 In the UK, the forensic examination of a recovered stolen motor vehicle might well be undertaken by a less qualified person than

someone who would forensically examine the scene of (say) an aggravated burglary. Consider why this might be so and the factors that would influence the skill required to conduct an appropriate forensic examination of different offence types.

5 INTERPRETING EVIDENCE

In the preceding chapters a number of commonly used forensic science disciplines have been described, along with an overview of the scientific analysis and recovery techniques associated with these forms of evidence. Each of these forensic techniques, and the many others not covered in this book, aim to provide police investigators and criminal courts with information relevant to a particular crime in order to assist with determining what occurred and who was involved, and ultimately to contribute to verdict decisions at trial. Results of forensic analyses are most likely to be among many pieces of information related to any particular incident, and therefore evidence cannot be considered in isolation but rather needs to be interpreted within the context of a dynamic investigation.

In the vast majority of police investigations, it is not known what exactly occurred before, during and after a criminal event took place and so all forms of relevant evidence help to piece together these unknown details. There is an abundance of uncertainty associated with any investigation and indeed with items of evidence, which makes decision making and reasoning complex and at risk of errors. Despite the fact that a particular forensic result may be based on rigorous scientific method (e.g. DNA analysis) and therefore may be presumed to be objective, the interpretation of the results in the context of a complicated investigation or trial remains a very subjective process. It is for this reason that attention has been drawn to the evaluation of evidence in the academic literature.

In this chapter we will explore the theoretical and philosophical perspectives that underpin the topic of reasoning and evidence interpretation. This will require consideration of probability theory and the use of likelihood ratios for quantifying and expressing confidence and evidential value. That will lead into a discussion of how the conclusions reached by forensic experts can be communicated to judges and juries during criminal trials. Finally, the chapter will also consider sources of error and bias in reasoning, and discuss some operational issues that may contribute to potential bias in the interpretation of forensic results. The topics covered in this chapter provide a good example of why it is important to take a multidisciplinary approach to studying and practising forensic science, and how a better understanding of it is achieved by the contribution of disciplines such as mathematics, physical and natural sciences, psychology and philosophy.

Reasoning about evidence

Reasoning about, and interpretation of, forensic evidence occur frequently during a criminal investigation, alongside other complicated decision-making processes that all contribute to the development of any potential prosecution. However, it is not only police investigators who interpret evidence, so it is important to remember that decisions are made based on the interpretation of evidence at various stages of the criminal justice process. This begins with the offender and the victim in many situations, and although their decisions are generally not considered in discussions of evidence interpretation, they can have a profound impact on the outcome of an investigation.

Consider, for example, an experienced offender who is committing a burglary and has previously been apprehended and charged as a result of leaving fingerprints behind at previous crime scenes. This offender may decide to take precautions in their future crimes to avoid leaving fingerprints, perhaps by wearing gloves (Beauregard and Martineau, 2014). This decision on the part of this offender will therefore have an impact on the types of evidence that CSIs are able to recover from the crime scene. Now let us consider a victim of a burglary, and their decisions and actions at the crime scene. On realising that their house has been broken into, some victims tidy up before the police arrive to search the scene for evidence. By failing to realise the potential for evidence to be present, and the impact that cleaning can have on the ability to recover that evidence, the victim's actions will have consequences for the forensic opportunities at the scene. Another common example of this is when a victim of sexual assault takes a shower before reporting that a crime has occurred, which can limit the effectiveness of evidence recovery during a medical examination.

Once a crime has been reported to the police, the investigative decision making begins. In cases of serious crime, CSIs will be dispatched to the crime scene. However, as we have seen in Chapter 4, this is not always the case for volume crimes such as theft from motor vehicles and burglaries. In some jurisdictions, finite resources do not allow all volume crime scenes to be attended by a CSI and so the first investigative decision is whether or not to request a scene visit. The procedure for allocating crime scene resources to volume crimes differs between jurisdictions, although some research has been conducted in order to compare different methods. A study by Lingwood et al. (in press) analysed recorded police data to determine whether screening of theft from motor vehicle crimes was more effective depending on whether the scene was assessed over the telephone or in person by a police officer. The results indicated that when scenes were assessed in person by a police officer, DNA and trace evidence were more likely to be recovered by the CSI. Conversely, when assessed over the phone, fingerprints were more likely to be recovered. This study indicates that the forensic opportunities at volume crime scenes may vary depending on the assessment procedures used, and therefore more research is needed to help maximise the police's use of CSIs in these cases.

Once the decision to deploy a CSI is made, the search of the crime scene involves many examples of reasoning about evidence. In Chapter 4 the process of crime scene examination and the collection of evidence were discussed. At this stage it is important to consider in further detail some of the factors that contribute to effective decision making at crime scenes.

Decision making during crime scene examination

As we have already seen in Chapter 4, in most cases crime scene investigators get only one chance to examine a scene while it is still in the state in which it was left after a crime has been committed. This means that although there may be opportunities to visit scenes subsequent to the initial examination, in most cases the availability of any further evidence will be limited by issues such as contamination and integrity of evidence (see Box 5.1). In other words, because there is usually only one chance to examine a scene, the decisions made during this initial examination need to be highlighted as crucial. To complicate matters further, resources such as time and money are limited, which poses further difficulties from a decision-making perspective. In an ideal, albeit hypothetical, world, everything at a crime scene could be recovered, packaged and analysed, which would ensure that nothing was missed and all opportunities for forensic evidence were realised. However, in real crime situations this is not the case, and CSIs need to exercise a great deal of discretion regarding what to recover during their limited time at a scene.

Box 5.1 Evidence integrity in the murder of Meredith Kercher

On 1 November 2007, Meredith Kercher was found murdered in her bedroom of the cottage she shared with three other women in Perugia, Italy. Kercher was a British student who was spending a year studying abroad. Soon after the crime was reported by Kercher's housemate Amanda Knox, the police began to suspect that Knox and her boyfriend Rafaelle Sollecito were involved in the crime. A full crime scene examination was conducted at the cottage as well as at Sollecito's apartment, and at the first trial the prosecution relied heavily on a number of key pieces of forensic evidence. One of these, which allegedly linked Sollecito to the crime scene, was a bra clasp belonging to the victim, which was reported to have had the victim's and Sollecito's DNA recovered from it. There were many other forensic exhibits entered into evidence at the trial, and the jury convicted Knox and Sollecito of murder and sentenced them to 26 and 25 years imprisonment, respectively. However, many aspects of the forensic evidence were challenged during an appeal and their convictions were overturned in 2011. One such piece of contested evidence was the bra clasp, which was not collected from the scene until 47 days after the crime occurred. Nevertheless, both Knox and Sollecito were reconvicted in a retrial in 2014.

Analysis: The bra clasp evidence in the Meredith Kercher murder trial was highly questionable on the grounds that it was not recovered during the initial crime scene investigation, and therefore the integrity of this piece of evidence could not be guaranteed. This highlights the importance of a thorough crime scene examination, as well as the dangers of contamination. This case also raises many issues relating to how forensic science can contribute to wrongful convictions (or at the very least, unsafe convictions), which will be discussed later in this chapter and further in Chapter 7.

Given the fact that many crime scenes are examined under time and resource constraints, the key to effective evidence collection is to make accurate decisions about what evidence is most likely to contribute to determining what happened and identifying the guilty offender(s). This feature of evidence is referred to as having *probative value*, and it describes the extent to which a piece of evidence is useful for proving facts in court. There are a number of features of evidence that determine its probative value, and it is awareness of these factors that contributes to effective decision making during crime scene examinations.

Imagine a straightforward, common volume crime scene such as a stolen vehicle. If a CSI is asked to examine the recovered vehicle for evidence that might link a suspect to this offence, they will be mindful of what evidence types might be most relevant and probative in this particular case. If the vehicle has a large amount of debris and rubbish in it, much of this is likely to belong to the owner of the car, so it is not probative and we would not want to collect all of it. However, if for instance it was known that the owner is not a smoker but a cigarette end is found inside the car, this might be a useful source of DNA, potentially belonging to the offender. Similarly, fingerprints recovered from the steering wheel of the car or the rear-view mirror would be useful for placing an individual inside the vehicle (and therefore would be of high probative value), while fingerprints on the outside of the car would be less useful (and therefore of lower probative value).

Another common issue relating to probative value concerns crime scenes in which a suspect has legitimate access to the location. Imagine a murder scene in which the victim's husband is a suspect, and the crime occurred in their house. There are many sources of potential evidence within the crime scene that could legitimately be linked to the suspect, since he lives at the premises. Therefore, items of probative value need to be carefully identified and collected. For example, it would not be particularly useful to place the husband in the house, or even in contact with the murder weapon if it was an item belonging to him. However, it might be useful to find his fingerprints (or footwear marks and so on) in the victim's blood at the scene if this would prove to be inconsistent with his version of events.

As outlined here, and also in Chapter 4, the determination of probative value and therefore the decisions made about what evidence to collect from crime scenes rely on careful decision making during the scene examination. We will see a little later in this chapter a number of methods for attempting to quantify the probative value of forensic evidence, and some of the difficulties associated with communicating these values in the courtroom.

Intelligence versus evidence

Forensic material and information gathered during police investigations can contribute to the resolution of criminal matters in a variety of ways. Investigators need to be strategic about how information gathered is utilised in order to maximise the usefulness of different evidence types. Awareness of these different uses of information is therefore an important part of the investigative decision-making process.

One distinction that it is important to make is the difference between intelligence and evidence. Police investigators collect information from many sources during complex investigations, and the distinction between whether a piece of information is useful as intelligence or evidence relies mainly on how that information is used. Police intelligence, which can include many evidence types including informants, eyewitnesses and forensic material, is gathered throughout an investigation in order to help build a picture of what happened and who may have been involved in a particular incident. However, what distinguishes intelligence from evidence is that intelligence is not intended to form the basis of the prosecution of an individual. In other words, only evidence is presented during a trial and therefore only evidence contributes to the prosecution of a defendant.

Investigators need to be mindful of the difference between intelligence and evidence, in order to ensure that critical pieces of information are collected and documented following correct protocol so that they will be admissible for presentation in the courtroom. Any information collected improperly or unlawfully is likely not to meet the rules of admissibility, and will therefore only be useful as intelligence, but not evidence (see Chapter 7 for a detailed discussion of admissibility criteria). In each jurisdiction, the police must follow detailed rules governing the rights of citizens and police powers to obtain evidence in various situations. In England and Wales, these rules are outlined in the Police and Criminal Evidence Act (PACE) 1984, while in some other countries the requirements are outlined in various sections of the Criminal Codes. The consequences of not gathering evidence properly can be significant, and Box 5.2 provides an example of a case in which improperly obtained evidence resulted in a successful appeal.

Box 5.2 R *v*. Nathaniel and the exclusionary rule

The defendant in this UK case, Nathaniel, was charged with rape, and the prosecution relied almost entirely on DNA evidence obtained from the crime scene, which 'matched' Nathaniel's DNA held on the National DNA Database. The sample obtained and loaded onto the database had been acquired by police during a previous rape investigation four years earlier, for which Nathaniel was a suspect. However, Nathaniel had been acquitted of this previous rape charge, and at the time of this case the legislation for retention of DNA required samples to be removed from the database if the suspect was not convicted. Therefore, Nathaniel's DNA should not have been retained after the first rape investigation, and he argued on appeal in the second trial that he had been assured that the DNA sample he provided during the first investigation would not be used for any other purposes and would be destroyed. The Court of Appeal ruled that the original DNA sample was illegally obtained in relation to the second rape investigation, and the charges against Nathaniel collapsed, with this evidence being deemed inadmissible at trial.

Analysis: This example highlights the importance of relying on lawfully obtained evidence, and also raises issues about the use of DNA databases for solving crime. We will see in Chapter 8 how recent changes in UK legislation (the Protection of Freedoms Act 2012) relating to the retention of DNA profiles on the NDNAD will have an impact on the usefulness of the database.

Determining probative value

We have seen how determining the usefulness of evidence, or its probative value, is a crucial aspect of a police investigation and the eventual prosecution of a defendant. This section will look more closely at some methods for quantifying the probative value of evidence, which helps us begin to articulate the usefulness and relative strength of various pieces of investigative information. Although these methods can be useful for forensic experts, the courts have been less enthusiastic about adopting such mathematical approaches, for reasons that we will discuss later in the chapter.

Probability

Many forensic science techniques rely on probabilities when interpretations of probative value are made. It is important therefore to review first some basic laws of probability, before looking at some forensic examples of how probabilities are used to express forensic results.

When we express a probability, we are stating a mathematical measure of the certainty that a particular event or outcome will occur. This measure of certainty is calculated based on a couple of assumptions about our situation: first, that we can express all possible outcomes quantitatively; and second, that all possible outcomes are equally likely to occur. In addition to these assumptions, we are also usually assuming that each event or outcome occurs independently of other outcomes (this assumption is problematic in forensic scenarios, for reasons that we will consider later). Probability values range from 0 (there is no chance of the event occurring) to 1 (100% certainty of the event occurring).

In order to calculate the probability of a particular event occurring, we need to know two values: the number of selected outcomes we are interested in; and the total number of possible outcomes that could occur. A simple formula to calculate the probability of any given outcome is

$$\textit{Probability of event A} = \frac{\textit{the number of outcomes producing event A}}{\textit{the total number of possible outcomes}}$$

A common, and very simple, example of calculating probabilities is to consider a six-sided die. If we want to calculate the probability of rolling the die and getting an even number as our outcome, we can use this formula. The numerator in this equation is 3, because there are three ways to roll an even number (we could roll a 2, 4 or 6), and the denominator is 6, as this is how many possible outcomes there are on a six-sided die. This gives us

$$\textit{Probability of rolling an even number} = \frac{3}{6} = \frac{1}{2} = .50$$

Therefore, the probability of rolling an even number is .50.

Now that we have reviewed how probabilities are calculated, there is another rule of probability that is particularly important in forensic calculations. This is called the *product rule,* and it allows us to calculate the probability of multiple, independent outcomes occurring. The product rule is expressed using the formula

$$\textit{Probability of A } \textbf{\textit{and}} \textit{ B} = (\textit{Probability of A}) \times (\textit{Probability of B})$$

If we go back to the example of rolling a die, we can calculate the probability of rolling a 6 on two consecutive rolls as

$$\textit{Probability of rolling two 6s in a row} = \frac{1}{6} \times \frac{1}{6} = \frac{1}{36} = .028$$

The final rule of probability to review here is how we calculate the probability that an event will not occur. Suppose we want to calculate the probability of *not* rolling a value of 6 on the die. We know that the probability of rolling a 6 is 1/6, or 0.17, so the probability of this outcome *not* happening is

$$\textit{Probability of } \textbf{Not} \textit{ rolling a } 6 = 1 - \textit{Probability of rolling a } 6 = 1 - .17 = .83$$

One of the most frequent examples of probabilities in the forensic sciences comes in those associated with DNA evidence testimony. Forensic DNA experts are often heard in court expressing very small probabilities in relation to the chances that the DNA analysed has not come from the defendant. Often these probabilities are in the range of '1 in many millions', and this particular calculation is referred to as the random match probability (RMP). The RMP is the probability that the crime sample tested 'matches' the defendant, if the defendant was not the source of the crime sample. In other words, it is the probability that the DNA match is a random coincidence. With current DNA technology, the discriminating power of DNA is so strong that the RMP is often an extremely small number. However, it is important to remember that this probability is never zero!

Bayesian reasoning

We have seen in the previous section that the calculation of probabilities is one way in which forensic results can be expressed and their respective probative values articulated. Throughout this chapter the complexity of investigations has been emphasised, therefore another important use of probabilities in an investigative context is to calculate our confidence in a particular proposition, given the emergence of new information. This concept is the hallmark of police investigations and criminal trials, as within both contexts we are required continually to update our beliefs based on new information or evidence that has been revealed.

This is where *Bayes' theorem* is applicable, 'a rule for updating degrees of belief on receiving new evidence' (Taroni et al., 2006, p. 7). This approach to probability is also applicable to forensic situations, because unlike the examples in the previous section, in which we assume independence of the outcomes, conditional probability allows us to recognise that situations in investigative contexts are rarely independent, and indeed that the probabilities of various pieces of evidence often relate on one another (or are *conditional* on each other).

Before moving on to see how Bayes' theorem works using an example, we need to consider its algebraic form. Suppose that A is an event whose probability we are considering and B is some piece of relevant evidence or information that we have obtained. Bayes' theorem states that the probability of A occurring, given that B is true (denoted as A|B), is

$$P(A|B) = \frac{P(B|A) \times P(A)}{P(B)}$$

If we were considering the guilt of a suspect (A) in the light of new evidence (B), then the equation above would be read as: 'The probability of the suspect being guilty, given the piece of evidence, is equal to the probability of the evidence occurring if the suspect were guilty multiplied by the prior probability of the suspect's guilt, divided by the probability of the evidence occurring.'

This type of reasoning is valid when we are able to accurately estimate the prior probability of a suspect's guilt, or the probability that a suspect is guilty before we know any of the evidence. Of course, this estimate is very difficult to make (in Chapter 3 we discussed how it can be difficult to make for some evidence types such as glass or fibres, for instance). Some people would argue that the 'innocent until proven guilty' premise of common law systems requires that the prior probability of guilt should be zero; however, this would result in our calculation always resulting in a zero outcome (as the numerator would always be 0).

Another option would be to assume that everyone in the relevant population is equally likely to be guilty, and therefore P(A) would be

$$\frac{1}{\textit{The size of the relevant population}}$$

Nevertheless, this reasoning is also logically flawed, as it is very unlikely that every member of the population of interest is equally likely to have committed a given criminal act. Finally, some commentators argue that perhaps assigning a value of .50 to the prior probability of guilt is most appropriate, although this is also problematic as it assumes that the suspect is as likely to be guilty as they are to be innocent.

In addition to these debates about how to assign prior probabilities correctly, the issue of the complexity of Bayes' theorem, and the fact that people do not intuitively think in conditional probability terms, has led to disagreement about whether this approach should be used in the courtroom, as the example in Box 5.3 demonstrates.

Box 5.3 Bayes theorem in the courtroom – the case of R *v.* Adams

Denis Adams stood trial in the UK in 1995 for rape, and the prosecution's case relied almost entirely on DNA evidence from the crime scene, which 'matched' Adams. The victim in the case failed to pick Adams out of an identification parade, and indeed her estimation of the age of her attacker ('in his 20s') was inconsistent with Adams, whom she described as looking in his 40s (he was 37 years old). During the trial, the defence disagreed with the random match probability presented by the prosecution DNA expert, and they called an expert witness to explain to the jury how to use Bayes' theorem to evaluate the strength of the DNA evidence against Adams correctly. The judge instructed the jury that they could use Bayes' theorem if they wished, and Adams was convicted of rape. The Appeals Court noted that that no alternative instructions were given to jurors if they did not wish to use Bayes' theorem, so it ordered a retrial. At the second trial Adams was again convicted, and his second appeal was rejected. However, the ruling was very critical of the use of Bayes' theorem, and the judge was quoted as saying: 'to introduce Bayes Theorem, or any similar method, into a criminal trial plunges the jury into inappropriate and unnecessary realms of theory and complexity deflecting them from their proper task.'

Analysis: This ruling conveyed a clear message about the court's views on the use of Bayes' theorem and the belief that jurors cannot understand such complicated mathematical approaches. We will see in Chapter 7 how psychological research has shed light on jurors' decision making and how this research has improved our understanding of how scientific and probabilistic evidence is integrated into jurors' verdict decisions.

Likelihood ratios

As we have seen in the previous section, Bayes' theorem offers a mathematical means to express the change in belief in a proposition, given new information (or evidence). However, it is a difficult, and for many people a counter-intuitive, way to make decisions in the context of a criminal investigation or trial. So another way of expressing the probative value of evidence that has increased in popularity in recent years is by using likelihood ratios. The usefulness of likelihood ratios can be seen in the equation

$$\textit{Prior odds} \times \textit{likelihood ratio} = \textit{Posterior odds}$$

The posterior odds are often what we need to know, and in the context of a criminal investigation these would represent the odds of the suspect having committed the offence given the prior odds and some new piece of evidence (with the probative value of the new evidence expressed as a likelihood ratio).

The likelihood ratio is a value that expresses the probative value of a particular piece of evidence. When we multiply the prior odds of a suspect having committed an offence by the likelihood ratio, a strong (or very probative) piece of evidence will produce posterior odds that are significantly higher than the prior odds. However, a piece of evidence with less strength will not quantitatively influence the prior odds so dramatically. In order to understand how the likelihood ratio for a piece of evidence is calculated, we need to consider two hypotheses:

1. H_p = the prosecution hypothesis that the defendant is the person who committed the crime.
2. H_d = the defence hypothesis that someone other than the defendant committed the crime.

With these two hypotheses in mind, the likelihood ratio for a piece of evidence (E) is expressed as

$$LR = \frac{P(E \mid H_p)}{P(E \mid H_d)}$$

The calculation of likelihood ratios to express the probative value of forensic evidence relies on our ability to express quantitatively the probability of the evidence corresponding to the suspect if they committed the crime, and also the alternative hypothesis in which someone other than the suspect committed the crime. For some evidence types, for which reliable frequency information exists, these calculations are possible and therefore likelihood ratios can be used as an expression of probative value. Examples of these evidence types include some aspects of footwear patterns, ballistics and certain forms of trace evidence comparisons. However, there are many other forms of evidence that are more difficult to evaluate quantitatively, and that therefore do not lend themselves to these types of probative value calculations. For example, if there is eyewitness evidence associated with a particular crime, it is not feasible to evaluate the veracity of this evidence using likelihood ratios. Similarly, investigative information provided by behavioural analysts (also known as criminal profilers) cannot accurately be expressed quantitatively.

In this section we have explored some quantitative, or mathematical, ways to interpret forensic evidence and determine its probative value. Although these methods provide some numerical measure of evidence strength, the calculations are not straightforward for many members of the criminal justice system and are therefore not intuitive methods for expressing probative value during criminal investigations or court proceedings. In order to avoid misunderstandings and subsequent misinterpretations, for instance by jurors, the forensic scientist must also be able to express their findings using terms and expressions that members of the public can understand. The next section considers how expert witnesses express probative value and levels of confidence during criminal trials.

Expressing expert opinion

As we have seen earlier in this chapter (see Box 5.3 for the R *v.* Adams ruling), the criminal courts consider Bayes' theorem and conditional probabilities to be too complicated and unlikely to assist juries in reaching legally correct verdicts. Indeed, decades of research into jury decision making have demonstrated that, on average, jurors do not logically integrate numerical information into their decisions. Therefore, forensic experts are required to communicate forensic conclusions during their court testimony using language that is intuitively simple to understand and interpret. Numerous attempts have been made to standardise the language used by experts and these have required continuous updating as new technologies emerge and the range of likelihood ratios encountered in case work has changed (Lucy, 2005).

One verbal scale, relating common language to various ranges of the likelihood ratio, has been suggested by Evett et al. (2000) and is reproduced in Table 5.1.

In Table 5.1 the language refers to situations where the likelihood ratio is greater than 1, which relate to instances where the evidence supports the prosecution's claims. However, the verbal equivalents are equally applicable to those where the likelihood ratio is less than 1, which would indicate support for the defence hypothesis. This attempt to standardise the language associated with likelihood ratio values has been adopted in a number of jurisdictions in various countries, and experts are encouraged to express their results using this terminology. However, some commentators argue that attempts to assign subjective terminology to the likelihood ratio calculation do not solve the problem of juries misinterpreting the meaning of the testimony. Terms such as 'weak', 'moderate' or 'strong' mean different things to different people, and are therefore unlikely to be uniformly interpreted by decision makers.

Forensic expert testimony struggles with semantic issues and (as we have seen in Chapter 2) perhaps no single word has caused as much controversy in recent years as the term 'match'. Historically, forensic

Table 5.1 Verbal equivalents to ranges of the likelihood ratio.

Likelihood ratio range	Verbal equivalent
1–10	Limited evidence to support
11–100	Moderate evidence to support
101–1000	Moderately strong evidence to support
1001–10 000	Strong evidence to support
>10 000	Very strong evidence to support

expert witnesses expressed various types of forensic analyses and conclusions as constituting a 'match' with an exemplar. However, the word 'match' conveys an extremely high level of confidence in the source of the evidence, to the exclusion of any other potential source. The shift towards expressing conclusions using probabilistic language demonstrates that the prior acceptance of absolute certainty is no longer scientifically or logically valid. The forensic sciences are now beginning to realise that conveying results using the definitive term 'match' overstates the level of confidence that the analyses can possibly provide, and therefore misrepresents the findings to the courts. Even DNA evidence, which has been described as the 'gold standard' of forensic analyses, accepts that absolute certainty (or a 100% match) is not possible; thus the inclusion of the random match probability in DNA expert testimony.

There are other commonly used phrases that need to be interpreted with caution in expert witness testimony. Robertson and Vignaux (1995) discuss frequent disagreement over the meaning of the term 'consistent with', which is commonly used to describe results in which comparison evidence techniques identify shared characteristics between samples. They claim that when scientists use the phrase 'consistent with', the intended meaning is simply that the evidence is not 'inconsistent with'. However, findings by Craddock et al. (as cited in Robertson and Vignaux, 1995) suggest that lawyers interpret 'consistent with' to mean 'reasonably strongly supporting' some proposition. It is not known what meaning juries attribute to this phrase, although it is possible that they may assume a meaning not intended by the forensic scientist. Box 5.4 presents an example of a miscarriage of justice that was partially attributed to the content of expert testimony regarding microscopic hair analysis.

Box 5.4 The wrongful conviction of Jimmy Ray Bromgard

On 20 March 1987 in Montana, USA, an 8-year-old girl was sexually assaulted by an intruder who broke into her home through a window. Jimmy Ray Bromgard became a suspect when a police officer who was familiar with him thought he looked similar to a composite sketch produced from the victim's description of the perpetrator. In an identification parade, the victim picked Bromgard from the line-up, but she expressed uncertainty about whether he was indeed the man who attacked her. Hairs recovered from the victim's bed formed the basis of the forensic evidence at Bromgard's trial. The forensic expert testified that the hairs from the crime scene were 'indistinguishable' from hairs belonging to Bromgard, and also that the chances were 1 in 10 000 that the hairs did not originate from him. The jury convicted Bromgard and he was sentenced to three 40-year terms, to be served consecutively.

Analysis: The jury was clearly compelled by the hair testimony, and the use of the word 'indistinguishable' seemed to imply a 'match'. However, the accompanying statistic of 1 in 10 000 used by the expert had no basis in science and was the result of a misuse of the product rule. This testimony was later found to be faulty, but not until 15 years later when Bromgard was exonerated through post-conviction DNA analysis. We will revisit this issue of faulty forensic science testimony, and its role in miscarriages of justice, in Chapter 7.

One of the most recent suggested changes to expert forensic testimony concerns fingerprint examination. Historically, fingerprints have been presented in court as conclusive 'matches' with the ability to identify individuals with levels of certainty not afforded to many other forensic techniques. However, recent high-profile miscarriages of justice caused by faulty fingerprint conclusions have contributed to new guidelines for fingerprint expert testimony. In the UK, the Scottish Fingerprint Inquiry was conducted in response to the erroneous identification of fingerprints belonging to Shirley McKie (this case study was featured in Box 2.13). In the USA, the arrest of Brandon Mayfield in connection with the Madrid bombings on the basis of an incorrect fingerprint identification also contributed to changes in fingerprint testimony (see Box 5.5). As a result of these cases, fingerprint testimony is now presented in court as evidence of 'opinion' rather than evidence of 'fact'. This change acknowledges the subjectivity of fingerprint examinations, and leaves room for interpretation by experts, police and triers of fact in the courtroom.

Box 5.5 The Madrid bombing investigation

In March 2004, bombs were detonated on commuter trains in Madrid, Spain, killing 191 people and injuring over 1800 others. A fingerprint was recovered by the Spanish National Police (SNP) from a plastic bag containing explosives detonators. The fingerprint was searched by INTERPOL, the FBI and other law enforcement agencies, which returned 20 potential 'matches'. An FBI fingerprint expert concluded that the latent print recovered from the bag belonged to Brandon Mayfield, a Muslim attorney in Portland, Oregon, USA. Despite there being no other evidence linking Mayfield to the bombings, covert surveillance was initiated and eventually he was arrested as a material witness. While three FBI fingerprint experts independently verified the fingerprint match, the SNP eventually identified Uohnane Daoud (an Algerian national) as the source of the fingerprint on the plastic bag. Mayfield was subsequently released, after spending over two weeks in custody.

Analysis: An inquest into this case raised important questions about fingerprint examinations, and forensic analyses in general, including how to avoid errors and faulty verifications in the future. There were similar issues raised in this inquest to those in the McKie case (Box 2.13), including the issue of human error and cognitive biases in forensic decision making, which is the topic of the rest of this chapter.

Although in both the McKie and Mayfield cases the erroneous fingerprint examinations did not ultimately result in a wrongful conviction, the fallibility of fingerprint conclusions was clearly recognised. There are a number of factors that may have contributed to these, and other, incorrect forensic conclusions, which are the topic of the next section.

Sources of bias and error in forensic science

Of particular interest in terms of potential sources of bias and error in the forensic sciences are those involving human factors, as opposed to analytical or technological issues. This area of research is rooted in cognitive psychology, but it is only recently that the cognitive factors relating to forensic examinations have been considered by the forensic community, therefore more research is needed in this area. This increasing interest in cognitive biases and errors is partly due to high-profile miscarriages of justice (such as those already mentioned). These issues were also highlighted in a National Academy of Sciences report entitled *Strengthening Forensic Science in the United States: A Path Forward* (2009).

This reviewed a number of common forensic science techniques and made recommendations to improve the validity and reliability of forensic analyses, including awareness of the role that human factors play in scientific conclusions.

Before we discuss some of the most influential cognitive biases in forensic science, it is important to differentiate between instances of misconduct or fraudulent forensic testimony and errors caused inadvertently by bias. There have been some cases in which forensic examiners have fabricated results, displayed incompetence or deliberately misrepresented their findings in the courtroom, and these are very serious instances of professional misconduct that are taken very seriously by the criminal justice system (see Box 5.6 for an example). However, errors caused by various types of cognitive bias are entirely different, particularly as the forensic examiner in these cases has no intention to deceive or produce erroneous results and conclusions. Therefore, in these examples blame should not be assigned to the individual examiner, but rather to the processes underlying forensic examinations, which need to be considered carefully in an attempt to minimise the opportunity for these errors to occur.

Box 5.6 Charles Smith – an example of incompetence in forensic medicine

Charles Smith was a prominent Canadian pathologist and former head Paediatric Forensic Pathologist at the Hospital for Sick Children in Toronto, Ontario (1982–2003). During this time, Dr Smith carried out hundreds of autopsies on children who had died suddenly or in suspicious circumstances. Many of these autopsies resulted in criminal charges and convictions of people thought to have been responsible for the deaths. However, in 2008 a public inquiry was launched to investigate 220 cases of 'shaken baby syndrome' originally investigated by Dr Smith. This concluded that in a number of these cases Dr Smith's forensic conclusions were not sound, and these had resulted in potential wrongful convictions of innocent people (often the parents of the children). In one such case, William Mullins-Johnson spent 12 years in prison for the rape and murder of his 4-year-old niece. Experts who reopened the case subsequently claimed that the victim was never sexually abused or strangled, and most likely died of natural causes. Charles Smith lost his licence to practise medicine in 2010.

Cases of professional malpractice such as this demonstrate the profound effect that such faulty forensic conclusions can have on the lives of those who are involved.

Analysis: It is clear from this and other similar examples that fraudulent forensic testimony is something that needs to be treated very seriously by the criminal justice system. However, it is important to note that it is almost never possible to know the ground truth in a given situation with certainty, so decisions need to be reached given the available evidence (just like any other criminal investigation and trial).

Confirmation bias

The idea that people tend to seek out and favour evidence that supports their pre-existing beliefs is not a new concept, and many years of psychology research demonstrate that this is a reliable and robust scientific finding. In addition to recognising it as a normal aspect of human decision making, it is also important to realise that this tendency does not always lead people to incorrect conclusions. However, it does compromise our ability to make truly objective decisions and judgements, therefore we need to be aware of this influence on human behaviour.

Psychologists have long been aware of a number of different sources of confirmation bias that have been demonstrated in the empirical literature. One of these relates to the role that our expectations play in our perception of various stimuli. In a criminal investigative context, assumptions and beliefs about the guilt of a suspect have been demonstrated to alter people's perceptions of various aspects of a case. Another influence that our expectations can have is on our processes of social perception. Of particular relevance to police investigations and forensic examinations, research has demonstrated that once people have formed a hypothesis about a situation (e.g. the likely guilt of a prime suspect), they actively seek out information and evidence that confirms their hypothesis, while simultaneously ignoring or explaining away evidence that is contradictory. This cognitive bias, often referred to as 'tunnel vision', can have serious limiting consequences for effective police investigations, although it occurs without conscious realisation and is thus difficult to avoid.

Kassin et al. (2013) outline what they refer to as the 'forensic confirmation bias', a series of confirmation bias effects that are of particular concern in a forensic context. The first of these refer to the effect that knowledge of the context of a criminal investigation can have on a forensic examiner's judgements and conclusions. A number of studies suggest that forensic conclusions can be affected by awareness of details about the crime or other evidence. For example, Dror et al. (2006) presented fingerprint experts with fingerprint evidence that they had previously examined in their case work and had concluded to be a 'match'. However, they were not aware that they had previously examined these fingerprints, and were told that they came from a high-profile case involving an incorrect identification. This context implied that the fingerprints did not match (although this was not their original conclusion) and indeed only one expert in five concluded that they matched. In other words, four of the five experts changed their original conclusions when presented with this contradictory contextual information. There is also empirical evidence to suggest that awareness of a suspect's confession can influence forensic conclusions (Dror and Charlton, 2006).

In addition to case details and evidence that may produce expectations with the potential to bias forensic conclusions, there are some organisational and procedural aspects of forensic examinations that may increase the risk of influence from cognitive biases. One of these issues – verification practices – was brought to the attention of the forensic community during cases such as the Brandon Mayfield erroneous identification (Box 5.5) and the Shirley McKie case (Box 2.13). In both of these cases, multiple fingerprint experts agreed with the conclusion, which implies that they all made the same mistaken identification. This seems highly implausible at first glance – how could multiple independent experts make exactly the same error? However, the contextual biases discussed above may help to explain, due to the fact that the verifications were not done independently and, more importantly, they were not 'blind'. In other words, an expert asked to verify a previous expert's opinion is most often aware of what the conclusion was. This information provides unnecessary, and potentially biasing, context (e.g. that a previous expert believes the prints to be a match) that may influence the verifier's conclusions. In turn, a third expert might be asked to verify and told that *two* previous experts concluded the fingerprints to be matches, which may be even more powerful context.

How to reduce the effects of bias in forensic science

Awareness of issues relating to context effects and confirmation biases in forensic science has been increasing in recent years, and is beginning to influence research agendas and policy decisions. This is a positive shift from the previous perception of forensic science as infallible and objective to recognising human factors and the potential for errors. However, this increased awareness alone is not sufficient to address the issue; indeed, advances in technology are working in the opposite direction by making the interpretation of forensic evidence more difficult for experts. For example, increasingly sophisticated and well-populated automated fingerprint databases produce lists of close matches for experts to consider, and with the ever-growing size of these databases the similarity between different fingerprints can be extraordinary. This was one of the factors to which the erroneous identification of Brandon Mayfield was attributed (Box 5.5), as his fingerprint and that belonging to the guilty person were extremely similar.

Given that cognitive biases are a feature of human nature, it is not feasible to attempt to rid forensic examiners of them, so steps should be taken to build protective features into forensic organisations and processes. Kassin et al. (2013) make a number of suggestions for reducing bias in forensic processes. These include ensuring that forensic examiners are not exposed to extraneous information about the case or the suspect that is not relevant to their specific analyses; implementation of blind verification procedures; and modelling pattern examinations after line-up procedures, such that experts examine an array of patterns consisting of the suspect and five plausible 'fillers'. In addition, these researchers suggest that the use of technology needs to reflect our knowledge of biases, for instance by randomising the order of lists of possible matches generated by automated databases. Finally, they highlight the importance of including basic psychology training in routine forensic education, in order to raise awareness of these issues among experts and change the current occupational culture of infallibility and objectivity.

Summary

This chapter has explored the complicated, and sometimes controversial, issue of evidence interpretation. Although the science involved in some of the forensic disciplines is based on robust and reliable methodology, interpretation of the probative value of evidence is a subjective process and is therefore prone to error and bias, just like any other human process. The consequences of these errors can be extremely serious, particularly in cases of wrongful conviction, therefore the forensic science community has an obligation to acknowledge these issues and attempt to implement strategies to reduce error. Following some recent policy documents and high-profile cases this has started to happen in recent years, but more research is needed in these areas to ensure continuous improvement.

Study questions

1 We have seen in this chapter the distinction between police evidence and intelligence, the key difference between which is the admissibility of the information to be relied on by the prosecution and presented in court. There have been cases of trials for serious crimes in which unlawfully obtained 'evidence' has been relied on by the police, and as a consequence the defendant has been acquitted. Consider whether you agree that only properly obtained evidence can be relied on, even in very serious cases when the police have in fact apprehended the guilty individual.

2 The Innocence Project (New York, USA) is a non-profit legal organisation that investigates claims of wrongful conviction through post-conviction DNA analysis. To date, over 300 wrongfully convicted individuals have been exonerated by the Innocence Project's work. While the leading cause of wrongful convictions in these cases has been mistaken eyewitness testimony, the second most common contributing factor is 'improper or unvalidated forensic science'. Visit the Innocence Project website at www.innocenceproject.org and read about some of these cases. Then consider how such errors may have occurred and how they might have been avoided.

6

FORENSIC SCIENCE IN THE POPULAR MEDIA

In October 2000, a new television series debuted in North America, featuring fictional storylines focused on the forensic investigation of crime. The show was called *CSI: Crime Scene Investigation* and its subsequent worldwide popularity fuelled the development of two spin-off series: *CSI Miami* and *CSI New York*. The *CSI* franchise continues to enjoy great success in many countries and since it introduced forensic fiction to the television viewing world, a number of television shows have capitalised on this trend by featuring forensic science in their plots, such as *Bones*, *NCIS* and *Body of Proof*. Despite differences in the focus of these various shows, they all share a common reliance on portrayals of forensic science, technology and crime scene investigators that tend to be extraordinarily inaccurate. This gap between forensic science fact and fiction is the topic of this chapter, and its potential to influence various people within the criminal justice system has been the subject of much debate over the last decade.

The popularity of forensic fiction

Before discussing the various ways in which forensic science is portrayed in the popular media, it is important to consider why this particular genre of programming has enjoyed such success in recent years. In his book *Reading CSI: Crime TV under the Microscope* (2007), Michael Allen suggests that the timing of the launch of the first *CSI* series in 2000 was integral to its subsequent success. It began 11 months before the World Trade Center terrorist attacks of 11 September 2001, and the show was elevated in the television ratings in the post–9/11 world of fear and increasing vulnerability in the USA. In this context, *CSI* offered 'certainty and unrelenting professionalism in the search for truth and justice' (Allen, 2007, p. 8).

However, we must remember throughout this chapter that *CSI* is not the only popular television show to focus on the fictional portrayal of forensic science; and indeed, that television is not the only form of media to feature forensic fiction. Many movies (particularly crime dramas) include forensic elements in their storylines, and often forgotten in these discussions is the long-term popularity of crime fiction novels, which also frequently describe forensic techniques contributing to the investigation of crime. So although *CSI* and television seem to have been the focus of academic and media discussions about the fictional portrayal of forensic science, many other sources of forensic fiction are consumed by the public.

Another factor to consider when attempting to explain the popularity of forensic science fiction on screen is the so-called 'reality TV craze', which describes the public's fascination with reality television in recent years. Sociologists have theorised about the reasons for people watching and enjoying reality TV shows, applying theories such as symbolic interactionism, functional analysis and conflict theory to the phenomenon. The specific details of these theories are not described here, as we are focusing on fictional television, not reality TV programmes. However, when we consider why forensic fiction is so appealing, it is useful to think about how these programmes advertise themselves to potential viewers. Despite being purely fictional, TV shows such as *CSI* are often advertised as based on real science and forensic techniques. In many cases this assumption is made implicitly, by featuring storylines based on (presumably real) science, while in other cases the claim is made explicitly. An example of explicit claims of realism would be when the police and legal procedural drama *Law and Order* claims to be featuring plots that are 'ripped from the headlines', which gives the false impression that the stories depict true events.

Now that we have considered some of the explanations for the popularity of these programmes, the next section outlines some aspects of forensic science fiction that are particularly different from the reality of forensic science practice.

Forensic reality versus forensic fiction

As already mentioned, the gap between forensic science fiction and reality is wide. This section outlines a number of aspects of forensic fiction that are particularly different from real-life forensic investigations. In addition to the procedural inaccuracies described in the following sections, the 'science' portrayed on television is also questionable. For instance, it has been estimated that 40% of the 'science' depicted on *CSI* does not exist (Schweitzer and Saks, 2007), and is instead purely science fiction for entertainment purposes. Real scientific techniques, such as those concerned with DNA, are often portrayed in forensic fiction, but they are frequently used in ways that would not be possible in real life. For example, the recovery of DNA from surfaces or materials from which it would not be possible to obtain a DNA profile is an example of real science being portrayed in unrealistic circumstances.

The role of the investigators and the portrayal of forensic facilities

One of the most striking differences between real forensic investigators and those depicted in fictional drama is the role of the crime scene investigator and their interaction with the criminal investigation. Fictional representations of crime scene investigators most often portray them involved in various aspects of the investigation, including (but not limited to) evidence collection and crime scene examination, analysis of evidence, interpretation of evidence, identification and arrest of suspects, interrogation of suspects, and in some cases even chasing down (and, most disturbingly, sometimes shooting at) fleeing persons of interest. While all of these activities are integral to real criminal investigations, in reality these roles are conducted by a range of different people who have distinct functions to serve within an investigation.

For example, in a real police investigation the arrest and interrogation of suspects would never be carried out by a crime scene investigator. The police officer in charge of the investigation (usually a detective) would conduct any necessary interviews with suspects, victims or witnesses; indeed, these police officers are specially trained to conduct investigative interviews effectively. Similarly, should the need arise to chase suspects or use force, this is most certainly something that is carried out solely by sworn police officers, and is not the role of the crime scene investigator (this is particularly true for jurisdictions where crime scene investigators are mainly civilian employees, for instance in the UK). This blurring of the boundaries between the role of the police officer and that of the crime scene investigator may give a false impression to viewers regarding the type of work that crime scene investigators do.

As outlined in Chapter 4, the role of the crime scene investigator is to search a crime scene systematically for various types of evidence, recover the evidence and package it using the most appropriate techniques and materials for transportation to the relevant forensic laboratory for analysis. During a real criminal investigation, this is generally where the role of the crime scene investigator ends. However, in forensic fiction they are often portrayed as being responsible for analysing and interpreting a wide range of evidence types. For example, it is not uncommon to see fictional crime scene investigators proceed to a chemistry or biology laboratory and employ sophisticated analytical techniques on the evidence, before reaching a conclusion about the results of the tests. In the real crime laboratory, these forensic science techniques are carried out by highly trained and specialised scientists. These real-life forensic scientists will be experts in a particular area of forensic science, such as chemistry or biology, and will have an educational background in the natural sciences at university level (Houck and Siegel, 2011).

In addition to confusing the roles of crime scene investigators and forensic scientists, forensic fiction also consistently portrays crime laboratories as well-funded, state-of-the-art facilities in which forensic analysts conduct their business shrouded in dim, blue lighting, seemingly unaffected by staffing or workload issues and mountains of evidence to process. In reality, however, forensic laboratories typically struggle with gaining sufficient funding, which makes it difficult to obtain the most up-to-date technology and equipment. In addition, forensic laboratories in busy jurisdictions are faced with increasingly large quantities of backlogged evidence – the US Department of Justice definition is that 'a case is backlogged if it remains in the laboratory for 30 days or more without the development of a report or analysis' (Edwards and Gatsonis, 2009, p. 39). These backlogs of cases make it difficult, perhaps impossible, for forensic laboratories to process current cases swiftly and efficiently, in contrast to the fictional portrayals. Furthermore, the crime laboratories in forensic fiction do not struggle with the staffing and workload issues faced by real forensic laboratories.

In the following sections, we will consider other specific aspects of forensic analyses that are exaggerated or ignored entirely in forensic fiction.

Collapsed investigative time frames

An episode of a television drama typically lasts for around 60 minutes, which is likely to contain approximately 45 minutes of the programme itself, as well as intermittent advertising breaks at various stages in the broadcast. In the case of crime dramas and forensic fiction, each episode tends to focus on a discrete criminal investigation (or in some cases, more than one) that is resolved during the course of the episode. This requires a great deal of creative licence in order to present the various stages of the investigation in a way that is easy for the viewer to follow, while maintaining a high level of dramatic entertainment value.

One of the ways in which the writers of these episodes manage to fit so much investigative activity into a 45-minute time slot is to speed up the various stages of the investigation in order to resolve the enquiry in such a short period. This allows for a more fast-paced portrayal of the investigation, and results in more interesting content. Nevertheless, it differs drastically from real-life investigative processes. It is fairly obvious why fiction is presented in this way, as it would not be particularly enthralling to watch investigators and police waiting days, weeks or even months for results from forensic laboratories!

Ley et al. (2012) conducted a content analysis of 51 episodes from the first six seasons of *CSI*, specifically analysing the portrayal of DNA evidence. One of the notable features of DNA analysis, as portrayed in these episodes, was the fact that it could be done with 'swiftness and relative ease' (2012, p. 59). This extraordinarily quick turnaround time was sometimes found to be referred to explicitly by the characters in the dialogue, or the elapsed time was conveyed implicitly, for example by having the analyst wearing the same clothes when they receive the sample, analyse it and report the findings, which implies a 24-hour time frame. The speed of these DNA processing times is wildly exaggerated compared with recent estimates of turnaround times in the USA (an average of 186 days) and the UK (average 3 days), although it is important to note that these estimates themselves vary widely depending on the specific jurisdiction and type of crime.

Another strategy used by crime dramas to exaggerate the time it takes to analyse forensic evidence is an over-reliance on automated technology. A good example of this is the portrayal of fingerprint identifications, which in fiction are often conducted by entering a crime scene fingerprint into an AFIS computer, which returns a 'match' instantaneously. While real-world fingerprint examiners do use AFIS technology to generate potential matches held in the database, as we have seen in Chapter 2 these similar fingerprints then need to be carefully examined by a number of fingerprint experts before any particular fingerprint is declared to be from the same person as the crime scene mark. It is the painstaking human examination of fingerprints that is eliminated from the process in forensic fiction, leading to the false conclusion that fingerprint examinations are entirely automated with instant, conclusive results.

Infallibility of forensic evidence

In addition to dramatically collapsed investigative time frames, a further inaccuracy relates to the portrayal of forensic science as infallible. During real police investigations, much of the evidence collected and used is not of a scientific nature. Perhaps one of the best examples of this is eyewitness testimony, which is regarded as crucial during police investigations. In contrast, fictional investigators often consider this type of non-scientific evidence to be of little use compared to scientific, physical evidence. This is often conveyed in the dialogue between characters in forensic fiction, as exemplified in quotes from *CSI* such as 'It is better to have one piece of forensic evidence than 10 witnesses' (Ley et al., 2012, p. 60).

As well as suggesting that scientific evidence is always preferred to other forms of evidence, forensic fiction promotes the message that science is entirely objective, and therefore that forensic science techniques are foolproof and certain to yield correct, conclusive and unbiased results. This perpetuates the myth that forensic evidence is always better than other forms of evidence, ignoring the subjectivity inherent in forensic analyses. As we have seen in Chapter 5, the interpretation of forensic results in real police investigations is a complicated and subjective process, requiring advanced knowledge of statistics and probability theory. The process is therefore at risk of various types of error, which is something that is not commonly discussed or shown in forensic fiction programmes.

The certainty of forensic results is conveyed in forensic dramas through the words used by the characters to describe various analytical conclusions. In particular, 'match' is almost always used in forensic fiction to describe similarity between forensic samples such as DNA, fingerprints, hair, fibres and tool marks. As discussed in Chapter 5, this overuse of 'match' is contrary to the current trend in the real world of forensics, in which experts instead favour expressions such as 'consistent with', 'likely to belong to' and 'cannot be excluded from' to convey their conclusions. By continuing to rely on 'matches' in forensic fiction, the myth of forensic evidence as an infallible and certain source of investigative information is maintained for the audience of these programmes.

Lack of courtroom procedures

A typical episode of any forensic drama takes the viewer through the crime scene examination, analysis of evidence, arrest and questioning of suspects, and the resolution of the case, usually culminating in charges being laid against the guilty person. In many of these episodes the perpetrator confesses during interrogation, which is often the result of their being faced with seemingly insurmountable forensic evidence proving their guilt. However, what is very rarely discussed or shown in forensic dramas is the trial process during which the defendant's guilt, and ultimately their fate, is decided. It may come as no surprise that these programmes do not portray criminal trials, as they are police and forensic procedural dramas, not courtroom dramas. By ignoring the fact that the criminal cases portrayed will need to be presented and argued in the courtroom, the subjective nature of criminal investigations (and forensic science specifically) is once again obscured for the viewer.

Ley et al.'s (2012) analysis of the portrayal of DNA evidence in episodes from the first six seasons of *CSI* found that the role of the evidence in trial proceedings was only mentioned in 17% of all cases. In this relatively small proportion of episodes, the characters often referred to the need for forensic evidence in order to convince a jury at trial ('For a conviction, we're going to need a DNA sample', 2012, p. 60) and in some cases reference was made to the superiority of physical evidence over other types of trial evidence ('It's her DNA, case closed', 2012, p. 60). Dialogue such as this in forensic fiction further perpetuates the myth of the conclusive nature of physical evidence, while simultaneously minimising the role of other important sources of investigative information and the trial process.

In the majority of episodes, no mention was made of the need for a criminal trial (Ley et al., 2012), which also sends a message to viewers about the cases portrayed in the show. In many episodes the suspect confesses to the crime(s) when faced with incriminating forensic evidence, leading to the assumption that denial is futile when the police present physical evidence. Interestingly, these portrayals of police interviews highlight further gaps between reality and fiction, as they often portray detectives relying almost entirely on the immediate presentation of forensic evidence at the outset of the interview. Recent research suggests that this is not the interview strategy utilised by the majority of police interviewers (Smith and Bull, 2013); indeed, early disclosure of evidence is not the ideal interview strategy according to a growing body of research (Moston and Engelberg, 1993; Hartwig et al., 2005; Dando and Bull, 2011). In the remainder of the episodes in which the suspect does not confess and there is no mention of a future criminal trial, the impression left on the viewer is that the forensic evidence is strong enough to secure a conviction, therefore discussions of the prosecution strategy at trial appears not to be necessary.

In this section we have discussed a number of ways in which forensic science as portrayed in fiction differs significantly from reality. In the next section the discussion will focus on how these unrealistic depictions of forensic science in the media may be influencing how various people within the criminal justice system behave.

The CSI Effect

The idea that the portrayal of forensic science in the popular media might be having an effect on the criminal justice system is a relatively new concept, and prior to 2006 only anecdotal evidence was available to suggest that there may be a problem. However, this issue has found its way into the academic literature and has resulted in mixed findings and a great deal of debate.

The term *CSI Effect* was coined by an article in *Time* magazine (Kluger, 2002), which reported that juries in the USA were demanding complex scientific evidence, of the sort seen in forensic fiction, during criminal trials. This was attributed to the popularity of *CSI* on television, and the article suggested that juries were reaching surprising (and perhaps incorrect) verdicts due to their fascination with forensic fiction. This initial article, and the new term CSI Effect, proceeded to feature in other news stories and prompted some legal professionals to come forward with anecdotal claims of trials that had perhaps gone wrong due to jurors expecting reality to be the same as television.

The idea that the media influences people's behaviour is not a new one and a number of theoretical perspectives have been used to explain the relationship between media and society. Much of the discussion focuses on the social construction of reality through the media (Robbers, 2008), an approach that has been used to address the relationship between news media portrayals of crime stories and the public's fear of crime. Another, more specific theory of media influence is cultivation theory, which is employed to explain how patterns in television viewing 'cultivate' the viewer's perceptions of reality, thereby influencing their attitudes and beliefs about the world around them (Podlas, 2006). So the possibility that forensic fiction may influence the criminal justice system through the CSI Effect does have roots in well-established social psychological theories. In the remainder of this chapter we will examine some of the available empirical evidence to see if there is any support for this effect.

The Prosecutor's Effect

Originally the CSI Effect referred to one specific possibility, which we will refer to here as the Prosecutor's Effect (Cole and Dioso-Villa, 2007): that jurors who watch forensic fiction have unrealistically high expectations regarding the presence of forensic evidence in a criminal trial. In reality, many criminal trials proceed without any forensic evidence available to support the prosecution's case. So the hypothesisis is that jurors who have these unrealistically high expectations are disappointed when they hear a trial with no forensic evidence, and are therefore less inclined to vote guilty in such cases. Cole and Dioso-Villa (2007) refer to this as the Prosecutor's Effect because this supposed increase in acquittals is thought to burden the prosecution in a trial, whose evidence does not satisfy these jurors.

One of the most often cited, anecdotal case examples of the Prosecutor's Effect is the Robert Blake trial (see Box 6.1 for a summary of this case and the subsequent trial). The first empirical test of this possible effect had less promising results, however. Podlas (2006) conducted a study in which participants were classified as either frequent or non-frequent viewers of *CSI* and their responses to a mock trial scenario depicting a rape trial (which included no forensic evidence) were compared. In particular, since the Prosecutor's Effect focuses on reasons for potentially wrongful acquittals, frequent and non-frequent viewers were compared with regard to their reported reasons for acquitting the defendant in the trial scenario. The results indicated that frequent and non-frequent viewers of *CSI* did not acquit for different reasons, therefore Podlas concluded that there was no evidence shown for the Prosecutor's Effect.

Box 6.1 The trial of Robert Blake

On 4 May 2001, Bonny Lee Bakley was murdered in Los Angeles, California, USA after dining with her husband Robert Blake at a suburban restaurant. According to Blake, who was charged with her murder, after dinner he and Bakley walked from the restaurant to their car, parked a short distance away. Blake realised that he had left his handgun in the restaurant (which he claimed to be carrying for protection, as his wife believed she was being stalked) and left Bakley in the car while he walked back to the restaurant. When he came back, he found Bakley in the passenger seat, bleeding from a bullet wound to the head, and he was unable to revive her. Police soon uncovered inconsistencies in Blake's story, and determined that he had motive to kill Bakley and had previously attempted to hire two hitmen to do so. Blake was arrested and charged with his wife's murder, and after a lengthy investigation and trial the jury began deliberations in March 2005. The jury's verdict was not guilty, which surprised many observers of this case. Some jurors subsequently spoke to the media about their decision and a number of them cited the lack of forensic evidence (particularly gunshot residue) in the prosecution's case.

Analysis: Due to the jury's reportedly high expectations for forensic evidence, this case is often cited in the media as one of the highest-profile examples of the Prosecutor's Effect. Of course, as we have seen in some of the other examples, it is not possible to know with any certainty whether or not Blake murdered his wife. However, some legal commentators felt that the prosecution proved Blake's guilt beyond a reasonable doubt, and therefore that this was a wrongful acquittal.

In a subsequent study by Shelton et al. (2006), participants were asked about their television viewing habits as well as their expectations about forensic evidence before completing a mock juror task. The results indicated that frequent viewers of *CSI* had higher expectations for forensic evidence in criminal trials compared with non-viewers. This would seem to suggest that the Prosecutor's Effect may exist, since perhaps these high expectations are the result of watching forensic fiction programmes. However, in the mock juror task the results showed no differences in verdict decision between viewers and non-viewers. Thus it seems that although viewers of forensic fiction have higher expectations for forensic evidence, this does not seem to result in different verdicts when compared with non-viewers. Despite not finding a direct relationship between viewing habits and verdict decisions, in a follow-up study Kim et al. (2009) reanalysed the same data and did find a significant indirect relationship between viewing habits, expectations and juror verdicts.

Some more recent studies suggest that one explanation for these inconsistent results may be the early focus on television viewing habits as the measure of interest (Smith and Bull, 2012, 2013). Measuring participants' exposure to forensic fiction in a meaningful way may be difficult to do with accuracy, so these recent studies shifted from focusing on television viewing to measuring the attitudes that people hold about forensic science. The results of these studies indicate that participants who reported high expectations for forensic evidence to be present in criminal investigations were significantly more likely than those who did not hold these expectations to vote 'not guilty' in mock trials that did not contain forensic evidence. While these findings suggest that the Prosecutor's Effect may have an influence in trials, the sources of people's attitudes (e.g. exposure to forensic fiction) were not confirmed.

Regardless of these mixed empirical findings, some attorneys have implemented strategies aimed at counteracting the CSI Effect, described in Box 6.2.

Box 6.2 The impact of the CSI Effect on prosecution and defence behaviour

Although there is yet to be any definitive empirical evidence to support the existence of the various versions of the CSI Effect, there is plenty of anecdotal evidence to suggest that prosecution and defence attorneys have changed the way they carry out their jobs in an effort to mitigate any potential CSI Effect. One way in which this is being done, particularly in the USA, is through the use of extensive pre-trial questioning of potential jurors. Pre-trial hearings, also known as *voir dire* from the French meaning 'to see to speak', provide both the prosecution and defence with an opportunity to identify any jurors who might be biased and unable to render a fair verdict, and to have them removed from the jury pool. Previously these hearings tended to focus on racial bias or strong opinions about the use of capital punishment, which may impair a juror's ability to be neutral during a trial. However, recently the questioning of potential jurors has also encompassed their television viewing habits. In addition to pre-trial questioning, criminal courts have also seen an increase in the use of so-called *negative evidence witnesses*. This practice is commonly seen in cases where the prosecution does not have forensic evidence, therefore a forensic expert witness is called to testify about the lack of evidence recovered and explain to the jury that it is not uncommon for there to be no forensic evidence. This is thought to mitigate the effects of unrealistically high expectations on the part of jurors. Finally, attorneys are also finding it necessary to address forensic fiction explicitly with juries and explain to them during trial how real life differs from the forensic science they see on television.

Analysis: Cole and Dioso-Villa (2007) have called these changes in prosecutor behaviour the Weak Prosecutor's Effect, and they provide anecdotal evidence that members of the legal system do believe that they must mitigate the CSI Effect by altering how they carry out their job. However, perhaps these reactions are not justified given the equivocal empirical findings relating to the existence of such an effect.

The Defence Effect

Although most of the early research in this area focused almost exclusively on the Prosecutor's Effect, there were some trials in which juries convicted defendants on the basis of seemingly weak evidence, which were also linked to the CSI Effect by some commentators in the media. In some of these trials the guilty verdicts were overturned by appellate courts, after being described as 'unsafe convictions' made on the basis of questionable forensic evidence (see Box 6.3 for a summary of the Barry George trial). These potentially wrongful convictions are referred to as the Defence Effect (Cole and Dioso-Villa, 2007), due to the fact that they burden the defence at trial.

Box 6.3 The trial of Barry George

On 26 April 1999, BBC television presenter Jill Dando was murdered outside her home in London, UK, with a single gunshot to the head. There were no witnesses to the shooting and police investigated a number of possible theories about suspects, although none produced any reliable leads. Eventually, a local man by the name of Barry George was arrested and charged with Dando's murder. The prosecution case during the trial relied heavily on circumstantial evidence, including George's apparent obsession with celebrities and his collection of military and gun-related material. However, it also presented two pieces of forensic evidence that were later believed to have misled the jury. The first was a single polyester fibre found on the victim's coat, which was reported to be consistent with trousers found in George's residence. The second was a single particle of gunshot residue recovered from inside George's jacket pocket, which was claimed by the prosecution to link George to the shooting.

Analysis: The jury voted guilty at the 2001 trial. George spent eight years in prison before being acquitted at a 2008 retrial on the basis that the original conviction had been 'unsafe' due to the ambiguous forensic evidence. The fact that the jury is believed to have overvalued the forensic evidence in this case makes it an often-cited example of the Defence Effect. Similar to the Robert Blake case discussed in Box 6.1, the truth is not known, but the ruling at the retrial highlighted the lack of proof beyond a reasonable doubt in this case.

The Defence Effect is based on the assumption that jurors who are exposed to forensic fiction have an exaggerated faith in forensic science, and therefore may place undue emphasis on weak or ambiguous forensic evidence when reaching their verdict and be more likely to vote guilty. In real police investigations, as opposed to fiction, not all forensic evidence is capable of proving the guilt of a defendant, and evidence with weak or ambiguous probative value needs to be carefully interpreted and considered before any judgements are made.

Despite some anecdotal claims to its veracity, this second version of the CSI Effect is generally ignored in the academic literature. However, some recent studies that have focused on jurors' attitudes to forensic evidence have included the types of attitudes that it hypothesises (Smith and Bull, 2012, 2013). This research found that participants with strong attitudes supporting the infallibility and capability of forensic science were more likely to vote guilty in a mock trial scenario where only weak forensic evidence was available, compared with participants who did not hold these attitudes. These findings suggest that the Defence Effect is plausible, although again the source of the attitudes was not identified.

Educating offenders

The CSI Effect is not thought to be operating only in the courtroom setting: some members of the criminal justice system believe that offenders are being educated by forensic fiction and as a result are demonstrating more forensic awareness and using more sophisticated techniques to avoid forensic detection while committing crimes. Cole and Dioso-Villa (2007) describe forensic investigators who report that certain behaviours at crime scenes are being recorded at an increasing rate, including the use of gloves, removal of cigarette ends and the use of bleach to remove blood. Other offender behaviours have also been reported to be occurring more frequently, such as the use of condoms during sexual assaults.

This possible version of the CSI Effect has not been extensively considered in the research literature, but Beauregard and Bouchard (2010) did conduct a study investigating the factors influencing offenders' forensic awareness and subsequent crime scene behaviours that exhibited the aim of avoiding forensic detection. Although this study did not link the forensic awareness of offenders to the source of their knowledge about forensic techniques (e.g. television), it nonetheless provided insight into their forensic strategies. The results indicated that offenders who are under the influence of drugs or alcohol are less likely to make attempts to avoid forensic detection (also found in Bond and Sheridan, 2007). Interestingly, the 2010 study found that a very small number of offenders in the sample of rape offences took precautions to avoid leaving DNA at the crime scene. If offenders are indeed learning forensic awareness from forensic fiction, one might expect that attempts to remove DNA from crime scenes would be more prevalent than the results of this study suggest.

Anecdotal claims by police investigators suggest that offenders may be demonstrating increasing forensic awareness during their crimes, and this is often blamed on the popularity of forensic fiction. However, this is an area that requires more research in order to reach any informed conclusions about the role of the media in shaping offender behaviour.

Influencing victim satisfaction

Victims of crime play a crucial role in its investigation, and police agencies are continually attempting to measure and manage victim satisfaction in order to ensure that members of the public are willing to engage with the police during and after criminal acts have occurred. Decades of research into consumer satisfaction highlight the importance of people's expectations; if a product or service does not meet or exceed a person's expectations, then they report being dissatisfied (Oliver, 2010). This concept can be extended to the situation in which a victim of crime reports the incident to the police, when they will hold a certain expectation for the level of service they will receive. If forensic fiction has indeed resulted in viewers having unrealistically high expectations about forensic evidence, this may have an impact on victims of crime and their reported satisfaction with the police, and crime scene investigators in particular.

Imagine a burglary has occurred, the victim reports the crime to the police and a crime scene investigator is deployed to the house to search for any available forensic evidence. If this burglary victim is a frequent consumer of forensic fiction, they may hold unrealistically high expectations that the investigator will recover large amounts of useful forensic evidence and that this will lead to the apprehension of the offender. What is most often the case is that the crime scene investigator is not able to recover any useful forensic evidence, and the victim's expectations are therefore not met. The victim may report being dissatisfied with their experience and may be less likely to engage with the police in the future.

The potential effect of forensic fiction on victim satisfaction has not yet been investigated in the literature, although a substantial body of research has focused on victim satisfaction and expectations more generally. While it is therefore theoretically plausible that this version of the CSI Effect is occurring in the criminal justice system, empirical research is required to determine the extent of the problem.

Educational effects of forensic fiction

The various possible versions of the CSI Effect described in this chapter are largely proposed to be having a negative effect on the criminal justice system. However, it is also possible that the popularity of forensic fiction has opened up the world of science to the general public and inspired people to pursue science education as a result. Partly thanks to forensic fiction, universities around the world have seen dramatic increases in the demand for undergraduate programmes in forensic science. It is not difficult to find a wide range of courses now offered linking traditional subjects, such as biology, chemistry, anthropology and psychology, with 'forensic' studies. These are very popular courses for undergraduate students, although despite the high numbers enrolling, there is also some evidence that a high proportion of students drop out of these courses. This low completion rate may be due to the disappointment felt by students whose expectations were unrealistically high based on forensic dramas on television.

The increase in forensic-themed courses is not necessarily beneficial to students who are hoping to work in the field of forensic science as a career. Some forensic practitioners, and indeed employers, worry that this rapid increase in demand for new courses has compromised the quality of the science content in these degree programmes. What forensic employers really want from new graduates is a solid grounding in core science knowledge and skills, so completing a more traditional natural science degree programme is still considered by many forensic employers as preferable to a course with forensic content and is likely to make a student a stronger candidate.

While not all consumers of forensic fiction are interested in pursuing an education and career in this area, some commentators have argued that this popular genre has educated lay people in scientific techniques and their application to the law. The creator of *CSI*, Anthony Zuiker, has been quoted as saying 'people know science now, they watch *CSI*'(Allen, 2007, p. 95), implying that the programme has raised awareness of science among the general population. This may be the case, for instance many people are likely to know what DNA is and why it is useful in criminal investigations, not from formal education in genetics but from exposure to the media. Nevertheless, as we have already seen, this 'education' includes significantly exaggerated depictions of the possibilities of science. Whether this effect is good or bad is not easy to determine, but it is difficult to deny that forensic fiction is functioning as an educator of the public to some degree.

Summary

In this chapter we have explored some of the ways in which forensic fiction differs substantially from the reality of criminal investigations.

Due to the overwhelming popularity of forensic dramas on television, and the inaccurate portrayal of forensic science that they contain, some members of the criminal justice system have expressed concern that there may be adverse effects on criminal trials. The CSI Effect has become the focus of empirical literature, although despite anecdotal support the research findings provide mixed conclusions about whether there really is any evidence of such an effect. Even so, attorneys have changed their trial strategies in order to address the perceived CSI Effect among juries. More research is needed to determine whether any other aspects of the criminal justice process might be affected by fictional portrayals of forensic science, but there is no doubt that *CSI: Crime Scene Investigation* and other shows in this genre have captured the imagination of millions of people worldwide.

This topic provides another example of how multidisciplinary approaches to forensic science can contribute to a better understanding of the role of science in the legal system and society more generally. In particular, researchers from disciplines such as psychology, criminology, media studies and sociology have begun to investigate the role of the media in shaping the public's perceptions of forensic science and how these beliefs may influence the criminal justice system. Through this improved understanding, it is hoped that forensic scientists and lawyers can be better prepared for the courtroom and that crime scene investigators can manage expectations more effectively.

Study questions

1 Consider some of the ways in which forensic fiction on television differs from reality. Why do you think that the popular media portrays forensic science in such an unrealistic manner?

2 There is the possibility that forensic fiction might be educating offenders in how to avoid detection by destroying forensic evidence or avoiding leaving it behind. Consider the possibility of this version of the CSI Effect in more detail. Do you think this is really something that should be a cause for concern?

7

FORENSIC SCIENCE IN THE COURTROOM

Once a police investigation has been completed and a suspect has been charged with the crime, the case will proceed to court if the evidence is deemed to be sufficient and the defendant does not plead guilty to the charges. It is then the court's job to decide whether the evidence presented against the defendant proves their guilt, beyond a reasonable doubt, and ultimately whether they should be found guilty or not guilty of the crime in question. Depending on the jurisdiction, criminal courts operate in very different ways, and this chapter will provide an overview of how some jurisdictions carry out criminal proceedings and in particular how forensic science features in these trials. Forensic evidence is typically presented at trial by expert witnesses, so the role of these witnesses and decisions about the admissibility of scientific evidence will also be discussed in this chapter. Similar to the previous chapters, this topic involves a number of academic disciplines, including psychology, physical sciences, philosophy and law, further highlighting the multidisciplinary nature of these debates.

Overview of various criminal court systems

It would require an entire book series to provide a detailed overview of all the different criminal court structures and procedures worldwide. In this section we will therefore focus on the broadest categories of legal systems and processes. There are two overarching models of procedural justice by which world court systems are commonly categorised: *adversarial* and *inquisitorial* systems. The features of these two systems are described here, although it is important to note that in practice no single court system is a pure representation of either model. Instead, it is useful to think of them as extreme ends of a continuum, with various court systems falling somewhere in between.

Adversarial legal systems

The main distinguishing feature of adversarial systems is the emphasis on cases being argued by two sides (or advocates), the defence representing the defendant and the prosecution representing the state. This structure requires the police to conduct an investigation, which provides the evidence used by the prosecution, followed by the defence gathering their own evidence and scrutinising the prosecution's case. The two advocates are then required to present their case to a neutral, impartial court where the final verdict is decided by a *trier of fact*. In adversarial systems, the trier of fact is usually a panel of lay people (a jury) or a judge. The role of the judge in this legal system is to act as a gatekeeper when deciding what evidence is admissible, and as a 'referee' to ensure that both advocates adhere to the rules of the law. This system of law is found mainly in 'common law' countries, consisting of the UK, those countries constituting the Commonwealth and others such as the USA.

An inherent element in adversarial systems is the presumption of innocence: the defendant is presumed innocent and must be proven to be guilty 'beyond a reasonable doubt' before they can be convicted at trial. This places the burden of proof on the prosecution, not the defence. It is rooted in the system's mistrust of the reliability of prosecution evidence, and the view that in order to reach fair and just verdicts the defence must be given the opportunity to challenge the evidence presented against the defendant. Therefore, the trial acts as a forum for determining whether there is reasonable doubt that the defendant committed the crime in question. It is important to remember that in this system the defence is not required to prove innocence; rather, the prosecution is required to prove guilt.

Inquisitorial legal systems

A defining feature of inquisitorial legal systems is the active role taken by the judge in criminal cases. Judges in these legal systems are primarily responsible for the investigation, collection of evidence, questioning of witnesses and ultimately the decision over the verdict. Therefore, in contrast to the adversarial system where the judge plays a gatekeeper role, judges in inquisitorial systems are fact gatherers. This system of law is found in some 'civil law' countries, dating back to Roman law, comprising many of those in mainland Europe as well as China and Japan.

Unlike in an adversarial system, much more confidence is placed in the integrity of the evidence gathered before the trial, and therefore by the time a case reaches trial in an inquisitorial system there is a much greater presumption of guilt. Juries do not tend to feature in inquisitorial systems, and the trial process itself is very different from the adversarial approach. The main feature of the process is the *case dossier*, which contains all the evidence and information gathered by the judge throughout the investigation. This dossier forms the basis of the decision-making process, and witnesses are called and questioned by the judge as required. The final verdict and sentencing decisions are then made by the judge, or sometimes a panel of judges, with very little (if any) participation from lay people.

Admissibility of evidence

Regardless of the type of legal system, evidence is required to be admissible if it is going to be presented at trial. In the case of adversarial systems, only evidence meeting certain admissibility requirements is heard by the jury at trial; in inquisitorial systems, only evidence deemed by the judge to be admissible will be included in the case dossier. Forensic science testimony is most likely to be presented to the court by an expert witness, and there are specific rules of law governing the admissibility of expert witnesses and their testimony. The exact rules of admissibility differ quite substantially between systems and jurisdictions, so this section will provide an overview of the criteria that forensic expert testimony needs to meet in the UK and the USA.

Expert testimony in the UK

In criminal courts in the UK, opinion evidence (such as forensic examinations) presented by an expert witness is considered to be admissible if it meets two basic criteria. First, the evidence must be related to an issue that is considered to be 'beyond the ordinary competence of the court' (Hannibal and Mountford, 2002, p. 355). Therefore, the expert must be presenting evidence on an issue that is likely to be outside the knowledge of an ordinary member of the public (e.g. referring to the knowledge of the fact finders: juries or magistrates). The second basic criterion is that the expert testimony must be capable of helping the court reach a decision on the case in question; in other words, the evidence needs to be relevant to the case. In terms of forensic science testimony, these basic requirements relate to the fact that the forensic expert witness needs to be testifying about technical or scientific knowledge that lay people are unlikely to possess, and it also needs to be directly relevant to deciding the guilt of the defendant.

In addition to the basic criteria of specialised knowledge and relevance, the court is also required to decide who qualifies as an 'expert' and is therefore allowed to give expert evidence. A witness's competence as an expert in their field is usually determined by the court's consideration of their qualifications and professional experience, and the burden to demonstrate expert status falls on the advocate who wishes to call the expert to testify. However, competence alone is not enough for the court to conclude that a potential witness is indeed an 'expert'. It is also necessary that the methods utilised by the expert are sound, and that they are well respected by other experts in the relevant field of study. So it could be the case that an expert has the required competences, but if they wish to testify about a technique or method that is not well accepted, then their evidence will not be admissible. See Box 7.1 for an example of an expert whose testimony was not accepted by the courts, despite his extensive experience and qualifications.

Box 7.1 R *v.* Gilfoyle

In June 1992, Paula Gilfoyle was found hanging in the garage of the house she shared with her husband Eddie Gilfoyle in Upton, Wirral, UK. A suicide note was found, and as there did not appear to be any suspicious circumstances, the police ruled her death a suicide and did not investigate any further. However, Paula's friends and family came forward after her death and provided information to the police that began to raise suspicion that perhaps her husband had murdered her and staged the scene to look like suicide. One strange piece of information provided was that Paula, who was heavily pregnant at the time of her death, had told friends that her husband was taking a suicide response class at the hospital where he worked, and that he had asked Paula to write a 'mock' suicide note to help with an assignment he had to submit. Eventually, Eddie Gilfoyle was charged with murder, for which he was convicted at trial. During the trial, the prosecution wanted to present a prominent forensic psychologist as an expert witness, who had prepared a report (referred to as a psychological autopsy) concluding that Paula's behaviour prior to her death was not consistent with someone who was suicidal, and that therefore in his professional opinion it was unlikely that she had killed herself. Despite the fact that the court agreed that this witness qualified as an expert on the basis of his qualifications and reputation, they chose not to allow this expert testimony on the grounds that the methods used to reach his conclusion were not based on acceptable scientific criteria. It was also stated that 'jurors do not need psychiatrists to tell them how ordinary folk who are not suffering from any mental illness are likely to react to the stresses and strains of life'.

Analysis: Eddie Gilfoyle served 18 years in prison before being released in 2010. He maintained his innocence throughout his time in prison, and his case is currently undergoing a review in the light of new evidence, including documentation alleging that Paula had previously attempted suicide. However, the victim's family have always insisted that she was murdered by her husband. This is an example of how tricky these cases can be; indeed, the Criminal Cases Review Commission has described the Gilfoyle case as one of the 'most complex' cases it has ever reviewed.

Expert testimony in the USA

In US federal criminal courts, and in the majority of states, the criteria used to determine the admissibility of scientific expert testimony are outlined in the Federal Rules of Evidence (FRE 702). Understanding the current version of FRE 702, most recently amended in 2000, requires a brief historical overview of the admissibility rules in the USA.

From 1923 to 1993 federal courts, and 45 states, used the Frye standard to determine the admissibility of expert testimony. This standard required that the evidence about which the expert wished to testify was based on 'generally accepted' scientific principles and that the reliability of the theory or technique was also generally accepted by the relevant scientific community. Although the Frye standard was superseded by the Federal Rules of Evidence and the Daubert ruling (outlined later in this section), some states have still not adopted these more recent rules and continue to use the Frye standard.

In 1974 the Federal Rules of Evidence were implemented to control evidentiary matters in the federal courts in the United States, and FRE 702 specifically outlines the criteria that expert testimony must meet in addition to the expert being considered to be sufficiently qualified and experienced:

- Similar to the UK's basic requirements, the testimony must contain 'specialised knowledge' that will help the trier of fact decide the facts of the case.
- The expert testimony must be based on sufficient facts or data. This criterion aims to ensure that testimony rests on reliable facts and a reasonable amount of data collected.
- The testimony must be the product of reliable principles and methods. Similar to the rules of admissibility in the UK, this criterion requires the expert's methods to be sound and scientific.
- The expert must have reliably applied the principles and methods to the facts of the case.

In 1991, the case of Daubert *v.* Merrell Dow Pharmaceuticals provided further guidance on the criteria that the courts could use when determining the admissibility of expert testimony, and in 2000 the Federal Rules of Evidence were amended to include the Daubert ruling. In particular, the Daubert case ruled that the judge would act as the gatekeeper for expert evidence considerations, and that this admissibility decision would be made at a pre-trial 'Daubert hearing'. Criteria that judges could consider, outlined by the Daubert ruling, include:

- whether the theory or technique can be, and has been tested;
- whether the theory or technique has been subjected to peer review and publication;
- the known or potential error rate of the technique;
- the existence of standards controlling the operation and use of the technique;
- whether the technique has widespread acceptance within the relevant scientific community

When interpreting these rules for the admissibility of expert testimony, the courts must consider what constitutes 'good science', in order to avoid admitting evidence that is based on unvalidated or faulty scientific methodology. This is generally done by determining whether the technique or method is falsifiable and testable, what the known or potential error rate is, the existence of standards for the technique, and the acceptance of the method by members of the scientific community (for example by determining whether it has been subjected to peer review). These tests (in any country) are extremely important in order to minimise the chances of wrongful convictions caused by faulty scientific testimony, as demonstrated in the example in Box 7.2.

Box 7.2 The wrongful conviction of Kennedy Brewer

In May 1992, 3-year-old Christine Jackson was abducted from her home in Mississippi, USA. She was found two days later in a shallow creek about 500 yards from the house, having been raped and murdered. Her mother's boyfriend, Kennedy Brewer, had been alone at home with Christine and his two other children the night she went missing and because there was no obvious sign of forced entry, he was charged with her murder. At Brewer's trial for capital murder and sexual battery, the prosecution presented a forensic odontologist who testified that 19 marks found on the victim's body were 'indeed and without doubt' bite marks inflicted by Brewer. During this testimony, the expert made claims of certainty and reliability that far exceeded the capabilities of bite mark analysis. The defence produced another dentistry expert who testified that the marks were not human bite marks, and were more likely to be the result of insect activity during the time that the victim's body was partially submerged in the creek. Regardless of this conflicting testimony, the jury found Brewer guilty largely on the basis of the questionable bite mark evidence, and he was sentenced to death.

Analysis: Brewer spent seven years on death row, and a further seven years in prison awaiting trial and appeals before the Innocence Project investigated his case. In 2008 Brewer became the first post-conviction DNA exoneree in Mississippi. The National Academy of Sciences forensic science review (see Chapters 2 and 8) concluded that bite mark evidence is not based on sufficient scientific research, and should therefore not be relied on for identifying individuals until further research is carried out to validate the technique.

The role of the expert witness

As we have seen previously, forensic experts are often called to testify about the technical and scientific aspects of the forensic analyses they have conducted, and to interpret their results in the context of a particular criminal case. However, at times the disciplines of science and the law find it difficult to understand one another, which can cause tension for expert witnesses.

Science and the law have been referred to as 'reluctant bedfellows' due to some fundamental differences between the disciplines. The first of these inherent differences refers to their goals: the goal of science is to seek objective truths about the world and the physical and natural laws that govern it, while the goal of the law is to seek justice. Although in some cases the 'truth' and 'justice' are one and the same, there are many instances where this is not the case. For example, imagine a trial in which the defendant pleads not guilty, but is in fact guilty of the crime in question. If the prosecution fails to prove the guilt of the defendant beyond a reasonable doubt, the correct and 'just' decision is for the jury to vote not guilty. In this case, the objective truth is that the defendant is guilty of the crime, but justice requires that the jury votes not guilty.

A second important difference between how scientists and lawyers carry out their work is evident in the way they communicate. Scientists communicate scientific findings through various media (journal articles, books, lectures and so on), but regardless of the format the communication involves trading facts with the scientific community. In the legal profession, facts are less important and the prevailing communication strategy is storytelling. Lawyers representing the two sides of a court case in an adversarial system communicate to the court through telling stories, which include some 'facts' that may be presented to the court by expert witnesses in the form of evidence.

Finally, science and the law also differ in their approach to results and conclusions. Scientists are required to remain open-minded about their findings, and to be willing to change their views and conclusions in the light of new discoveries and results. Historically, the physical sciences have witnessed dramatic paradigm shifts as a result of emerging evidence and research findings. The law, however, aims for more definitive closure wherever possible. Of course, there are mechanisms in place within the law for revisiting cases in the light of new evidence (e.g. appeals procedures), but there are also features of the legal system that promote closure (e.g. statutes of limitations legislation).

Expert witnesses are therefore scientists who are required to participate in the legal system, which operates in ways that are sometimes contradictory to how scientists are accustomed to working. Despite these tensions, the role of the expert witness is to remain an unbiased, neutral witness by communicating to the court the results of rigorous forensic analyses. The importance of neutrality cannot be overstated, and it is vital that witnesses do not perceive themselves to be 'on the side' of either adversary in a trial. This requires experts to maintain strict ethical standards when conducting expert examinations, as there can be an implicit expectation that they will find results that will support the side of the case that has retained their services. However, this is not the true situation, and courts require experts to uphold this ethical duty in every trial.

Defence versus prosecution experts

Forensic scientists are most likely to appear in court to present the results of forensic analyses on behalf of the prosecution, due to the fact that most forensic analysis is conducted at the request of the police during their investigation. Although the defence also has the option to have evidence examined by their own experts, they are often at a significant disadvantage compared to prosecution experts. First, forensic analyses conducted during the police investigation often compromise the integrity of the evidence, which disadvantages any subsequent experts who wish to examine that evidence. For example, some forensic techniques are invasive, which means that they alter or destroy the evidence in some way, therefore once they have been carried out the evidence is no longer in the same state as it was when it was recovered (see Chapters 2 and 3). This often makes it impossible for alternative analyses to be conducted, which leaves defence experts only able to verify the results of the prosecution's witness by reviewing their notes, photographs, reports and so on.

A second disadvantage facing the defence lawyer is that forensic examinations are cost prohibitive, and not all defendants have funds available to cover costly analyses. This limits the opportunities for the defence to have another expert provide a second opinion on the forensic findings, and in some cases this lack of verification can lead to errors. This has been particularly relevant in cases where questionable forensic techniques are admitted to trial by the prosecution, and the defence is not able to secure an appropriate expert to provide a critical analysis of the technique and associated testimony. However, it is also important to note that even in cases where a defence expert is presented to the court, juries often still feel compelled to favour prosecution witnesses. This is demonstrated by the cases of Kennedy Brewer (Box 7.2) and David Shawn Pope, described in Box 7.3.

Box 7.3 The wrongful conviction of David Shawn Pope

In July 1985, a woman in Texas, USA was awoken in the morning to find a man in her bedroom holding a knife to her throat. He proceeded to rape the victim and flee the apartment. Following the attack, and after reporting it to the police, the victim received a number of phone calls from the attacker, some of which police assisted her in recording. David Shawn Pope became a suspect in this case after being seen by police in the apartment complex and subsequently being charged with driving infractions. Pope was thought to resemble the description of the attacker, and was picked by the victim from a live line-up parade (although she had previously been shown a photo of him in a photo line-up and failed to identify him). At Pope's trial, the prosecution presented an expert witness who testified that he had analysed the sound waves of the recorded messages left by the attacker and had been able to match them uniquely to 'voiceprints' of Pope's voice. The defence also called an expert, who testified that so-called voice spectrographic analysis was not scientific and could not be relied on. However, the jury was convinced by this evidence and convicted Pope to 45 years in prison.

Analysis: Pope spent 15 years in prison before being exonerated by DNA analysis in 2001. In many cases defendants are at a significant disadvantage in relation to challenging prosecution evidence with their own expert witnesses: faulty forensic science was used by the prosecution expert witness, but despite the defence presenting a challenging expert, the jury was still convinced by the prosecution's evidence. This case also highlights the importance of keeping 'junk science' out of the courtroom, and it is the judge's gatekeeper role that is crucial in this regard. However, judges are not required to have any scientific training or knowledge, so how can they act as effective gatekeepers in criminal cases involving scientific expert testimony?

Fact finders: Judges and juries

Earlier in this chapter, we explored the two main types of legal system and the philosophical and practical differences between them. You will recall that in an adversarial system the verdict is often determined by a deliberating jury, while in the inquisitorial model it is typically decided by a professional judge (or panel of judges). Different jurisdictions around the world operate in a wide variety of ways, and in some courts verdicts are reached by a mixed panel of lay people and professionals. Regardless of the system, however, the fact finders in the court are not required to have any minimum science qualification, therefore their experience and knowledge of interpreting scientific analyses are likely to be limited. It is thus important to consider how scientific evidence is understood by the triers of fact and to be aware of some of the common misunderstandings that can occur in order to avoid them as much as possible. This part of the chapter will concentrate largely on juries as decision makers, as this is where the majority of the empirical literature has been focused.

Juries in the adversarial system

In the USA, criminal defendants have a constitutional right to be tried by a jury of their peers, which implies that this is a feature of the justice system that should be viewed as favourable by the public and defendants alike. Nevertheless, the majority of prosecutions in the USA are not resolved through jury trials, as most defendants do not invoke their right to a jury trial and instead agree to a *plea bargain* with the prosecution. In other words, the defendant avoids a jury trial by pleading guilty to a lesser charge in exchange for a reduced sentence. This tendency to favour plea bargaining over trials results in an estimated 149 000 jury trials per year, of which approximately 66% are criminal trials (National Center for State Courts, 2007).

Similarly, in the UK relatively few criminal cases (1–2% of trials) are heard by juries, but for different reasons. There is no constitutional right to jury trial to uphold (Hope and Memon, 2006); instead, jury trials are reserved for serious offences in the Crown Court, while most criminal charges are presented in a Magistrates' Court, where juries are not used. The situation is very similar in Australia and New Zealand, where juries are reserved for only the most serious indictable offences, amounting to approximately 1% of all criminal trials (Goodman-Delahunty and Tait, 2006).

With such small numbers of trials in these jurisdictions being decided by juries, you may be wondering why psychology and legal researchers have spent the last five decades investigating juror's decision-making strategies. However, although jury trials may represent a small proportion of all criminal trials, they are most likely to be used in the most serious and complicated trials. So it is important to understand the jury decision-making process in order to utilise juries more effectively.

How do jurors make decisions?

The majority of psychology research relating to juries since the 1980s has focused on understanding more about how jurors reach decisions, particularly in complicated trial situations. There are two levels of decision making relating to the jury process: the individual decision-making process undertaken by each individual juror; and the collective decision-making process undertaken during the jury's deliberation process.

The basic premise underlying the juror's decision-making process is that each juror arrives at trial carrying with them their own unique combination of life experience, education, attitudes, beliefs and biases. In other words, no two jurors will share exactly the same combination of background characteristics, therefore each juror will be watching the trial through a unique lens representing their own life and circumstances. Recognising that jurors are not blank slates when a trial begins has helped to shape decades of psychology research and theory into the decision-making process. Early research largely focused on the influence on verdict preference of demographic characteristics, such as age, gender and political affiliation. However, none of these characteristics are reliable predictors of jurors' decisions and therefore the focus shifted to understanding the cognitive processes underlying those decisions.

The most famous and robust theory of how jurors interpret and organise large amounts of trial information was proposed by Pennington and Hastie (1986) and is referred to as the *Story Model*. This differed from earlier models in two important ways: it emphasised the importance of the individual juror's personal experiences, attitudes and beliefs; and it focused on the use of narratives (or stories) as a method of organising and remembering information. The Story Model explains the juror decision-making process in three steps. The first step involves the interpretation and integration of all the trial evidence and information into a dynamic narrative, which is constantly updated as new trial evidence is presented. By the end of the trial, jurors who have constructed a story that supports the guilt of the defendant will be inclined to vote 'guilty'. The second stage requires the juror to determine the decision alternatives that are available to them, including which charges the defendant is facing and the various verdict options. The final stage requires the juror to consider their verdict options and decide which is best suited to the story that they have constructed. This then forms the basis of each juror's pre-deliberation judgement, which is taken into the deliberation process.

So the key to the Story Model is the construction of a plausible story to explain the criminal case and the associated information and evidence. Pennington and Hastie (1992) identified a number of sources of information that contribute to the development of a story. The first source of information is the evidence presented at trial by the prosecution and the defence, including all witnesses called to testify. This is the only legally relevant information that jurors can use to construct their stories, although there are other sources of information on which we know jurors rely as well. The first is their general knowledge about the world, attitudes and beliefs about relevant people and situations, and their expectations of the criminal justice system. In addition, research has also indicated that extra-legal factors such as the demeanour of the defendant and victim, and the performance of the prosecutor and defence lawyer, contribute to shaping a juror's perception of the trial and their resulting story.

It is important to note that relying on prior experience, attitudes and beliefs is not necessarily an inherently poor strategy for reaching decisions. In fact, our ability to make quick decisions throughout our daily lives, and to avoid getting overwhelmed by relatively simple and repetitive decision making, depends on our making use of prior knowledge. These mental shortcuts that we perform all day long are referred to as *heuristics*, and they feature most prominently in decisions that are complex or involve significant amounts of uncertainty. So it is no wonder that heuristics are an important part of jury decision making. However, these shortcuts can also result in faulty decisions when the prior knowledge, attitudes and beliefs are incorrect or not based on accurate information, which will be discussed in more detail later in this chapter.

After a trial ends, and each juror has considered the case individually and reached their own conclusions about what the verdict ought to be, the jury as a group must reach a consensus on what verdict to declare.

The specific rules of deliberation and verdict differ between jurisdictions, but most juries must either reach a unanimous verdict or meet minimum majority standards, depending on the size of the jury. Psychological research has investigated the effectiveness of group decision making and the social psychology of group dynamics, which are relevant to jury deliberations. The research findings indicate that there are positive and negative effects of group deliberations on decision making, some of which are particularly relevant to jury deliberations (Devine et al., 2010).

Juror decision making about forensic science testimony

There is a large body of research literature investigating the general cognitive aspects of juror decision making and the influence of pre-trial beliefs, attitudes and experiences on the process of reaching a verdict. A smaller subset of this research has focused specifically on how jurors reach decisions about forensic science testimony presented during trials, and in particular how well they understand complicated scientific evidence in the context of the criminal trial. Remember, members of the jury are not required to have any prior knowledge of scientific techniques or theories, therefore it is of concern that they may be required to make life-changing decisions based, at least in part, on scientific information.

One area of concern that has been a focus of this research literature is the quantification of scientific evidence presented during forensic testimony. In particular, as we saw in Chapter 5, it is common practice for expert witnesses to express forensic results using probabilities and frequencies. For example, when an expert presents a DNA 'match' to the court, it is accompanied by the random match probability (RMP), representing the probability of that match being purely coincidental. In other words, the RMP is the probability that the DNA profile matches a particular person, if that person was not actually the source of the DNA. With the discriminating power of modern DNA technology, it is not uncommon to have an RMP of one in many millions (or billions), which would mean that the probability of a match being coincidental is very small (although never completely impossible).

The question raised by researchers is whether probabilities and frequencies are understood by jurors, and how they influence the decision-making process. Generally, what the research indicates is that probabilities and statistics are difficult for jurors to understand, and that a number of errors can occur in decisions made about these evidence types. Schklar and Diamond (1999) describe two main types of error that often occur when DNA evidence is evaluated by jurors. First, jurors can make mathematical errors when interpreting a probability or statistic, and therefore fail to update their perception of the defendant's guilt correctly in the light of the evidence presented (referred to as a *misaggregation error*). Alternatively, jurors can rely on inaccurate background beliefs or attitudes about certain evidence types, which may result in faulty decision making (referred to as a *misperception error*).

In addition to errors caused by a lack of understanding of complicated probabilities and statistics, the language used by expert witnesses and legal advocates can have an impact on how jurors perceive forensic evidence. The *exemplar cueing theory*, proposed by Koehler (2001), argues that how a piece of evidence is framed when it is presented will have a significant impact on how it is perceived by a juror. When evidence is framed in a way that highlights the uniqueness of the evidence (e.g. by presenting a very small RMP), then jurors find the evidence compelling. However, if the same piece of evidence is presented in a way that draws attention to the existence of alternative explanations (e.g. stating that 100 other people in the population would share these characteristics with the defendant), then it is perceived as weaker evidence.

Exemplar cueing theory demonstrates how the language used by the expert witness, as well as that used by the prosecution and defence, can influence the impact that a piece of evidence has on jurors. This is particularly worrying, as it has been established that jurors do not have a good understanding of probabilities and statistics and therefore struggle to notice when something is being misrepresented during a trial. It is therefore not uncommon for prosecutors and defence attorneys to exploit these potential errors for their own benefit during criminal trials. For example, a prosecutor would find it advantageous to frame a piece of incriminating evidence to highlight uniqueness (and therefore make it appear more compelling), while the defence would benefit from highlighting alternative explanations in order to reduce the perceived probative value of the same evidence. This is not the only source of potential errors in jurors' interpretations of forensic evidence, as we will see in the next section.

Common courtroom fallacies regarding forensic science testimony

In this final section, two common errors in reasoning about forensic science testimony will be described. Both of these errors occur quite commonly, and spontaneously, when people are trying to reason about probabilities. However, in the context of a criminal trial, they can be explicitly stated by the expert witness during examination by the prosecution or defence representatives, or indeed by judges in their summation to the jury at the end of the trial. Therefore, awareness of these errors in judgement is crucial in order to be able to avoid falling prey to them when considering the strength of forensic testimony.

The prosecutor's fallacy

The first of these common errors is often referred to as the *prosecutor's fallacy*, due to the fact that this type of misunderstanding of probability in forensic testimony tends to favour the prosecution's case. In other words, this particular error has the potential to cause misinterpretation of evidence that can lead to the wrongful conviction of a defendant. Due to the fact that this fallacy seems quite counter-intuitive, it has been documented in a number of criminal trials, an example of which is described in Box 7.4.

Box 7.4 The prosecutor's fallacy

The UK case of Sally Clark highlights a number of statistical and mathematical errors that can plague criminal proceedings, of which the prosecutor's fallacy is only one example. In September 1996, Sally Clark gave birth to a baby boy (Christopher) and 11 weeks later the baby was found dead in his cot of 'natural causes'. In November 1997, Sally and Steve Clark had a second baby boy (Harry) and 8 weeks later he suddenly collapsed, apparently of natural causes. Following an autopsy, retina and brain damage attributed to abuse were recorded and baby Christopher's death was also investigated and evaluated to have been a possible case of smothering. Police arrested Sally Clark and she was charged with murdering both her children. The prosecution presented a medical expert who was asked to testify about the prevalence of sudden infant death syndrome (SIDS) and to comment on the likelihood of this being the cause of both babies' deaths. It was this expert testimony that caused controversy about the use of statistics in the courtroom, as the expert testified that the probability of a family having two babies die of SIDS was 1 in 73 million. It is assumed by many commentators that the jury's guilty verdict relied heavily on the misinterpretation of this statistic, although the calculation of this statistic was later ruled invalid by the Royal Statistical Society.

Analysis: It is thought that the jury may have fallen into the prosecutor's fallacy and wrongly equated the figure of 1 in 73 million with the likelihood of Sally Clark's not having murdered her children. Sally Clark was convicted by a 10–2 majority vote and sentenced to life imprisonment. On a review of the trial evidence, her conviction was overturned on appeal in January 2003. The prosecutor's fallacy is not the only type of faulty reasoning that may have occurred in this case, as it is also an example of a misinterpretation of the product rule and statistical independence (see also Box 5.4).

The prosecutor's fallacy is particularly prevalent in relation to the evaluation of RMP testimony, which you will recall from earlier in this chapter and Chapter 5. In the language of formal logic, the probability of the DNA being a match (E) if the defendant is not the source of the DNA (H) is expressed as

$$P(E|H)$$

In plain English this expression is read as the probability (P) of the evidence (E = DNA match) given the hypothesis that the defendant is innocent (H).

There is nothing wrong with the logic so far, but the prosecutor's fallacy arises when the RMP is interpreted as also being the probability that the defendant is innocent of the crime in question. That is not the same as what the expert testifies when they report the RMP. The probability (P) of the defendant being innocent (H) given a DNA match (E) is expressed formally as

$$P(H|E)$$

So the prosecutor's fallacy can be expressed formally as

$$P(E|H) \neq P(H|E)$$

It now becomes clear why this mistake (which is easily made) would favour the prosecution's case. If an expert witness testified that DNA from the crime scene matched the defendant's DNA profile and the RMP was reported as 1 in 5 million, the prosecution would be happy with jurors who thought that this was the same as saying that there is a 1 in 5 million chance that the defendant is innocent! In fact, sometimes the prosecution is able to frame its examination questions in such a way that expert witnesses make this mistake in their testimony, so it is no wonder that jurors are known to commit this error in reasoning.

The defendant's fallacy

It is not only the prosecution that can benefit from common misunderstandings about the interpretation of probabilities and statistics in the courtroom. The *defendant's fallacy* is an example of a commonly occurring error in judgement that can potentially benefit the defence case, and we have already seen in this chapter why this fallacy occurs (see the earlier discussion of exemplar cueing theory). This particular error occurs most commonly when an expert witness testifies about some evidence type, and provides statistics to help the jury understand the frequency of the evidence in the population. For example, a prosecution witness might testify that blood evidence recovered from the crime scene 'matches' the defendant, and that this evidence has characteristics that would be shared by one in a million other individuals. This might be considered compelling odds that the defendant is indeed likely to be the source of the blood, but in a city with a population of 10 million the defence might argue that there are ten people who could have contributed the blood, of which the defendant is only one. Therefore they might further argue that there is only a 10% (or 1 in 10 possible guilty people) chance that the defendant is guilty – put another way, a 90% chance that the defendant is innocent.

This type of error in reasoning was documented a number of times during the O.J. Simpson murder trial (Box 4.3). Blood evidence from the crime scene was reported to be consistent with the defendant's blood, but the characteristics would also have been shared by approximately 1 in 400 people. The defence team used this to argue that if you took everyone in Los Angeles with those same blood characteristics, they would fill a football stadium, and therefore urged the jury to consider this evidence irrelevant.

The problem with the defendant's fallacy and this line of argument is that it ignores all other relevant evidence, and assumes that everyone in the population is equally likely to have committed the crime in question. This is obviously not a valid argument to make in these circumstances, but the argument is still used by defence attorneys during trials, and can be considered compelling by jurors who do not spot the error in logic.

Summary

This chapter has described the two main models of judicial process, the adversarial and inquisitorial systems, and considered how expert evidence is evaluated for admissibility as well as some of the issues related to prosecution and defence witnesses. It has also discussed jury decision making, the topic of five decades of legal psychology research. The Story Model of juror decision making highlights the importance of a juror's prior knowledge, attitudes and beliefs and provides a theoretical basis for discussions relating to how well jurors understand scientific evidence presented in the courtroom. Research has concluded that jurors are often not capable of understanding the intricacies of scientific analyses; in particular, statistical or probabilistic evidence poses significant problems in the courtroom. It is therefore extremely important that expert witnesses, as well as attorneys and judges, are well aware of these errors in logic and hold to their ethical requirements when testifying in court. Awareness of these common errors should be used to educate the triers of fact, rather than employed to exploit errors in reasoning for the advocates' benefit during trial.

Study questions

1 A significant disadvantage facing defendants in criminal trials is related to forensic science, due to the fact that most forensic analyses are requested on behalf of the police (and therefore usually the prosecution) during the investigation of the crime. This means that the defence has very limited opportunities to analyse evidence independently because of missed opportunity and also the cost-prohibitive nature of forensic testing. Think about some scenarios where this might cause significant problems, possibly even resulting

in miscarriages of justice. How could the system possibly be improved in order to address this risk?

2 Juries in criminal trials are considered by some countries to be a fundamental right of the defendant and a necessary feature of a democratic legal system. Other countries argue that placing such serious decisions, with such significant consequences, in the hands of untrained lay people is unfair and increases the chances of problematic verdicts. Given the discussion in this chapter of research suggesting that, on average, jurors have only a poor understanding of complicated scientific testimony, do you think that jury trials are the best way to achieve justice in criminal trials?

8

ISSUES IN CONTEMPORARY FORENSIC SCIENCE AND JUSTICE

This final chapter considers some of the current issues in forensic science and criminal justice, and looks forward to the future of forensic research, technology and practice. These issues expand on the knowledge of forensic practice and related criminal justice topics that you have encountered in the preceding chapters, and the chapter calls attention to a few of the 'hot topics' in the field.

The first section examines new forensic technology, primarily in the areas of fingerprint and DNA advances, and considers how these emerging technologies might be used by law enforcement as well as other issues that they raise. The second section discusses the need for accreditation and international standards in forensic laboratories. These issues bring together the theory and practice presented in Chapters 2, 3 and 5 and stress the importance of maintaining high levels of quality and standardisation in forensic laboratories.

The third section discusses biometric databases and the privacy and ethical issues that are raised through the use of such databases to detect crime. Different jurisdictions have various approaches to the collection and retention of personal information (including DNA and fingerprints), so a number of different countries will be mentioned as well as new legislation recently enacted in the UK and USA. Finally, the issue of international standards for forensic databases and the impact of databases on the policing of cross-border and transnational crime will be discussed.

New technology

From previous chapters it can be seen that there already exists a comprehensive range of techniques to analyse all manner of forensic exhibits irrespective of their type and origin. However, law enforcement agencies continue to look for new ways in which forensic material can be analysed and this is particularly true when trying to analyse ever smaller amounts of material (such as DNA) or surfaces known to be difficult (such as recovering fingerprints from fabrics). A great deal of effort is being put into investigating these and other areas to broaden the occasions on which forensic evidence can be recovered, analysed and interpreted for the courts. This work might be viewed as an incremental advance, slowly increasing the range of exhibits from which useful forensic material can be recovered. In parallel with this, what have been described as alternative technologies are being developed, with the aim of adding value over and above the current possibilities for the recovery and analysis of material.

Recovering fingerprints from difficult surfaces

Two surfaces from which latent fingerprints are difficult to recover are both likely to be encountered together at the crime scene, namely skin and fabric. Offences involving contact between victim and offender, such as robbery or violence, mean that, from Locard's Exchange Principle, there will be an exchange of material between the skin and clothing of both offender and victim. While this offers the potential to recover trace evidence such as fibres, we have seen already that identification evidence (DNA and fingerprints) also offers the advantage of enabling the identification of an unknown offender. Recovery of fingerprints from the skin and clothing of a homicide victim (especially one who had been involved in a struggle or died from manual strangulation) would especially be of value when the identity of the offender was unknown.

Fabric

Until recently, radioactive sulphur dioxide was suggested as offering the best possibility of fingerprint development on fabric, although success rates were known to be low (Bowman, 2004). Fraser et al. (2011) have explored the potential for *vacuum metal deposition* (*VMD*) to enhance such fingerprints on fabric. VMD is a well-known, highly sensitive technique for the enhancement of sweat fingerprints on smooth, non-porous surfaces such as plastics (e.g. polythene carrier bags) and is known to be particularly successful if the fingerprint is old or the plastic has been wetted (Bowman, 2004). Originally introduced as a technique for depositing metal coatings onto glass to form mirrors (Philipson and Bleay, 2007), VMD is a process in which thin layers of metal (typically gold followed by zinc) are sequentially thermally evaporated onto the surface of the sample in a partial vacuum (Fraser et al., 2011). Fingerprint sweat deposits were taken by Fraser et al. (2011) from donors who, in turn, grabbed a sample of fabric with a hand for 10 seconds. Results showed that greater ridge detail was revealed on shinier, tighter-weave materials like nylon. Duller, more porous fabrics like cotton showed only 'empty' fingerprints (i.e. no ridge detail present) or only grab marks. Fraser et al. (2011) noted that samples where an empty fingerprint was revealed might prove useful for more targeted swabbing for cellular DNA material, thus making the recovery of DNA evidence on such samples less speculative.

Skin

Like fabric, skin is thought to be one of the most difficult surfaces from which to recover fingerprint sweat impressions (Champod et al., 2004). Attempts to enhance fingerprints on skin have included (Trapecar and Balazic, 2007) examination with light sources (visible and ultraviolet), direct lifting with adhesive tape and fuming with cyanoacrylate (superglue). Trapecar and Balazic (2007) have considered fingerprint recovery from skin on both living subjects and cadavers. They investigated magnetic black, Swedish Black (soot) and Silver Special powders and, in addition, both cyanoacrylate fuming and *ruthenium tetroxide* (*RTX*) on cadavers. Enhancement was carried out within 2 hours of fingerprint deposition and the cadavers had been deceased for 20 to 30 hours and stored for at least 12 hours at 6°C. Identifiable fingerprints were enhanced by magnetic black and Swedish Black powders on both living subjects and cadavers and with RTX on cadavers. The quality of the fingerprints was not influenced by the initial contact time during donation or whether the subject was alive or dead. As was noted for fabrics, identification of areas of finger contact on skin might prove useful for more targeted swabbing for cellular DNA material.

More recently, Trapecar (2009) has extended this work and shown that silicone (a casting material, applied to the enhanced fingerprint after mixing with a hardener) and white fingerprint gelatine (a thick, low-adhesive gelatine layer with a carrier of linen rubber) were the best materials to recover the enhanced fingerprint from the skin.

For both fabric and skin, attempts to recover identifiable fingerprints have shown the possibility of using this technology also to target areas for DNA swabbing. We have already seen, in Chapter 2, that cellular DNA represents the most difficult DNA specimen type from which to obtain a full, single, SGM+ profile, so speculatively looking for fingerprints on skin and fabric in this way may remove the need to speculatively search for cellular DNA on such items, thereby increasing the potential to obtain a full, single, SGM+ profile of the offender.

Alternative technologies to enhance fingerprints

Non-invasive fingerprint visualisation

One area of research that offers an additional dimension to fingerprint enhancement is *non-invasive fingerprints*. Non-invasive means that there is no physical or chemical interaction between the method of enhancement and the item (substrate) or fingerprint deposit. Such techniques are favoured by law enforcement agencies since, being non-contact, they do not exclude subsequent enhancement by some other technique or to search for another evidence type. For example, consider a rifle recovered from a crime scene that is required for both fingerprint enhancement and test-firing. A common fingerprint enhancement technique for the rifle would be cyanoacrylate fuming. However, exposing the rifle to superglue vapour would most likely inhibit a subsequent successful test-firing. Alternatively, if the rifle were test-fired first there would be a real possibility of destroying any fingerprint ridge detail on the surface of the rifle during handling and firing.

Such a dilemma is a constant headache for those involved in the forensic examination of exhibits. Currently, an exhibit such as the rifle would first of all be examined for fingerprints by cyanoacrylate fuming, with areas required for test-firing (such as the end of the barrel and the trigger mechanism) protected from the superglue vapour. As mentioned in Chapter 2, in relation to major crime such a staged process as this (fingerprint examination followed by test-firing) is known as a sequence of treatments. If, however, we had access to a fingerprint enhancement technique that was non-invasive, then the weapon could be examined for fingerprints without compromising a subsequent test-firing.

Williams (2010) has demonstrated fingerprint visualisation on metals using a *scanning Kelvin microprobe* (*SKP*), a device used to detect imperfections and defects in the surface of a metal. Williams measured the electrical potential difference arising between a wire probe and a metal surface containing a fingerprint deposit due to differences in their respective *work functions*, where work function is defined as the energy required to remove an electron from a solid. The magnitude of this potential difference is affected by the fingerprint deposit and fingerprint corrosion of the metal surface. By measuring this variation in potential, the fingerprint is visualised in terms of potential difference. The usefulness of visualising fingerprint corrosion has been demonstrated on fingerprints deposited beneath layers of soot or paint and also on spent brass cartridge cases where fingerprints were deposited pre-firing (Bond, 2008, 2011).

A growing method of non-invasive visualisation is illustrated in the work of Crane et al. (2007), who employed *Fourier transform infrared micro spectroscopy (FTIR)*. This technique is a development from infra-red spectroscopy and uses, in addition, Fourier filtering of the detected infrared signal to remove substrate images with periodic patterns, such as might be encountered on bank notes. Crane et al. (2007) also revealed the presence of associative evidence within a fingerprint deposit in the form of a material fibre that was spectroscopically analysed along with the fingerprint. They asserted that an invasive fingerprint visualisation technique may have interfered with the spectral image obtained from the fibre.

Intelligent fingerprinting

Leggett et al. (2007) have described the detection of drug metabolites present in eccrine sweat secretions, deposited as a latent fingerprint. Specifically, they detected the presence of cotinine, a metabolite of nicotine, from individuals who smoked tobacco products. Leggett et al. (2007) fabricated gold nanoparticles (16 nm in diameter), functionalised with multiple anti-cotinine antibodies, to enhance the reaction between the antibody and the cotinine antigen within the fingerprint deposit. Leggett et al. (2007) concluded that, in addition to identifying metabolites of drugs, their metabolite-enhanced image of the fingerprint deposit was sufficient to identify the fingerprint donor. They noted that the ultimate sensitivity of this detection technique had still to be determined, but that the potential functionalisation of nanoparticles with other antibodies might enable more general illicit drug screening or medical diagnoses. Thus, as well as being able to visualise fingerprint ridge detail, this technique also gave an insight into the social activity of the donor (e.g. that they were a smoker). Technologies such as these that can not only visualise the fingerprint but also give information about endogenous and exogenous material present on the finger at the time of deposition are referred to as *intelligent fingerprinting*.

More recently, sensitive *surface science analytical technology* has been employed, which collects material removed from the surface of a specimen (Szynkowska et al., 2010; Bradshaw et al., 2012). This has enabled identification of both exogenous and endogenous material deposited as a fingerprint, including gunpowder residues, gunshot primer residues and MDMA (ecstasy). In addition to the identification of these trace amounts of exogenous substances, which do not naturally occur in fingerprint sweat, the presence of these contaminants enabled visualisation of the fingerprint ridge lines.

Acceptance of new technology by the courts

Many of these alternative technologies rely on fingerprint visualisation by exploiting a physical property of the fingerprint deposit or background substrate to produce contrast between the two that is not visible to the naked eye, for example measuring infrared wavelength absorption or electrical potential difference. To produce the required contrast and visualisation requires processing of the measured data, for example the potential difference between different points on the surface of a substrate. This is achieved using different colours or shades of grey to represent different values of potential difference, the result being a digital image of the fingerprint with similar colours or shades occurring where the physical property being measured (potential difference) has similar values (such as where the fingerprint deposit is present). While this produces an image of the fingerprint, it is a departure from more traditional means of fingerprint visualisation, in which the enhancement technique produces an image of the fingerprint on the surface of the substrate that is visible to the eye. As we have seen earlier, examples of this would include powdering and ninhydrin. The product of these traditional enhancement techniques is an image of the fingerprint that could, if required, be viewed by a jury. As the image of the fingerprint visualised in, for example, potential difference exists only as a digital image, demonstrating the existence of the fingerprint on an exhibit to a jury is more problematic and requires acceptance by the jury that the image is a faithful representation of the ridge detail of the fingerprint that they cannot see on the exhibit. This acceptance can be achieved by proper analysis and testing of a new fingerprint visualisation technique to demonstrate that the image produced is a faithful representation of the original fingerprint.

The robustness of this analysis is, ultimately, tested in court where the accuracy and reliability of the technique are examined. We have seen in Chapter 7 how rules of admissibility of expert testimony require that techniques meet certain standards before they are permitted to be heard by the court (Keierleber and Bohan, 2005; Taylor and Blenkin, 2011a, b). It has been argued that the Daubert standard is concerned, essentially, with the trustworthiness of an expert witness, and this is best determined through an understanding of the error within the expert's testimony. Haug and Baird (2011, p. 754) proposed that scientific evidence should be accepted in court if 'an expert can account for the measurement error, the random error, and the systematic error in his evidence'. Measurement error can be thought of as precision, random error as reliability or consistency and systematic error as validity or accuracy (Haug and Baird, 2011).

A detailed consideration of the errors involved in forensic science testimony has also been undertaken by Jabbar (2010), who proposed that error rate should be the primary (if not the sole) consideration for a court when determining whether to admit scientific evidence. However, neither Haug and Baird (2011) nor Jabbar (2010) actually describe how error rates for scientific measurements for a range of forensic evidence types might be calculated or validated. We will explore in more detail in the next section some of the difficulties involved in error rate measurement and probative value calculation for a range of evidence types, which can make the fulfilment of admissibility criteria problematic.

The value of alternative technologies

In developing technology that offers a new method of visualising fingerprints, for it to be of value to law enforcement agencies the researcher must consider a number of factors. First, what is the development likely to offer over existing technology? It might be that it gives improved fingerprint visualisation over current technology, as does the scanning Kelvin microprobe, or it might provide a new dimension to fingerprint visualisation, as does intelligent fingerprinting, or it might simply provide a quicker, cheaper or more effective means of recovering fingerprints. Whatever the motivation, it is essential that the researcher demonstrates the advantages to the police of developing this new technology. Much is written in the scientific press on new techniques to visualise fingerprints but, while demonstrating the feasibility of a technique, not all research considers what benefit the technique offers over existing methods (Bersellini et al., 2001). Without such consideration, it is unlikely that new technology will be adopted for use by law enforcement agencies. In the UK, the government-funded *Centre for Applied Science and Technology* (*CAST*) has provided detailed information on the validity of techniques and determined under what circumstances they might usefully be employed, especially in a sequence of treatments. For fingerprint enhancement, this manual is now provided online (https://www.gov.uk/government/publications/fingerprint-sourcebook). By following the protocols contained within the manual, those enhancing fingerprints are provided with a justification for the methodology they have used, should this be challenged in court.

DNA technologies

It might be supposed that since the introduction of SGM+ in 1999 with a discrimination of 1 in 1 000 000 000, there would be little else to improve with regard to DNA profiling for law enforcement. However, as with any other discipline in forensic science, there is the desire to produce quantifiable results from ever smaller and more degraded amounts of material. In addition to this, research is being undertaken to try to reduce significantly the time taken to process DNA material in order to produce a profile suitable for loading to and searching on a computerised database. Unlike fingerprint identification evidence, where the time taken to load a fingerprint onto a database for searching is largely determined by the time taken for a fingerprint examiner to mark up minutiae present on the fingerprint, DNA profiling requires time for a number of processes to complete. These include DNA isolation, quantification and amplification (of STR), which can all slow down the time taken to analyse a specimen. Thus, to reduce the time taken to search a DNA profile on a database requires these DNA process times to be reduced.

Rapid processing of DNA

There are two routes by which the rapid processing of DNA can occur (Verheij et al., 2012). The first is DNA profiling without prior DNA extraction, directly onto a biological stain (Linacre et al., 2010), and the second by speeding up the process to obtain an interpretable DNA profile (Giese et al., 2009). For the second route, Verheij et al. (2012) have recently published a protocol for rapid PCR amplification on DNA material recovered from items that might be encountered at a crime scene. These included non-porous surfaces such as cups, bottles, watches, car door handles, gear controls, steering wheels and porous surfaces such as clothing, shoe laces, cigarette ends, plasters and tissues. Non-porous surfaces were swabbed with cotton swabs moistened with water, while DNA was recovered from porous surfaces using tape-lift stubs. Verheij et al. (2012) were able to reduce the DNA processing time to six hours and provided a protocol for DNA processing within this time scale. They found this protocol to be most successful for single-source DNA samples such as saliva, blood, semen and hair roots; that is, not the problematic cellular specimen type.

Reducing the time taken to process DNA material recovered from the crime scene in this way then allows two routes by which the DNA profile might be obtained. The first is to continue to use the improved technology and protocol in a controlled laboratory environment, and the second is to undertake rapid DNA processing at the crime scene itself (Liu et al., 2008; Hopwood et al., 2010; Bienvenue et al., 2010). The second route has given rise to *lab on a chip* technology, designed for use at the crime scene. Portable DNA detectors now exist that can be used at the crime scene or in a police station. Using rapid DNA technology, devices the size of a briefcase can perform STR analysis in a few hours (Liu et al., 2012). However, as we have seen in Chapter 2, innocent contamination is a real issue for DNA processing. With the contamination issues known to exist in a controlled laboratory environment, how likely is it that these same controls could be exercised at the crime scene or in a police station? Perhaps a realistic approach to lab on a chip technology at the crime scene is to see this as intelligence rather than evidence gathering. That is, successful profiling of a DNA sample at the crime scene might yield the name of a potential offender to the police, but this would then need evidential corroboration by reprocessing the DNA sample in a controlled laboratory. However, this would require the retention of some of the original sample for future processing, which would no doubt add to the complexity of the operation being performed at the crime scene.

Next-generation DNA processing

An obvious extension to the current national DNA databases is to produce an international database. The *European Network of Forensic Science Institutes* (*ENFSI*) has made recommendations to use an expanded set of 12 loci for DNA testing in an effort to minimise adventitious associations, which is known as the *European Standard Set* (*ESS*; Gill et al., 2006). In the USA, the FBI has formed the CODIS Core Loci Working Group to expand the STR loci set to include 20 loci that are required and 3 loci that are highly recommended for inclusion by kit manufacturers in a single next-generation multiplex (Hares, 2012a, b). The challenge is to be able to process efficiently both reference samples and crime scene samples, the latter often being recovered in a degraded condition. Meeting this challenge will enable expanded STR multiplexes and loci sets to be used for routine forensic testing.

In the longer term, new methods of DNA sequencing, collectively known as *next-generation sequencing* (*NGS*), are being developed for biological and medical applications. NGS offers a considerably higher throughput coupled with lower-cost processing and the sequencing of several human genomes in a single run in a matter of days (Berglund et al., 2011). Using NGS for forensic DNA processing will enable other areas of the genome to be analysed, an issue that will require legislative changes and public debate and would change the concept of the original UK DNA database, for which only small areas of the human genome were analysed in order to provide discrimination for criminal justice purposes. Would improving the accuracy and process time for DNA evidence warrant an expansion of the DNA identity of an individual that was stored on an international database?

An emerging application of DNA technology

The use of DNA profiling to assist in solving or preventing crime continues to expand into new areas, for example wildlife crime (Johnson and Wilson-Wilde, 2014). As with human DNA profiling, accreditation and certification protocols are essential in the forensic wildlife community (Wetton et al., 2003).

The need for accreditation

We saw in Chapter 2, in relation to fingerprint evidence, how in 2009 the US National Academy of Sciences (NAS) reported on a study of the state of forensic science in the US entitled *Strengthening Forensic Science in the United States: A Path Forward* (Edwards and Gatsonis, 2009). However, the report went much further than examining merely fingerprint evidence and found serious deficiencies in the US forensic science system in many disciplines and across many areas of application. It concluded that, with the exception of nuclear DNA analysis, no forensic discipline had been tested rigorously to show a consistent and highly probable connection between crime scene evidence and that recovered from an individual. As a new discipline introduced in the 1980s, nuclear DNA analysis enjoyed this position since its scientific method had been subject to much scrutiny and the likelihood of an (innocent) error occurring during interpretation (an adventitious association) has been quantified. In general, the report found that disciplines requiring some form of laboratory analysis and measurement (such as glass, fibre or toxicological evidence) had a stronger scientific basis than those disciplines requiring subjective comparison or identification (such as tool mark or fingerprint evidence).

The full implications of the NAS report and the inability of many evidence types currently to meet the courtroom admissibility criteria become clear if we consider the report in the context of the many case-study boxes presented throughout this book. The overwhelming majority of these case studies have illustrated the use of evidence types other than DNA, which the NAS report would argue fail to meet the required standard for scientific method and interpretation of evidential value. While these case studies have presented some of the facts of the case and explained why the jury may have accepted a prosecution interpretation of forensic evidence, what if that interpretation for the jury was flawed? Ultimately, the truth of what occurred at a crime scene is unknowable and the conviction or acquittal of a defendant depends on a jury's acceptance or rejection of the interpretation of the value of the evidence. Thus, forensic science is, essentially, the application of scientific method to enable an interpretation that is intended to get as close as possible to the truth of what occurred at the crime scene, rather than an analysis that leads to only one possible interpretation of the evidence. As we have seen in Chapter 5, there are always two competing hypotheses for the jury to consider and evaluate, even with evidence that meets admissibility standards.

We saw in Chapter 2, in relation to fingerprints, that the NAS report suggested that a probabilistic approach could be undertaken along the same lines as is currently employed for DNA evidence. This is perhaps understandable as, from the work of Francis Galton and from experience, we know that the distribution of minutiae on a fingerprint is very specific. However, what about other evidence types such as tool or footwear impressions or ballistic marks? The evidential or probative value of these evidence types is determined by the distribution of features that occur, either randomly (such as with footwear impressions) or through contact with another object (such as with tool impressions and ballistic marks). The occurrence of these features and the likelihood of their agreement with features on another object (for instance, associating a footwear impression with a shoe) can be examined using the techniques described in Chapter 5.

Since the publication of the NAS report, many of these evidence types have become the subject of research to enable a statistical or Bayesian approach to the interpretation of their evidential value (Lock and Morris, 2013; Bunch & Wevers, 2013; Petraco et al., 2012; Skerrett et al., 2011). In addition, other evidence types that display characteristic features of an individual, such as voice analysis (Rose, 2013) and handwriting analysis (Taroni et al., 2012; Hepler et al., 2012), have also been the subject of research to establish likelihood ratios for evidential value. However, what about other evidence types such as glass, fibres or soil? While these evidence types require comparison (for instance, associating glass from a broken window with glass fragments found on an item of clothing), as we have seen in Chapter 3, they additionally require knowledge of the frequency of their occurrence and resistance to transference or shedding. For example, consider fibres recovered from an item of clothing belonging to a suspect. In order to fulfil the admissibility criteria, the scientist must investigate not only how often those fibres occur, but also how easily they might be shed from the originating garment and how easily they might be retained by the garment under examination. All of these factors will affect the likelihood ratio, and hence the evidential or probative value of the evidence, related to the finding of these fibres on the suspect's clothing.

Establishing the true likelihood ratio in these circumstances and then explaining it to a jury can be problematic, which is why texts that explain the calculation of likelihood ratio for, say, fibre evidence often state in a worked example that it relates to an *isolated community*, thereby artificially restricting the occurrence of a particular fibre in that community (Adam, 2010). Clearly, the need to establish these factors and their error rate adds to the complication of satisfying the admissibility criteria and hence gaining acceptance for scientific testimony. Since the publication of the NAS report, an increasing amount of work is being undertaken to investigate the validity and reliability of likelihood ratios for different types of forensic evidence (Alberink et al., 2013; Abraham et al., 2013; Morrison, 2011; Lyle, 2010).

The NAS report also discouraged the use of zero error rates with, for example, fingerprint evidence, and argued that suggesting to a court near or complete infallibility in the scientific method or skill of the examiner was, in itself, unscientific (Cole, 2005). The report felt that forensic science method was often divorced from traditional scientific method, a view previously expressed by Thornton and Peterson (2002), who commented that forensic scientists are rarely trained in scientific method and hence do not understand the implications of not adhering to it. The report also expressed the need to separate forensic science from police culture with both practitioners and public forensic science laboratories becoming independent from police and prosecutors, a view presented earlier by Cooley and Turvey (2007, p. 79).

To achieve a strong sense of direction and focus, the NAS report recommended the establishment of a new and independent National Institute of Forensic Science to lead research, establish and maintain standards and oversee forensic science education (Mnookin et al., 2011). It expressed the view that the new institute should be strongly rooted in science, with strong ties to the forensic science community, and not be part of a law enforcement agency, and that it must be led by people who are skilled and experienced in developing and executing national strategies and plans for standard setting; managing accreditation and testing processes; and developing and implementing rule-making, oversight and sanctioning processes. The recommendation to establish a new and independent National Institute of Forensic Science was perceived as reflecting the historical failure of both the FBI Crime Laboratory and the National Institute of Justice to improve and strengthen forensic scientific method (Giannelli, 2011) and poor working practice in other, state-funded laboratories (Goldstein, 2011). However, the feasibility and political will to establish such a new federal agency have been challenged (Risinger, 2010). The NAS report also stimulated debate outside the USA (Julian et al., 2011), leading to a call for the establishment of forensic science as a distinct scientific discipline, 'identifying and associating traces for investigative and security purposes, based on its fundamental principles and the case assessment and interpretation process that follows with its specific and relevant mode of inference' (Crispino et al., 2011). Although it is difficult to see how a scientific method could be decoupled from its core discipline and then inserted into a new forensic science discipline, the underlying premise of Crispino et al. (2011) is the need to recognise the special interpretation required of scientific analysis when applied to the legal system.

Responding to this need - ISO 17025

The suggestion by the NAS report to set up a National Institute of Forensic Science had, to some extent, already been enacted in the UK. In 2008 the UK Home Office established a new position of Forensic Science Regulator to set, monitor and maintain quality standards in forensic science provision. This move was partly a governmental response to cases of poor evidence analysis and interpretation (such as the case-study examples of fingerprint misidentification, Boxes 2.12 and 2.13) and poor evidence processing (such as the case-study example of DNA misidentification, Box 2.8). Although sponsored by the Home Office, the Regulator is a public appointee and operates independently of the Home Office on behalf of the criminal justice system as a whole. The business plan for the Regulator states that by the end of March 2017 all aspects of forensic science in the criminal justice system should be operating to a single quality standards framework, based on the Regulator's codes of practice and conduct (Forensic Science Regulator, 2013). These codes of practice and conduct (Forensic Science Regulator, 2012) align with the International Organization for Standardization standard ISO 17025, which specifies the requirements for a management system for laboratory forensic science services to demonstrate an ability to deliver consistently products and services that meet the requirements of the criminal justice system.

The *United Kingdom Accreditation Service* (*UKAS*) accredits against ISO 17025, which in the UK is seen as an integral part of the quality framework and an expectation for those supplying forensic science services to the police and criminal justice system. ISO 17025 is a standard for laboratory competence and was developed for application in any laboratory that performs testing and calibration. As well as laboratory accreditation, the Forensic Regulator codes of practice and conduct also cover crime scene examination and strategy; the recovery, transport and storage of exhibits; testing carried out at the crime scene; and the method by which exhibits are selected for forensic analysis.

In the USA, the American Society of Crime Laboratory Directors Laboratory Accreditation Board (ASCLD/LAB) decided in 2009 to move to ISO 17025 accreditation, with a complete transition accomplished in March 2014, although ASCLD/LAB continues to support those laboratories operating under the previous standard (ASCLD/LAB Legacy Accediation Program). In Canada, the Standards Council of Canada offers accreditation to laboratories that undertake forensic testing; while in Australia, ISO 17025 is administered through the National Association of Testing Authorities.

Although ISO accreditation will answer some of the issues raised by the NAS report, particularly related to working practices and adherence to protocols (Giannelli, 2011; Goldstein, 2011), it will not address issues related to the interpretation of forensic evidence and meeting the Daubert standard, the special requirements for using scientific analysis to provide evidence in a court.

Private or public? The move to privately funded laboratories

The separation of forensic science from police culture recommended by the NAS has also taken place in the UK, albeit through the requirement to save money rather than a perceived need to remove the forensic scientist from the police investigator and prosecutor. In 2010, the UK government announced the closure of the government-run Forensic Science Service (FSS), responsible for the majority of forensic science provision to the 43 police forces in England and Wales. In the years leading up to this announcement, the private sector had slowly become more attracted to an involvement with forensic science and had, at times, been accused by the FSS and the police service of 'cherry picking' those pieces of the business that required little capital investment to undertake, thereby leaving the FSS to maintain expensive laboratories and facilities with an increasingly uncertain income. The final justification for closure of the FSS was that in 2010 it was losing about £2 million a month (Dyer, 2011; Limb, 2011).

The impending closure of the FSS brought expressions of concern from the scientific community over the future of forensic research in the UK. Among these was Professor Sir Alec Jeffreys, who pioneered DNA profiling in the 1980s at the University of Leicester, work from which the FSS set up the first national DNA database in 1995. Despite these concerns, the FSS did close in 2012, leaving a small number of private companies to provide the police service with its forensic science needs. In July 2013, the UK government Science and Technology Committee, which had opposed the closure of the FSS three years earlier, held an inquiry into the current state of forensic science in the country. It found that the revenue of the private forensic providers was diminishing as more and more of the 43 police forces in England and Wales were undertaking 'low-level' evidence processing and screening in-house, mainly as a result of austerity measures imposed on the police service by the government. This in-house work mainly comprises screening exhibits (such as clothing for DNA) and trace evidence recovery (such as glass, hair and fibres). The Committee found that many of these police forces were struggling to meet the requirements of the Forensic Regulator in terms of minimum standards and ISO 17025 accreditation. Thus, the private laboratories were finding themselves in the same situation that some of them had earlier placed the FSS, in that parts of the forensic process requiring low investment (in terms of equipment or overheads) were being taken away from them by the police.

Clearly, the growing trend for police forces to undertake forensic examination of exhibits within police premises is contrary to the need expressed by the NAS report to separate forensic science from police culture in order to maintain a truly independent forensic service, distinct from both police investigators and prosecutors. A concern of the Science and Technology Committee inquiry in 2013 was that there is a real possibility that breaking up the forensic examination process between the police and private-sector providers could increase the possibility of a vital piece of forensic evidence being missed or links between different pieces of evidence not being established. The result of this could be that evidence would be lost, resulting in a miscarriage of justice. To maintain an effective forensic science capability outside of the police service, there is a need to explore how the private (or public) sector can best meet the needs of the police, while ensuring an optimal scale of operation to provide a cost-effective service (Speaker, 2013).

The future of forensic research in the UK

As the Science and Technology Committee and scientists like Sir Alec Jeffreys had warned in 2010, there appeared to be no strategy for the provision of forensic science research in the UK. This is, however, being addressed by the government. A review in 2011 of research and development in forensic science in the UK conducted by Professor Bernard

Silverman, Chief Scientific Adviser to the Home Office (Silverman, 2011), considered how forensic research might be conducted in a post-FSS world and recommended that the Forensic Science Regulator should act as a facilitator to bring together a consortium of appropriate representative bodies and other parties to organise a regular cross-disciplinary forensic science conference. As a result, in 2013 the *Forensic Science Special Interest Group* (*ForSIG*) was established under the auspices of the *Technology Strategy Board* (*TSB*). The latter was set up by the government in 2006 to generate innovative solutions within UK businesses across a variety of disciplines. TSB is located on the same site as many of the UK research councils and works closely with both academia and the private sector. ForSIG is chaired by the Forensic Regulator and has a number of work streams designed to enable closer networking and better communication between forensic science end users, suppliers of products and services, academics and other researchers and policy makers, to achieve improved research and development. An example of where ForSIG is innovating is in the production of a document for researchers concerning how to innovate for the criminal justice system (Tully et al., 2013). This document tackles the special issues that a researcher has to understand and address in order to produce new equipment or methodology for use in the judicial process.

The ethics of biometric databases

Current technology and computer capabilities enable large amounts of information to be uploaded, stored and searched by agencies worldwide. This includes the storage and searching of biometric information, which for the purposes of this chapter will refer mainly to fingerprints and DNA. In the previous chapters we have seen the unquestionable forensic potential of biometric information, and it is certain that these forms of identification evidence have revolutionised policing over the last century. However, the very reason that these evidence types are so useful as forensic evidence (i.e. their ability to identify individuals) is also the cause of controversy due to the inherently personal and private features of biometric information.

Much of the current debate about biometric databases is focused on DNA, which is perhaps understandable due to its uniqueness and the ability to determine various genetic markers and information about an individual from their full DNA profile. In contrast with the controversies over DNA databases, fingerprint databases have largely been forgotten in the ethical and privacy debates, although much of the relevant legislation covers the acquisition and retention of both DNA and fingerprints by criminal justice agencies. The legislation that allows law enforcement agencies to utilise DNA in criminal investigations is specific to each jurisdiction, so a few examples of DNA databases are provided here.

It seems fitting to review the UK National DNA Database (NDNAD) first, as the UK is the home of DNA profiling techniques and was the first country to implement a national database. The NDNAD is also an interesting starting point for this discussion since some very recent new legislation has drastically changed the retention laws in the UK, as we will see shortly. It was established in 1995 and the legislation facilitating the development of the database allowed DNA from convicted offenders to be retained as well as crime scene samples. By 2002 the NDNAD contained over 1.5 million profiles, and in an effort to expand the database further new legislation in 2001 allowed the police to retain DNA from anyone who was charged with a recordable offence (regardless of whether they were subsequently convicted). By March 2005 the NDNAD had expanded to over 3 million profiles, and another change in legislation in 2004 extended police powers to retaining DNA profiles from anyone arrested for a recordable offence. By September 2012 (the latest figures available) the NDNAD contained DNA profiles from 5.68 million individuals and per capita is the largest national database in the world.

The ability to obtain DNA samples from all arrestees, and to retain these profiles indefinitely regardless of whether the individual is charged or convicted of the offence, was considered by some to be an effective strategy for policing and maximising the potential for DNA to solve crimes in the UK. There were even supporters of a further expansion programme proposing to collect mandatory DNA samples from all members of the public. This followed the reasoning that the bigger the database, the more effective it would be, and that if everyone's DNA were included many more crimes could be solved much more efficiently. However, other commentators argued that the benefit of expanding the NDNAD further was not justified by the massive costs involved, since such a small percentage of the solving of all crime in England and Wales is assisted by DNA evidence.

The biggest challenge to face the NDNAD, and the associated legislation, was in the form of two individual cases that together challenged the policy of retaining DNA indefinitely. These cases are jointly referred to in the literature as 'S and Marper' because, although the cases and defendants were not related to one another, they were heard together by the European Court of Human Rights (ECHR). Box 8.1 outlines the background to both of these cases; as you can see, in the case of S the defendant was found not guilty of robbery and in the case of Marper the suspect did not go to trial for harassment. Although both were legally innocent, they were both required to provide DNA and fingerprints on arrest and they both argued to the ECHR that the retention of their DNA violated Article 8 of the European Convention of Human Rights (the right to a private life).

Box 8.1 The cases of S and Marper

In the first of these cases, the defendant (referred to only as 'S' as he was a juvenile at the time of the offence) was charged with robbery at the age of 11. He was subsequently acquitted of these charges, but when he was arrested his fingerprints and DNA were obtained by the police, and would lawfully be held indefinitely. In the case of Marper, the defendant was charged with harassing his ex-partner, although the charges were dropped before going to trial when he and his partner reconciled. Similar to S, Marper's fingerprints and DNA were obtained on arrest and were to be held indefinitely in the respective databases. In 2004, the Court of Appeal upheld that retention of the DNA and fingerprints was lawful and their information was not authorised for removal from the police databases.

Analysis: Both S and Marper continued to argue that it was in violation of their human rights to have their DNA and fingerprints held on the national databases, in light of the fact that neither of them was convicted of the crime for which he was accused. While the legislation in the UK at the time of these cases led the UK Court of Appeal to rule that the retention of their biometric data was lawful, S and Marper went on to argue that this legislation violated their human rights, and their case was heard by the European Court of Human Rights (ECHR) in 2008.

In 2008, the 17 judges of the ECHR unanimously ruled that indefinite retention of DNA and fingerprints from innocent people violates their right to a private life. Part of the court decision was the statement that 'keeping the information could not be regarded as necessary in a democratic society'. This decision sent a very clear message about the human rights implications of retaining DNA and fingerprints from innocent individuals and it required the UK to introduce new legislation in 2012 to address these concerns. The Protection of Freedoms Act 2012 now requires consideration of the seriousness of the offence and the age of the offender in the determination of retention rules for cases where the suspect is not charged or convicted of the offence. This new legislation will only allow indefinite retention of DNA and fingerprints from adult offenders who are convicted or juvenile offenders convicted of serious offences. There is also a requirement that profiles of innocent people need to be removed from the NDNAD retrospectively in order to meet the standards of the ECHR ruling.

While the UK has seen a shift to more conservative DNA retention policies, other countries may be moving in a different direction. In the USA the *National DNA Index System (NDIS)*, part of CODIS, contains DNA contributions from federal, state and local law enforcement agencies. DNA legislation in the USA is much more complicated than that in the UK, due to the state and federal law systems, which means that different states have varying legislation regarding police use of DNA. Until very recently, US jurisdictions were not permitted to obtain DNA samples from arrested individuals, so the NDIS consisted only of DNA from convicted individuals and crime scene samples. However, a 2013 Supreme Court ruling made it legal for police to obtain a DNA sample from individuals arrested of serious offences. This change resulted from the case of Maryland *v.* King, in which King was charged in 2009 with assault and was required to provide a DNA sample by the Maryland DNA Collection Act. His DNA matched a crime scene sample from a 2003 unsolved rape, of which he was subsequently convicted. On appeal, King argued that taking his DNA was in violation of the Fourth Amendment (protecting citizens from unreasonable searches and seizures). He lost his appeal on the grounds that non-intimate samples of DNA (such as cheek swabs) are lawfully obtained when someone is charged with a violent offence.

An even more drastic comparison can be made between the UK or US approach and that of other countries such as Canada. The Canadian National DNA Data Bank is maintained by the Royal Canadian Mounted Police, and at the end of July 2013 it contained only 361 278 profiles, of which only 274 095 were from offenders. These comparably small numbers of offender profiles are a result of the national legislation in Canada (Bill C-3), which enables a judge to authorise collection of DNA samples from offenders who have been convicted of designated offences. In a separate piece of legislation (Bill C-104), a Judge can also issue a warrant allowing police to take DNA from a suspect in some cases. This approach to DNA databases in Canada, in which only convictions for designated offences allow a DNA profile to be taken, has resulted in a very modest database that appears to favour the privacy of individuals' personal information over the massive expansion of the DNA database programme for law enforcement purposes.

The Genetics Policy Initiative (www.dnapolicyinitiative.org), a collaboration between GeneWatch UK (www.genewatch.org), Privacy International (www.privacyinternational.org) and the Council for Responsible Genetics (www.councilforresponsiblegenetics.org), reports that currently there are 60 countries with operational DNA databases, and a further 34 countries working to establish or expand their DNA database use. Organisations such as these have a mandate to openly debate the ethics and privacy issues raised by the use of DNA databases, and they believe that a balance can be struck between the law enforcement benefits of DNA databases and the rights and privacy of citizens and their personal information. There is a fine line to walk between public safety and law enforcement concerns and the ethical and privacy issues raised by biometric databases, and it is even more difficult to evaluate the effectiveness of one approach in this area over another.

Transnational crime and forensic science

Improvements in communication and information technology, particularly the proliferation of the internet, have made the commission of transnational crimes much easier and therefore more prevalent. Crimes that cross jurisdictional boundaries, whether they are local, regional or national boundaries, are particularly difficult to investigate effectively due to the geographical and bureaucratic nature of policing agencies. However, there are some successful cooperative agreements in place that improve the ability of police agencies to share information and, most relevant to this chapter, forensic evidence and intelligence.

The first obstacle impeding efficient cross-border police cooperation during criminal investigations relates to differences in legislation between countries. What may be considered a criminal act in one jurisdiction may not be legislated against in another, therefore police powers and information-gathering procedures will not be compatible in these circumstances. Legislative differences refer not only to criminal acts but also to law governing the collection and retention of biometric and forensic information. Indeed, even when similar laws allow evidence and information to be collected and retained in two jurisdictions, issues relating to the compatibility of information technology may make the sharing of this information difficult, or even impossible. Lemieux (2010) observes that this issue of incompatibility in IT systems is particularly pronounced in attempts made to cooperate between northern- and southern-hemisphere countries, where the use of the latest technology is disproportionately implemented in northern-hemisphere nations. Issues of technology can also relate to the analysis and storage of forensic information, such as DNA, which can make uploading and searching of suspect or crime scene samples problematic between countries.

In order to overcome some of these difficulties, formal and informal agreements are in place between many nations in an effort to tackle organised and transnational criminal activity more effectively. Perhaps the best examples of formal, international agencies are INTERPOL and EUROPOL, which were established as 'data and analysis centres providing a framework built on pooling of resources and expertise' (Lemieux, 2010, p. 3). A less formal but powerful European initiative is the *Schengen Agreement*, which is not an agency in its own right but provides a framework for international security cooperation in Europe. This framework was introduced in order to compensate for the 'security deficit' caused by the abolition of EU member states' internal border controls (den Boer, 2010). European partners who have signed up to Schengen have agreed to allow international police agencies to conduct investigative operations across borders, as well as to share access to forensic information. In May 2005 some Schengen signatory countries signed the Prüm Treaty, which included requirements on member states to establish DNA databases as well as expanding the collection and sharing of biometric information between members.

INTERPOL has been actively supporting the sharing of forensic information between European countries through its biometric databases. The INTERPOL AFIS fingerprint database holds 198 000 fingerprint records (as at December 2013), and member countries can upload finger marks as well as gain access to records online. The DNA Gateway, which was started in 2002, provides access to DNA profiles for member countries and is hosted by INTERPOL. By the end of 2013 it held 140 000 DNA profiles (from 69 countries) and it is capable of sharing data with CODIS in the USA and Canada in certain cases. Box 8.2 provides details of a case in which the DNA Gateway led to the arrest of members of an international organised crime gang.

Box 8.2 The DNA Gateway and the Pink Panthers

The Pink Panthers group is an international organised crime syndicate thought to be responsible for high-value jewellery thefts in Europe, North America, the Middle East and Asia. It has been operating since 1999, and INTERPOL estimates the value of its robberies to be in excess of €330 million. As this criminal gang operates internationally, linking its crimes and identifying its members is very difficult for policing agencies, which makes sharing of information such as fingerprints, DNA and photographs particularly important. DNA samples recovered from crime scenes in France, Liechtenstein, Switzerland and the United Arab Emirates established links between various crime types (including robbery, prison escape and forgery of travel documents) and a group of individuals, leading to the arrest between 2005 and 2008 of three members of the Pink Panthers.

Analysis: This case is often used as an example of the success of INTERPOL's DNA Gateway programme and the international sharing of forensic information in organised crime investigations. Without cross-border and international agreements in place, it is very unlikely that the DNA samples from various countries would have led to the successful arrest of these offenders.

While North American police agencies can request forensic information from agencies such as INTERPOL, the USA, Canada and Mexico also have information-sharing agreements with one another to assist in crimes transcending their shared borders. Compatibility between AFIS for fingerprints and CODIS for DNA enables sharing of biometric information where required, and makes linking of cases and identification of individuals easier during cross-border investigations. As well as being important for investigating illegal immigration and human trafficking, post–9/11 attention has shifted to the importance of these cooperative agreements in the investigation and prosecution of terrorism offences worldwide.

While this section has highlighted some successes in tackling international crime and the importance of sharing forensic and biometric information between nations, barriers to effective transnational police investigations still exist. There is potential for these to be reduced if more countries adopt compatible legislation and forensic technology, but with an increase in information sharing comes the opportunity for more intense debate about privacy and ethical concerns relating to personal information.

Study questions

1. Current developments in fingerprint enhancement tend to concentrate on recovering identifiable fingerprints from difficult surfaces, whereas DNA research tends to focus on more rapid processing from more degraded samples. Consider whether these research strategies amount to achieving the same goal for these two evidence types, or whether there are potential flaws in this approach for either fingerprints or DNA.
2. There is no question that DNA has revolutionised the way in which the police investigate crime and the use of forensic science. However, as we have seen in this chapter, the implementation of national DNA databases causes controversy relating to ethical and privacy issues. The expansion of DNA databases to include mandatory samples from all members of society would surely lead to more frequent 'hits' with crime scene material, but innocent people would also be required to be on the database. Do you think that the goal of public safety should outweigh the right to privacy in this case?

REFERENCES

Abraham, J., Champod, C., Lennard, C. and Roux, C. (2013) 'Modern statistical methods for forensic science examination: A critical review', *Forensic Science International*, **232**: 131–150.

Adam, C. (2010) *Mathematics and Statistics for Forensic Science*, Chichester: Wiley.

Aditya, S., Sharma, A.K., Bhattacharyya, C.N. and Chaudhuri, K. (2011) 'Generating STR profile from touch DNA', *Journal of Forensic and Legal Medicine*, **18**: 295–298.

Alberink, I., Bolck, A. and Menges, S. (2013) 'Posterior likelihood ratios for evaluation of forensic trace evidence given a two-level model on the data', *Journal of Applied Statistics*, **40**: 2579–2600.

Allen, M. (2007) *Reading CSI: Crime TV under the Microscope*, London: I.B. Tauris.

Alwi, A.R. and Kuppuswamy, R. (2004) 'Studies on the layer structure of paint flakes collected from motor vehicles in Kuala Lumpur', *Journal of Forensic Sciences*, **54**: 645–652.

Andalo, F.A., Calakli, F., Taubin, G. and Goldenstein, S. (2011) 'Accurate 3D footwear impression recovery from photographs', 4th International Conference on Imaging for Crime Detection and Prevention 2011 (ICDP 2011), Nov 3–4, London.

Attinger, D., Moore, C., Donaldson, A., Jafari, A. and Stone, H.A. (2013) 'Fluid dynamics topics in bloodstain pattern analysis: Comparative review and research opportunities', *Forensic Science International*, **231**: 375–396.

Baber, C. and Butler, M. (2012) 'Expertise in crime scene examination: Comparing strategies of expert and novice crime scene examiners in simulated crime scenes', *Human Factors*, **54**: 413–424.

Baron, M., Gonzalez-Rodriguez, J., Croxton, R., Gonzalez, R. and Jimenez-Perez, R. (2011) 'Chemometric study on the forensic discrimination of soil types using their infrared spectral characteristics', *Applied Spectroscopy*, **65**: 1151–1161.

Beauregard, E. and Bouchard, M. (2010) 'Cleaning up your act: Forensic awareness as a detection avoidance strategy', *Journal of Criminal Justice*, **38**: 1160–1166.

Beauregard, E. and Martineau M. (2014) 'No body, no crime? The role of forensic awareness in avoiding police detection in cases of sexual homicide', *Journal of Criminal Justice*, **42**: 213–220.

Beavan, C. (2002) *Fingerprints*, London: Fourth Estate.

Berglund, E.C., Kiialainen, A. and Syvänen, A. (2011) 'Next-generation sequencing technologies and applications for human genetic history and forensics', *Investigative Genetics*, **2**, doi:10.1186/2041-2223-2-23.

Berry, J. and Stoney, D.A. (2001) 'History and development of fingerprinting', in H.C. Lee and R.E. Gaensslen (eds), *Advances in Fingerprint Technology*, New York: Elsevier, pp. 2–40.

Bersellini, C., Garofano, L., Giannetto, M., Lusardi, F. and Mori, G. (2001) 'Development of latent fingerprints on metallic surfaces using electropolymerisation processes', *Journal of Forensic Sciences*, **46**: 871–877.

Biedermann, A. and Taroni, F. (2013) 'On the value of probability for evaluating results of comparative pattern analyses', *Forensic Science International*, **232**: E44–E45.

Bienvenue, J.M., Legendre, L.A., Ferrance, J.P. and Landers, J.P. (2010) 'An integrated microfluidic device for DNA purification and PCR amplification of STR fragments', *Forensic Science International: Genetics*, **4**: 178–186.

Bille, T.W., Cromartie, C. and Farr, M. (2009) 'Effects of cyanoacrylate fuming, time after recovery, and location of biological material on the recovery and analysis of DNA from post-blast pipe bomb fragments', *Journal of Forensic Sciences*, **54**: 1059–1067.

Bleay, S.M., Sears, V.G., Bandey, H.L. et al. (2012) *Fingerprint Source Book*, London: Home Office.

Bodziak, W.J. (2000) *Footwear Impression Evidence, Detection, Recovery and Examination*, 2nd edn, Boca Raton, FL: CRC Press.

Bond, J.W. (2007a) 'Value of DNA evidence in detecting crime', *Journal of Forensic Science*, **52**: 128–136.

Bond, J.W. (2007b) 'Maximising the opportunities to detect domestic burglary with DNA and fingerprints', *International Journal of Police Science and Management*, **9**: 287–298.

Bond, J.W. (2008) 'Visualization of latent fingerprint corrosion of metallic surfaces', *Journal of Forensic Sciences*, **53**: 812–822.

Bond, J.W. (2009) 'The value of fingerprint evidence in detecting crime', *International Journal of Police Science and Management*, **11**: 77–84.

Bond J.W. (2011) 'Optical enhancement of fingerprint deposits on brass using digital colour mapping', *Journal of Forensic Sciences*, **56**: 1285–1288.

Bond, J.W. (2013) 'Advances in the use of latent finger marks', in G.N. Rutty (ed.), *Essentials of Autopsy: Advances, Updates and Emerging Technologies*, London: Springer, pp. 131–148.

Bond, J.W. and Brady, T.F. (2013) 'Physical characterization and recovery of corroded fingerprint impressions from post-blast copper pipe bomb fragments', *Journal of Forensic Sciences*, **58**: 776–781.

Bond, J.W. and Sheridan, L. (2007) 'The relationship between the detection of acquisitive crime by forensic science and drug dependent offenders', *Journal of Forensic Science*, **52**: 1122–1128.

Bossler, A.M. and Holt, T.J. (2013) 'Assessing officer perceptions and support for online community policing', *Security Journal*, **26**: 349–366.

Bowman, V. (2004) *Manual of Fingerprint Development Techniques*, Sandridge: Home Office.

Bradshaw, R., Rao, W., Wolstenholme, R., Clench, M.R., Bleay, S. and Francese, S. (2012) 'Separation of overlapping fingermarks by Matrix Assisted Laser Desorption Ionisation Mass Spectrometry Imaging', *Forensic Science International*, **222**: 318–326.

Brewer *v* State, 725 So. 2d 106, 134 (Miss. 1998).

Buffoli, B., Rinaldi, F., Labanca, M. et al. (2014) 'The human hair: From anatomy to physiology', *International Journal of Dermatology*, **53**: 331–341.

Bull, P.A., Parker, A. and Morgan, R.M. (2006) 'The forensic analysis of soils and sediment taken from the cast of a footprint', *Forensic Science International*, **62**: 6–12.

Bullock, K. (2013) 'Community, intelligence-led policing and crime control', *Policing and Society*, **23**: 125–144.

Bunch, S. and Wevers, G. (2013) 'Application of likelihood ratios for firearm and tool mark analysis', *Science and Justice*, **53**: 223–229.

Carey, A., Rodewijk, N., Xu, X.M. and van der Weerd, J. (2013) 'Identification of dyes on single textile Fibres by HPLC-DAD-MS', *Analytical Chemistry*, **85**: 11335–11343.

Champod, C., Lennard, C., Margot, P. and Stoilovic, M. (2004) *Fingerprints and Other Ridge Skin Impressions*, New York: CRC Press.

Charlton, D. (2009) 'Fingerprints', in R. Sutton and K. Trueman (eds), *Crime Scene Management Scene Specific Methods*, Chichester: Wiley, pp. 100–130.

Chatterton, C. and Kintz, P. (2014) 'Hair analysis to demonstrate administration of amitriptyline, temazepam, tramadol and dihydrocodeine to a child in a case of kidnap and false imprisonment', *Journal of Forensic and Legal Medicine*, **23**: 26–31.

Chumbley, L.S., Morris, M.D., Kreiser, M.J. et al.(2010) 'Validation of tool mark comparisons obtained using a quantitative, comparative, statistical algorithm', *Journal of Forensic Sciences*, **55**: 953–961.

Cole, S.A. (2004) 'Grandfathering evidence: Fingerprint admissibility rulings from Jennings to Llera Plaza and back again', *American Criminal Law Review*, **41**: 1189–1276.

Cole, S.A. (2005) 'More than zero: Accounting for error in latent fingerprint identifications', *Journal of Criminal Law and Criminology*, **95**: 985–1078.

Cole, S.A. (2010) 'Who speaks for science? A response to the National Academy of Sciences report on forensic science', *Law, Probability and Risk*, **9**: 25–46.

Cole, S. & Dioso-Villa, R. (2007) 'Symposium: The CSI effect: The true effect of crime scene television on the justice system. CSI and its effects: Media, juries, and the burden of proof', *New England Law Review*, **41**: 435–469.

Cook, R. and Wilson, C. (1986) 'The significance of finding extraneous fibres in contact cases', *Forensic Science International*, **32**: 267–274.

Cooley, C. and Turvey, B. (2007) 'Observer effects and examiner bias: Psychological influences on the forensic examiner', in W.J. Chisum and B. Turvey (eds), *Crime Reconstruction*, Boston, MA: Elsevier Science, pp. 61–90.

Crane, N.J., Bartick, E.G., Perlman, R.S. and Huffman, S. (2007) 'Infrared spectroscopic imaging for noninvasive detection of latent fingerprints', *Journal of Forensic Science*, **52**: 48–53.

Crispino, F. (2008) 'Nature and place of crime scene management within forensic sciences', *Science and Justice*, **48**: 24–28.

Crispino, F., Ribaux, O., Houck, M. and Margot, P. (2011) 'Forensic science – a true science?' *Australian Journal of Forensic Sciences*, **43**: 157–176.

Crown, D.A. (1969) 'The development of latent fingerprints with ninhydrin', *Journal of Criminal Law, Criminology and Police Service*, **60**: 258–264.

Croxton, R.S., Baron, M.G., Butler, D., Kent, T. and Sears, V.G. (2010) 'Variation in amino acid and lipid composition of latent fingerprints', *Forensic Science International*, **199**: 93–102.

Curran., J.M., Triggs, C.M., Almirall, J.R., Buckleton, J.S. and Walsh, K.A.J. (1997) 'The interpretation of elemental composition measurements from forensic glass evidence', *Science and Justice*, **37**: 241–249.

Dalby, O., Butler, D. and Birkett, J.W. (2010) 'Analysis of gunshot residue and associated materials – a review', *Journal of Forensic Sciences*, **55**: 924–943.

Daly, D.J., Murphy, C. and McDermott, S.D. (2012) 'The transfer of touch DNA from hands to glass, fabric and wood', *Forensic Science International*, **226**: 41–46.

Dando, C. and Bull R. (2011) 'Maximising opportunities to detect verbal deception: Training police officers to interview tactically', *Journal of Investigative Psychology and Offender Profiling*, **8**: 189–202.

De Alcaraz-Fossoul, J., Mestres Patris, C., Balaciart Muntaner, A., Barrot Feixat, C. and Gene Badia, M. (2013) 'Determination of latent fingerprint degradation patterns – a real fieldwork study', *International Journal of Legal Medicine*, **127**: 857–870.

Devine, D., Clayton, L., Dunford, B. Seying, R. and Pryce, J. (2010) 'Jury decision making: 45 years of empirical research on deliberating groups', *Psychology, Public Policy and Law*, **7**: 622–727.

Den Boer, M. (2010) 'Towards a governance model of police cooperation in Europe: The twist between networks and bureaucracies', in F. Lemieux (ed.), *International Police Cooperation: Emerging Issues, Theory and Practice*, Devon: Willan Publishing, pp. 42–61.

De Wael, K., Fabrice, G.C., Gason, S.J., Christiaan, A., and Baes, V. (2008) 'Selection of an adhesive tape suitable for forensic fibre sampling' *Journal of Forensic Sciences*, **53**: 168–171.

Di Maio, V.J.M. (1999) *Gunshot Wounds, Practical Aspects of Firearms, Ballistics, and Forensic Techniques*, 2nd edn, Boca Raton, FL: CRC Press.

Dror, I. and Charlton, D. (2006) 'Why experts make errors', *Journal of Forensic Identification*, **56**: 600–616.

Dror, I., Charlton, D. and Peron, A. (2006) 'Contextual information renders experts vulnerable to making erroneous identifications', *Forensic Science International*, **156**: 174–178.

Dyer, C. (2011) 'MP's lambast government for haste in closing down Forensic Science Service', *British Medical Journal*, **343**: d4210.

Edwards, H. and Gastonis, C. (2009) *Strengthening Forensic Science in the United States: A Path Forward*, Washington, DC: National Academies Press.

Edwards, H., Munshi, T., Scowen, I., Surtees, A. and Swindles, G.T. (2012) 'Development of oxidative sample preparation for the analysis of forensic soil samples with near-IR Raman spectroscopy', *Journal of Raman Spectroscopy*, **43**: 323–325.

Elspeth, L. and McVicar, M. (2011) 'Passive exposure and persistence of gunshot residue (GSR) on bystanders to a shooting: Comparison of shooter and bystander exposure to GSR', *Canadian Society of Forensic Science*, **44**: 89–96.

Erol-Kantarci, M. and Mouftah, H. T (2013) 'Smart grid forensic science: Applications, challenges and open issues', *IEEE Communications Magazine*, **51**: 67–73.

Evett, I., Jackson, G., Lambert, J.A. and McCrossan, S. (2000) 'The impact of the principles of evidence interpretation on the structure and content of statements', *Science and Justice*, **40**(4): 233–239.

Faulds, H. (1880) 'On the skin-furrows of the hand', *Nature*, **22**: 605.

Forensic Science Regulator (2012) *Forensic Science Regulator Codes of Practice and Conduct*, London: Home Office.

Forensic Science Regulator (2013) *Forensic Science Regulator Business Plan 2012 to 2017*, London: Home Office.

Found, B. and Ganas, J. (2013) 'The management of domain irrelevant context information in forensic handwriting examination casework', *Science and Justice*, **53**: 154–158.

Fraser, J., Sturrock, K., Deacon, P., Bleay, S. and Bremner, D.H. (2011) 'Visualisation of fingermarks and grab impressions on fabrics. Part 1: Gold/zinc vacuum metal deposition', *Forensic Science International*, **208**: 74–78.

Gallop, A. and Stockdate, R. (1998) 'Trace and contact evidence', in P. White (ed.), *Crime Scene to Court: The Essentials of Forensic Science*, Cambridge: RSC, pp. 47–72.

Giannelli, P.C. (2011) 'Daubert and forensic science: The pitfalls of law enforcement control of scientific research', *University of Illinois Law Review*, **1**: 53–90.

Giese, H., Lam, R., Selden, R. and Tan, E. (2009) 'Fast multiplexed polymerase chain reaction for conventional and microfluidic short tandem repeat analysis', *Journal of Forensic Sciences*, **54**: 1287–1296.

Gill, P., Fereday, L., Morling, N. and Svhneider, P.M. (2006) 'The evolution of DNA databases – recommendations for new European STR loci', *Forensic Science International*, **156**: 242–244.

Girard, J.E. (2013) *Criminalistics: Forensic Science, Crime and Terrorism*, Burlington, MA: Jones & Bartlett.

Girod, A., Ramatowski, R. and Weyermann, C. (2012) 'Composition of fingermark residue: A qualitative and quantitative review', *Forensic Science International*, **223**: 10–24.

Goldstein, R.M. (2011) 'Improving forensic science through state oversight', *Texas Law Review*, **90**: 225–258.

Goodman-Delahunty, J. and Tait, D. (2006) 'Lay participation in legal decision making in Australia and New Zealand: Jury trials and administrative tribunals', in M. Kaplan and A. Martin (eds), *Understanding World Jury Systems through Social Psychological Research*, Hove: Psychology Press, pp. 47–70.

Goray, M., Mitchell, R.J. and Van Oorschot, R.A. (2010) 'Investigation of secondary DNA transfer of skin cells under controlled test conditions', *Legal Medicine*, **12**: 117–120.

Graham, E. (2008) 'DNA reviews: Low level DNA profiling', *Forensic Science, Medicine and Pathology*, **4**: 129–131.

Graham, J. (2009) *Cyber Fraud*, Boca Raton, FL: CRC Press.

Haber, L. and Haber, R.N. (2008) 'Scientific validation of fingerprint evidence under Daubert', *Law, Probability and Risk*, **7**: 87–109.

Haglund, W.D. (2001) 'Archaeology and forensic death investigations', *Historical Archaeology*, **35**: 26–34.

Hannibal, M. and Mountford, L. (2002) *The Law of Criminal and Civil Evidence: Principles and Practice*, Harlow: Pearson Education.

Hares, D.R. (2012a) 'Expanding the CODIS core loci in the United States', *Forensic Science International: Genetics*, **6**: E52–E54.

Hares, D.R. (2012b) 'Addendum to expanding the CODIS core loci in the United States', *Forensic Science International: Genetics*, **6**: E135.

Harrison, K. (2006) 'Is crime scene examination science, and does it matter anyway?' *Science and Justice*, **46**: 65–68.

Harroun, S.G., Bergman, J., Jablonski, E. and Brosseau, C.L. (2011) 'Surface-enhanced Raman spectroscopy analysis of house paint and wallpaper samples from an 18(th) century historic property', *Analyst*, **136**: 3453–3460.

Hartwig, M., Granhag, P.A., Stromwall, L.A. and Vrij, A. (2005) 'Detecting deception via strategic disclosure of evidence', *Law and Human Behavior*, **29**: 469–484.

Haug, M. and Baird, E. (2011) 'Finding the error in Daubert', *Hastings Law Journal*, **62**: 737–756.

He, J., Lv, J.G., Ji, Y.J., Feng, J.M. and Liu, Y. (2013) 'Multiple characterizations of automotive coatings in forensic analysis', *Spectroscopy Letters*, **46**: 555–560.

Heard, B. (2008) *Firearms and Ballistics*, Chichester: Wiley.

Hepler, A.B., Saunders, C.P., Davis, L.J. and Buscaglia, J. (2012) 'Score-based likelihood ratios for handwriting evidence', *Forensic Science International*, **219**: 129–140.

Her Majesty's Inspectorate of Constabulary (2000) *Under the Microscope*, London: Home Office.

Her Majesty's Inspectorate of Constabulary (2002) *Under the Microscope, Refocused*, London: Home Office.

Herschel, W.J. (1880) 'Skin furrows of the hand', *Nature*, **23**: 76.

Hicks, T., Vanina, R. and Margot, P. (1996) 'Transference and persistence of glass fragments on garments', *Science and Justice*, **36**: 101–107.

Hockmeister, M., Budowle, B., Borer, U.V., Comey, C.T. and Dirnhofer, R. (1991) 'PCR-based typing of DNA extracted from cigarette butts', *International Journal of Legal Medicine*, **104**: 229–233.

Holland, M.M. and Parsons, T.J. (1999) 'Mitochondrial DNA sequence analysis – validation and use for forensic casework', *Forensic Science Review*, **11**: 22–49.

Hope, L. and Memon, A. (2006) 'Cross-border diversity: Trial by jury in England and Scotland', in M. Kaplan and A. Martin (eds), *Understanding World Jury Systems through Social Psychological Research*, Hove: Psychology Press, pp. 31–46.

Hopwood, A.J., Hurth, C., Yan, J. et al. (2010) 'Integrated microfluidic system for rapid forensic DNA analysis: Sample collection to DNA profile', *Analytical Chemistry*, **82**, 6991–6999.

Houck, M.M. (2013) 'Trace evidence', in J. Fraser and R. Williams (eds), *Handbook of Forensic Science*, Cullompton: Willan, pp. 166–195.

Houck, M. and Siegel, J.A. (2011) *Fundamentals of Forensic Science*, 2nd edn, Oxford: Elsevier.

Jabbar, M. (2010) 'Overcoming Daubert's shortcomings in criminal trials: Making the error rate the primary factor in Daubert's validity inquiry', *New York University Law Review*, **85**: 2034–2064.

Jackson, A.R.W. and Jackson, J.M. (2011) *Forensic Science*, Harlow: Prentice Hall.

James, J.D., Pounds, C.A. and Wilshire, B. (1991) 'Flake metal powders for revealing latent fingerprints', *Journal of Forensic Science*, **36**: 1368–1375.

Jamieson, A. (2004) 'A rational approach to the principles and practice of crime scene investigation: I. Principles', *Science and Justice*, **44**: 3–7.

Jelly, R., Lewis, S.W., Lennard, C., Lim, K.F. and Almog, G. (2008) 'Lawsome: A novel reagent for the detection of latent fingermarks on paper surfaces', *Chemical Communications*, **35**: 13–15.

Jelly, R., Patton, E.L.T., Lennard, C., Lewis, S.W. and Lim, K.F. (2009) 'The detection of latent fingermarks on porous surfaces using amino acid sensitive reagents: A review', *Analytica Chimica Acta*, **652**: 128–142.

Jobling, M.A. and Gill, P. (2004) 'DNA in forensic analysis', *Nature Review Genetics*, **5**: 739–751.

Johns, S. & Kahn, R. (2004) *Status and Needs United States Crime Laboratories*, Largo, FL: American Society Crime Laboratory Directors.

Johnson, M. and Reynolds, S. (2006) 'General crime scene considerations and documentation', in E. Stauffer and M. Bonfanti (eds), *Forensic*

Investigation of Stolen Recovered and Other Crime Related Vehicles, Burlington, MA: Academic Press, p. 37–57.

Johnson, R.N. and Wilson-Wilde, A.L. (2014) 'Current and future directions of DNA in wildlife forensic science', *Forensic Science International: Genetics*, **10**: 1–11.

Julian, R.D., Kelty, S.F., Roux, C. et al. (2011) 'What is the value of forensic science? An overview of the effectiveness of forensic science in the Australian criminal justice system project', *Australian Journal of Forensic Sciences*, **43**: 217–229.

Kashyap, V.K., Sitalaximi, T., Chattopadhyay, P. and Trivedi, R. (2004) 'DNA profiling technologies in DNA analysis', *International Journal of Human Genetics*, **4**: 11–30.

Kassin, S.M., Dror, I.E. and Kukucka, J. (2013) 'The forensic confirmation bias: Problems, perspectives, and proposed solutions', *Journal of Applied Research in Memory and Cognition*, **2**: 42–52.

Kaur, S., Krishan, K., Chatterjee, P.M. and Kanchan, T. (2012) 'Analysis and identification of bitemarks in forensic casework', *Oral Health and Dental Management*, **12**: 127–131.

Keierleber, J.A. and Bohan, T.L. (2005) 'Ten years after Daubert: The status of the states', *Journal of Forensic Sciences*, **50**: 1154–1163.

Kim, Y., Barak, G. and Shelton, D. (2009) 'Examining the CSI Effect in the cases of circumstantial evidence and eyewitness testimony: Multivariate and path analysis', *Journal of Criminal Justice*, **37**: 452–460.

Kind, S. & Overman, M. (1972) *Science against Crime*, New York: Doubleday.

Klein, A., Nedivi, L. and Silverwater, H. (2000) 'Physical match of fragmented bullets', *Journal of Forensic Sciences*, **45**: 722–727.

Kluger, J. (2002) 'How science solves crimes', *Time*, 21 October.

Koehler, J. (2001) 'When are people persuaded by the DNA match statistics?' *Law and Human Behavior*, **25**: 493–513.

Komarinski, P. (2005) *Automated Fingerprint Identification Systems (AFIS)*, Burlington, MA: Elsevier.

Koons, R.D. and Buscagalia, J. (2002) 'Interpretation of glass composition measurements: The effects of match criteria on discrimination capability', *Journal of Forensic Sciences*, **47**: 505–512.

Krishan, K. (2008) 'Estimation of state from footprint and foot outline dimensions in Gujjars of North India', *Forensic Science International*, **175**: 93–101.

Langan, P. and Levin, D. (2002) 'Recidivism of prisoners released in 1994', *Bureau of Justice Statistics Special Report*, **15**: 58–65.

Lawson, T.F. (2003) 'Can fingerprints lie: Re-weighing fingerprint evidence in criminal jury trials', *American Journal of Criminal Law*, **31**: 1–66.

Lee, C.S., Sung, T.M., Kim, H.S. and Jeon, C.H. (2012) 'Classification of forensic soil evidences by application of THM-PyGC/MS and multivariate analysis', *Journal of Analytical and Applied Pyrolysis*, **96**: 33–42.

Leggett, R., Lee-Smith, E.E., Jickells, S.M. and Russell, D.A. (2007) '"Intelligent" fingerprinting: simultaneous identification of drug metabolites and individuals using antibody-functionalized nanoparticles', *Angewandte Chemie International Edition*, **46**: 4100–4103.

Lemieux, F. (2010) *International Police Cooperations: Emerging Issues, Theory and Practice*, Cullompton: Willan Publishing.

Lennard, C. (2007) 'Fingerprint detection: Current capabilities', *Australian Journal of Forensic Sciences*, **39**: 55–71.

Ley, B., Jankowski, N. and Brewer, P. (2012) 'Investigating CSI: Portrayals of DNA testing on a forensic crime show and their potential effects', *Public Understanding of Science*, **21**(1): 51–67.

Limb, M. (2011) 'Experts warn that marketisation of Forensic Science Service will leave crimes unsolved', *British Medical Journal*, **342**: d1935.

Linacre, A., Pekarek, V., Swaran, Y.C. and Tobe, S.S. (2010) 'Generation of DNA profiles from fabrics without DNA extraction', *Forensic Science International: Genetics*, **4**: 137–141.

Lingwood, J., Smith, L.L. and Bond, J.W. (in press) 'Amateur vs professional: Does the recovery of forensic evidence differ depending on who assesses the crime scene?' *International Journal of Police Science and Management*.

Liu, P., Greenspoon, S.A., Yeung, S.H.I., Scherer, J.R. and Mathies, R.A. (2012) 'Integrated sample cleanup and microchip capillary array electrophoresis for high performance forensic sample STR profiling', *Methods in Molecular Biology*, **830**: 351–365.

Liu, P., Yeung, S.H.I., Crenshew, K.A., Crouse, C.A., Scherer, J.R. and Mathies, R.A. (2008) 'Real-time forensic DNA analysis at a crime scene using a portable microchip analyzer', *Forensic Science International: Genetics*, **2**: 301–309.

Lock, A.B. and Morris, M.D. (2013) 'Significance of angle in the statistical comparison of forensic tool marks', *Technometrics*, **55**: 548–561.

Locke, J. and Unikowski, J.A. (1991) 'Breaking of flat glass – part 1: Size and distribution of particles from plain glass windows', *Forensic Science International*, **51**: 251–262.

Lowe, A., Murray, C., Whitaker, J., Tully, G. and Gill, P. (2002) 'The propensity of individuals to deposit DNA and secondary transfer of low level DNA from individuals to inert surfaces', *Forensic Science International*, **129**: 25–34.

Lucy, D. (2005) *Introduction to Statistics for Forensic Scientists*, Chichester: Wiley.

Ludwig, A., Fraser, J. and Williams, R. (2012) 'Crime scene examiners and volume crime investigations: An empirical study of perception and practice', *Forensic Science Policy and Management*, **3**: 53–61.

Lyle, J.R. (2010) 'If *error rate* is such a simple concept, why don't I have one for my forensic tool yet?' *Digital Investigation*, **7**: S135–S139.

Marriott, C., Lee, R., Wilkes, Z. et al. (2014) 'Evaluation of fingermark detection sequences on paper substrates', *Forensic Science International*, **236**: 30–37.

McDonald, P. (1993) *Tire Imprint Evidence*, Boca Raton, FL: CRC Press.

McQuillan, J. and Edgar, K.A. (1992) 'Survey of the distribution of glass on clothing', *Journal of the Forensic Science Society*, **32**: 333–348.

Meuwly, D. (2006) 'Forensic individualisation from biometric data', *Science and Justice*, **46**: 205–213.

Midkiff, C.R. (1993) 'Lifetime of a latent fingerprint. How long? Can you tell?', *Journal of Forensic Identification*, **43**: 386–392.

Mnookin, J.L., Cole, S.A., Dror, I.E. et al. (2011) 'The need for a research culture in the forensic sciences', *UCLA Law Review*, **58**: 725–779.

Mohan, J., Kumar, C.D. and Simon, P. (2012) 'Denture marking as an aid to forensic identification', *Journal of the Indian Prosthodontic Society*, **12**: 131–136.

Mohandie, K. and Meloy, J.R. (2013) 'The value of crime scene and site visitation by Forensic Psychologists and Psychiatrists', *Journal of Forensic Sciences*, **58**: 719–723.

Moore, R., Kingsbury, D., Bunford, J. and Tucker, V. (2012) 'A survey of paint flakes on the clothing of persons suspected of involvement in crime', *Science and Justice*, **52**: 96–101.

Morgan, J., Ponikiewski, N. and Dunstan, E. (2004) *The Processing of Fingerprint Evidence after the Introduction of the National Automated Fingerprint Identification System*, Home Office Online Report 23/04, London: Home Office.

Morgan, R.M., Allen, E., King, T. and Bull, P.A. (2014) 'The spatial and temporal distribution of pollen in a room: Forensic implications', *Science and Justice*, **54**: 49–56.

Moriarty, K., Smith, L.L. and Bond, J.W. (in press) 'Assessing the effectiveness of forensic screening procedures for the detection of theft from motor vehicle crimes', *International Journal of Police Science and Management*.

Morrison, G.S. (2011) 'Measuring the validity and reliability of forensic likelihood-ratio systems', *Science and Justice*, **51**: 91–98.

Moston, S. and Engelberg, T. (1993) 'Police questioning techniques in tape recorded interviews with criminal suspects', *Policing and Society* **3**: 223–237.

Muehlethaler, C., Massonnet, G., Deviterne, M. et al. (2013) 'Survey on batch-to-batch variation in spray paints: A collaborative study', *Forensic Science International*, **229**: 80–91.

Napier, T. (2009) 'Marks', in J. Fraser and R Williams (eds), *Handbook of Forensic Science*, Cullompton: Willan, pp. 196–228.

Naples, V.L. and Miller, J.S. (2004) 'Making tracks: The forensic analysis of footprints and footwear impressions', *Anatomical Record Part B*, **279B**: 9–15.

National Center for State Courts (2007) *State-of-the-States Survey of Jury Improvement Efforts*, Williamsburg, VA: National Center for State Courts.

Negrusz, A. and Cooper, G.A.A. (eds) (2013) *Clarke's Analytical Forensic Toxicology*, 2nd edn, London: Pharmaceutical Press.

Neuhasuser, S. (2013) 'Phonetic and linguistic principles of forensic voice comparison', *International Journal of Speech and Language and the Law*, **20**: 325–330.

Oliver, R.L. (2010) *Satisfaction: A Behavioural Perspective on the Consumer*, New York: ME Sharpe.

Osterburg, J.W., Parthasarathy, T., Raghaven, T.E.S. and Scolve S.L. (1977) 'Development of a mathematical formula for the calculation of fingerprint probabilities based on individual characteristics', *Journal of the American Statistical Association*, **72**: 722–778.

Pang, B.C.M. and Cheung, B.K.K. (2007) 'Double swab technique for collecting touched evidence', *Legal Medicine*, **9**: 181–184.

Pennington, N. and Hastie, R. (1986) 'Evidence evaluation in complex decision making', *Journal of Personality and Social Psychology*, **51**: 242–258.

Pennington, N. and Hastie, R. (1992) 'Explaining the evidence: Tests of the Story Model for juror decision making', *Journal of Personality and Social Psychology*, **62**: 189–206.

Petraco, N.D.K., Shenkin, P., Speir, J. et al. (2012) 'Addressing the National Academy of Sciences' challenge: A method for statistical pattern comparison of striated tool marks', *Journal of Forensic Sciences*, **57**: 900–911.

Philipson, D. and Bleay, S. (2007) 'Alternative metal processes for vacuum metal deposition', *Journal of Forensic Identification*, **57**: 252–273.

Pizzamiglio, M. Mameli, A., My, D. and Garofano, L. (2004) 'Forensic identification of a murderer by LCN DNA collected from the inside of the victim's car', *Progress in Forensic Genetics*, **1261**: 437–499.

Podlas, K. (2006) 'The CSI Effect: Exposing the media myth', *Fordham Intellectual Property, Media and Entertainment Law Journal*, **16**: 429–465.

Pope *v*. State 756 S.W.2d 401 (1988).

Prime, R. and Hennelly, L. (2003) *Effects of the Processing of DNA Evidence*, London: Home Office.

R *v*. Adams [1996] 2 Cr. App. R 467, 469.

R *v*. Clark [2003] EWCA Crim 1020.

R *v*. Gilfoyle [2001] 2 Cr App R5.

R *v*. Nathaniel [1995] 2 Cr. App. R 565.

Ramotowski, R.S. (2001) 'Composition of latent print residue', in H.C. Lee and R.E. Gaensslen (eds), *Advances in Fingerprint Technology*, New York: Elsevier, pp. 63–104.

Ramatowski, R.S. (2012) 'Amino acid reagents', in R.S. Ramatowski (ed.), *Lee and Gaensslen's Advances in Fingerprint Technology*, Boca Raton, FL: CRC Press, pp. 17–54.

Raymond, J.J., Walsh, S.J., Van Oorschot, R.A., Gunn, P.R. and Roux, C. (2004) 'Trace DNA: An underutilised resource of Pandora's box? A review of the use of trace DNA analysis in the investigation of volume crime', *Journal of Forensic Sciences*, **54**: 668–686.

Reid, L., Chana, K., Bond, J.W., Almond, M.J. and Black, S. (2010) 'A comparison of gunshot residue collection techniques', *Journal of Forensic Sciences*, **55**: 753–756.

Reidy, L., Bu, X.X., Godfrey, M. and Cizdziel, J.V. (2013) 'Elemental fingerprinting of soils using ICP-MS and multivariate statistics: A study for and by forensic chemistry majors', *Forensic Science International*, **233**: 37–44.

Ribaux, O., Baylon, A., Roux, C. et al. (2010a) 'Intelligence led crime scene processing. Part 1: Forensic intelligence', *Forensic Science International*, **195**: 10–16.

Ribaux, O., Baylon, A., Roux, C. et al. (2010b) 'Intelligence led crime scene processing. Part II: Intelligence and crime scene examination', *Forensic Science International*, **199**: 63–71.

Risinger, D.M. (2010) 'The NAS/NRC report on forensic science: A path forward fraught with pitfalls', *Utah Law Review*, **225**: 236–239.

Robbers, M. (2008) 'Blinded by science: The social construction of reality in forensic television shows and its effect on criminal jury trials', *Criminal Justice Policy Review*, **19**: 84–102.

Roberts, K., King, M., Mancuso, G., Bartick, E., Morgan, S. and Goodpaster, S. (2012) 'Forensic fibre examination: Can fibre evidence be individualized?' *Abstracts of Papers of the American Chemical Society*, **243**: Meeting Abstract: 338-CHED.

Robertson, B. and Vignaux, G.A. (1995) *Interpreting Evidence: Evaluating Forensic Science in the Courtroom*, Chichester: Wiley.

Rose, P. (2013) 'More is better: Likelihood-ratio based forensic voice comparison with vocalic segmental cepstra frontends', *International Journal of Speech Language and the Law*, **20**: 77–116.

Rosenburg, M.B. and Dockery, C.R. (2008) 'Determining the lifetime of detectable amounts of gunshot', *Applied Spectroscopy*, **62**: 1238–1241.

Ruwanpura, P.R., Perera, U.C.P., Wijayaweera, H.T.K. and Chandrasiri, N. (2006) 'Adaptation of archaeological techniques in forensic mass grave exhumation: The experience of "Chemmani" excavation in northern Sri Lanka', *Ceylon Medical Journal*, **51**: 98–102.

Saferstein, R. (2014) *Criminalistics: An Introduction to Forensic Science*, 10th edn, Harlow: Pearson.

Saks, M.J. and Koehler, J.J. (2008) 'The individualization fallacy in forensic science evidence', *Vanderbilt Law Review*, **61**: 199–219.

Sammons, J. (2012) *The Basics of Digital Forensics*, Waltham, MA: Elsevier.

Schklar, J. and Diamond, S. (1999) 'Juror reactions to DNA evidence: Errors and expectancies', *Law and Human Behavior*, **23**: 159–184.

Schweitzer, N. and Saks, M. (2007) 'The CSI Effect: Popular fiction about forensic science affects the public's expectations about real forensic science', *Jurimetrics*, **47**: 357–364.

Schwoeble, A.J. and Exline, D.L. (2000) *Current Methods in Forensic Gunshot Residue Analysis*, Boca Raton, FL: CRC Press.

Shelton, D., Kim, Y. and Barak, G. (2006) 'A study of juror expectations and demands concerning scientific evidence: Does the "CSI Effect" exist?' *Vanderbilt Journal of Entertainment and Technology Law*, **9**: 331–368.

Sildo, J., Zummerova, A., Sikuta, J., Mikulas, L., Kuruc, R. and Moravansky, N. (2011) 'The significance of external body examination during crime scene investigation', *Romanian Journal of Legal Medicine*, **19**: 253–258.

Silverman, B. (2011) *Research and Development in Forensic Science: A Review*, London: Home Office.

Skerrett, J., Neumann, C. and Mateos-Garcia, I. (2011) 'A Bayesian approach for interpreting shoemark evidence in forensic casework:Accounting for wear features', *Forensic Science International*, **210**: 26–30.

Smith, L.L. and Bull, R. (2012) 'Identifying and measuring juror pre-trial bias for forensic evidence: Development and validation of the forensic evidence evaluation bias scale', *Psychology, Crime and Law*, **18**: 797–815.

Smith, L.L. and Bull, R. (2013a) 'Exploring the disclosure of physical evidence in police interviews with suspects', *Journal of Police and Criminal Psychology*, doi: 10.1007/s11896/013/9131.

Smith, L.L. and Bull, R. (2013b) 'Validation of the factor structure and predictive validity of the forensic evidence evaluation bias scale for robbery and sexual assault trial scenarios', *Psychology, Crime and Law*, doi: 10.1080/1068316x.2013.793340.

Speaker, P.J. (2013) 'Forensic science service provider models: Data-driven support for better delivery options', *Australian Journal of Forensic Sciences*, **45**: 398–406.

Suzuki, Y., Kasamatsu, M., Sugita, R., Ohta, H., Suzuki, S. and Marumo, Y. (2003) 'Forensic discrimination of headlight glass by analysis of trace impurities with synchrotron radiation X-ray fluorescence spectrometry and ICP-MS', *Bunseki Kagaku*, **52**: 469–474.

Sweet, D. and Hildebrand, D. (1999) 'Saliva from cheese bite yields DNA profile of burglar: A case report', *International Journal of Legal Medicine*, **112**: 201–203.

Szynkowska, M.I., Czerski, K., Rogowski, J., Paryjczak, T. and Parczewski, A. (2010) 'Detection of exogenous contaminants of fingerprints using ToF-SIMS', *Surface Interface*, 42: 393–397.

Taroni, F., Aitken, C., Garbolino, P. and Biedermann, A. (2006) *Bayesian Networks and Probabilistic Inference in Forensic Science*, Chichester: Wiley.

Taroni, F., Marquis, R., Schmittbuhl, M., Biedermann, A., Thiery, A. and Bozza, S. (2012) 'The use of the likelihood ratio for evaluative and investigative purposes in comparative forensic handwriting examination', *Forensic Science International*, **214**: 189–194.

Taylor, M. and Blenkin, M. (2011a) 'Forensic identification scientific evidence since Daubert: Part I – A quantitative analysis of the exclusion of forensic identification scientific evidence', *Journal of Forensic Sciences*, **56**: 1180–1184.

Taylor, M. and Blenkin, M. (2011b) 'Forensic identification scientific evidence since Daubert: Part II – Judicial reasoning in decisions to exclude forensic identification evidence on grounds of reliability', *Journal of Forensic Sciences*, **56**: 913–917.

Thomas, P. and Farrugia, K. (2013) 'An investigation into the enhancement of fingermarks in blood on paper with Genipin and Lawsone', *Science and Justice*, **53**: 315–320.

Thomasma, S.M. and Foran, D.R. (2013) 'The influence of swabbing solutions on DNA recovery from touch samples', *Journal of Forensic Sciences*, **58**: 465–469.

Thornton, J.I. and Peterson, J.L. (2002) 'The general assumptions and rationale of forensic identification', in D. Faigman, D. Kaye, M. Saks and J. Sanders (eds), *Science in the Law: Forensic Science Issues*, St. Paul, MN: West, pp. 29–37.

Tjin-A-Tsoi, T.B.P.M. (2013) *Trends, Challenges and Strategy in the Forensic Science Sector*, The Hague: Netherlands Forensic Institute.

Trapecar, M. (2009) 'Lifting techniques for finger marks on human skin previous enhancement by Swedish Black powder – A preliminary study', *Science and Justice*, **49**: 292–295.

Trapecar, M. and Balazic, J. (2007) 'Fingerprint recovery from human skin surfaces', *Science and Justice*, **47**: 136–140.

Trzcinska, B., Zieba-Palus, J. and Koscielniak, P. (2013) 'Examination of car paint samples using visible microspectrometry for forensic purposes', *Analytical Letters*, **46**: 1267–1277.

Tully, G., Sullivan, K., Vidaki, A. and Anjomshoaa, A. (2013) *Taking Research and Development to Market*, London: Home Office.

Verheij, S., Harteveld, J. and Sijen, T. (2012) 'A protocol for direct and rapid multiplex PCR amplification on forensically relevant samples', *Forensic Science International: Genetics*, **6**: 167–175.

Vinceti, M., Salomone, A., Gerace, E. and Pirro, V. (2013) 'Application of mass spectrometry to hair analysis for forensic toxicological investigations', *Mass Spectrometry Reviews*, **32**: 312–332.

Wallace-Kinkell, C., Lennard, C., Stoilovic, M. and Roux, C. (2007) 'Optimization and evaluation of 1,2- Indanedione for use as a fingermark reagent and its application to real samples', *Forensic Science International*, **168**: 14–26.

Wargacki, S.P., Lewis, L.A. and Dadmun, M.D. (2007) 'Understanding the chemistry of the development of latent fingerprints by superglue fuming', *Journal of Forensic Science*, **52**: 1057–1062.

Webb, B., Smith, C., Brock, A. and Townsley, M. (2005) 'DNA fast tracking', in M.J. Smith and N. Tilley (eds), *Crime Science: New Approaches to Preventing and Detecting Crime*, Cullompton: Willan Publishing, 167–190.

Wetton, J.H., Higgs, J.E., Spriggs, A.C., Roney, C.A., Tsang, C.S.F. and Foster, A.P. (2003) 'Mitochondrial profiling of dog hairs', *Forensic Science International*, **133**: 235–241.

Williams, G. (2010) 'Visualisation of fingerprints on metal surfaces using a scanning Kelvin probe', *Fingerprint Whorld*, **36**: 51–60.

Wu, D. and Chrichton, J. (2010) 'DNA swabs from vehicles: A study on retention times, locations, and viability of identifying the most recent driver', *Journal of Forensic Identification*, **60**: 308–319.

Yamashita B. and French M. (2014) 'Latent print development', in E.H. Holder Jr., L.O. Robinson and J.H. Laub (eds), *The Fingerprint Sourcebook*, Washington, DC: NIJ, pp. 155–222.

Yoon, C.K. (1993) 'Botanical witness for the prosecution', *Science*, **260**: 894–5.

Zhang, C.L., Morrison, G.S., Ochoa, F. and Enzinger, E. (2013) 'Reliability of human-supervised formant-trajectory measurement for forensic voice comparison', *Journal of the Acoustical Society of America*, **133**: EL54–EL60.

Zieba-Palus, J. and Trzcinska, B.M. (2013) 'Application of infrared and Raman spectroscopy in paint trace examination', *Journal of Forensic Sciences*, **58**: 1359–1363.

Zieba-Palus, J., Michalska, A. and Weselucha-Birczynska, A. (2011) 'Characterisation of paint samples by infrared and Raman spectroscopy for criminalistic purposes', *Journal of Molecular Structure*, **993**: 134–141.

GLOSSARY

ACPO Association of Chief Police Officers (UK).

adenine a nucleotide base found in DNA, often abbreviated to A.

adversarial legal system a type of legal system characterised by advocate attorneys and often juries of lay people.

AFIS Automated Fingerprint Identification System, a generic name for computerised storage of fingerprint records.

AFR Automated Fingerprint Recognition system, introduced in Scotland in 1991.

allele a version of a gene that gives rise to variations such as blood type.

anagen phase the first stage of hair growth when it is actively growing (*see also* catagen phase and telogen phase).

apocrine sweat glands restricted to regions of the body such as armpits and genital areas.

arches a fingerprint pattern found in approximately 5% of fingerprints.

ASCLD American Society of Crime Laboratory Directors.

attendance criteria criteria used by police forces to determine whether a particular crime warrants attendance by a CSI.

base pair a pair of bases that link together the two DNA strands.

basic yellow 40 a dye used in conjunction with cyanoacrylate to enhance fingerprint sweat on non-porous surfaces (*see also* rhodamine).

Bayes' theorem a particular form of conditional probability calculation often used in forensic science.

biometric databases measurements and statistical information about biological features that can be used to uniquely identify individuals.

birdshot the small metal pellets or shot that are fired from a shotgun (*see also* buckshot).

bore/gauge for a shotgun, the weight of a solid sphere of lead that will just pass along the inside of the barrel, expressed as a fraction of a pound (*see also* calibre).

breech the end of a firearm chamber furthest from the muzzle (*see also* breech marks).

breech marks marks caused when the cartridge case is forced backwards towards the end of the chamber furthest from the muzzle. These are a negative impression of any marks present on the face of the breech (*see also* breech).

buccal scrape also called buccal swab, a method of obtaining DNA by collecting cells from a person's inner cheek.

buckshot the small metal pellets or shot that are fired from a shotgun (*see also* birdshot).

calibre the approximate internal diameter of the barrel of the firearm (such as 0.22 inch or 9 mm calibre) (*see also* bore/gauge).

cartridge the ammunition that is used in a firearm to produce a bullet projectile.

case dossier a collection of information and testimony relating to a criminal or civil case, which is presented to the judge (in inquisitorial legal systems).

CAST Centre for Applied Science and Technology, a UK Home Office–funded institution, which provides the Home Office with detailed information on all science and technology matters related to Home Office activities and constitutes an interface between government, suppliers and end users. In a forensic context, CAST examines the validity of forensic techniques and determines under what circumstances they might usefully be employed, especially in a sequence of treatments.

catagen phase the second stage of hair growth when the growth of the hair slows down (*see also* anagen phase, telogen phase).

cellular DNA DNA material that is not present as a visible stain, e.g. skin cells rubbed off in sweat.

centre fire a firearm in which the firing pin strikes the centre of the cartridge case (*see also* rim fire).

chambering marks marks caused to the side of a cartridge case by the action of loading it into the chamber of a firearm.

chromatographic techniques a series of related laboratory techniques for separating mixtures, such as the dyes used in fibre production.

CODIS Combined DNA Index System.

common approach path the route taken by all those entering or leaving the scene of a major incident, usually different to the path taken by the victim and offender.

comparison evidence types of evidence that can be compared in order to determine whether they have common characteristics and a potential shared origin.

comparison microscope an instrument that has two identical stages under which two items for comparison can be placed (one item per stage).

conditional e.g. conditional probability, when the likelihood of two (or more) events are related to one another, e.g. the outcomes are not independent.

contemporaneous notes notes of an activity that are made at the time the activity is taking place, e.g. the forensic examination of a crime scene.

continuity label a label designed to be fixed to the outmost layer of packaging of an exhibit to show who had possession of the exhibit at any time.

cortex contained within the cuticle and gives hair its strength, elasticity and curl (*see also* cuticle, medulla).

CSE crime scene examiner, more commonly known as CSI.

CSI crime scene investigator.

CSM crime scene manager, the supervisory CSI at (usually) a major crime scene.

cuticle the outside covering of the hair (*see also* cortex, medulla).

cyanoacrylate ethyl cyanoacrylate is the chemical used to enhance fingerprint sweat on non-porous surfaces (also known as superglue fuming).

cytosine a nucleotide base found in DNA, often abbreviated to C.

Daubert standard a standard used in the USA to determine the admissibility of expert evidence during a criminal trial, based on the Daubert ruling.

defendant's fallacy an error in reasoning caused by misrepresenting the population of interest during evidence interpretation.

DFO 1,8-diazafluoren-9-one, a chemical used to enhance fingerprint sweat on porous surfaces by reacting with amino acids.

DNA deoxyribonucleic acid.

eccrine sweat glands found on the hands and soles of the feet.

ENFSI European Network for Forensic Science Institutes, a Europe-wide organisation with the aim of sharing knowledge and cooperating in the field of forensic science. ENFSI has 61 members in 34 countries.

ESLA electrostatic lifting apparatus, which can be used on a variety of surfaces such as linoleum and carpet to recover footwear impressions onto a Mylar film.

ESS European Standard Set of loci for DNA testing. Intended to minimise adventitious matches.

EUROPOL the European Union's law enforcement agency.

evidence an item seized or recovered by the police during an investigation, or the result of an examination of an item, which may be introduced in court. Evidence is not restricted to items of forensic interest (*see also* evidential value, intelligence and intelligence value).

evidence bag a bag, usually of paper or polythene, designed to hold forensic evidence securely and to avoid contamination (*see also* evidence tape).

evidence box a cardboard box used to securely hold forensic evidence, such as a footwear lift (*see also* evidence tape).

evidence tape tape used to seal evidence bags, usually marked with the name of the originating police force (*see also* evidence bag, evidence box).

evidential value also known as probative value, the ability of an exhibit (a piece of evidence) to contribute to the police investigation in a way that would permit the results of any analysis to be introduced in court (*see also* evidence, intelligence and intelligence value).

exemplar cueing theory a theory describing how the framing of a piece of evidence at trial can affect how probative the jury perceives it to be.

external ballistics the examination of firearms discharge evidence at the crime scene, e.g. bullet trajectories (*see also* internal ballistics, terminal ballistics).

extraction marks formed by the pulling from a firearm chamber of the casing by an extractor claw that engages with the extractor groove of the cartridge (*see also* extractor claw, extractor groove).

extractor the device used to extract a used cartridge casing from a firearm (*see also* extractor claw, extractor groove, extraction marks).

extractor claw part of the device to extract a used cartridge casing from a firearm (*see also* extractor groove, extraction marks).

extractor groove part of the device to extract a used cartridge casing from a firearm (*see also* extractor claw, extraction marks).

familial searching searching DNA databases for a profile that shares characteristics with a crime scene sample, in order possibly to identify someone who may be related to the offender.

FBI Federal Bureau of Investigation, in the USA.

firing pin the firing pin of a firearm strikes the primer cup, which contains the primer, thereby igniting the primer (*see also* primer cup, primer).

fluorescence the emission of light by a substance that has absorbed light, used with certain chemicals to enhance fingerprint deposits.

FOA first officer attending, the first police officer to arrive at a crime scene.

follicle the part of the skin that grows hair.

forensic relating to legal proceedings, e.g. forensic science refers to scientific disciplines that assist in the resolution of legal and courtroom proceedings.

ForSIG The TSB Forensic Science Special Interest Group (UK; *see also* TSB).

Fourier transform infrared micro spectroscopy a development from infrared wavelength spectroscopy using Fourier filtering of the detected infrared signal to remove substrate images with periodic patterns, such as might be encountered on bank notes.

FSS Forensic Science Service (UK).

gelatine lifter a colourless, black or white tacky gelatine layer that is applied over a footwear impression to recover it.

gene a sequence of base pairs that determine human characteristics.

gravity mark the name given to the orientation mark on a recovered fingerprint (known as a fingerprint lift).

GSR gunshot residue.

guanine a nucleotide base found in DNA, often abbreviated to G.

Henry classification system a means of classification for storing and retrieving a person's finger and palm impressions.

heuristic a mental shortcut, which helps people make decisions efficiently.

IAFIS Integrated Automated Fingerprint Identification System, introduced by the FBI in 1999.

IBIS a generic name for Integrated Ballistics Identification Systems.

IDENT1 the second generation UK fingerprint computer system that replaced NAFIS.

identification evidence evidence types that can identify individuals (e.g. DNA and fingerprints).

impressed action marks marks that occur during the loading, firing and ejection process of the cartridge casing of a firearm.

inner cordon a small area marked out in the immediate vicinity of a major incident and protected.

inquisitorial legal system a type of legal system characterised by a judge who is active in the criminal investigation and the lack of a jury.

intelligence information gathered during a criminal investigation, which provides insight to the police but is not intended to be used during trial. An item seized or recovered by the police during the investigation, the result of an examination of an item, or information that cannot be introduced in court but may assist in identifying an offender. Intelligence is not restricted to items of forensic interest (*see also* evidence, evidential value, intelligence value).

intelligence value forensic information that falls below the standard required for evidence but is still useful to the police. The ability of an exhibit (a piece of evidence) to contribute to the police investigation in a way that would not permit the results of any analysis to be introduced in court, but might provide the police with information to assist in identifying an offender (*see also* evidence, evidential value and intelligence).

intelligent fingerprints fingerprint enhancement that also gives information about substances secreted by the donor.

internal ballistics the pattern of markings imparted to a bullet and cartridge case by the firearm during the firing process (*see also* external ballistics, terminal ballistics).

INTERPOL the world's largest international police organisation, with 190 member countries.

intimate sample a sample (such as for DNA) that cannot be taken without the consent of the donor, e.g. a penile swab.

ISO 17025 an international quality standard that specifies the requirements for a management system for laboratory forensic science services (*see also* UKAS).

isolated community used to give explanatory examples of the use of statistics and likelihood ratios in determining evidential (or probative) value by assuming that a crime has been committed in a community with a limited (and known) opportunity to commit it.

lab on a chip technology designed to give portable DNA analysis at the crime scene.

latent fingerprint a fingerprint deposited in sweat and generally not visible to the naked eye.

LCN low copy number DNA processing, obtained by applying more than the normal number of cycles for PCR (34 instead of 28; *see also* PCR).

likelihood ratio a means of expressing the probative value of evidence.

Livescan an electronic means of capturing an arrestee's finger and palm impressions, usually in the custody suite of a police station.

Locard's exchange principle theory that contact results in transfer of material.

locus the position of a gene within the DNA molecule, plural loci.

loops a fingerprint pattern found in approximately 60% of fingerprints.

mechanical fit proving an association between two items by showing that, at one time, they were joined together as one item (*see also* physical fit).

medulla occurs in the centre of the hair shaft and is not present in all hair (*see also* cortex, cuticle).

minutiae characteristics of fingerprint ridges, used to make a fingerprint identification.

misaggregation error an error in reasoning in which a mathematical error is made when interpreting a statistic or probability.

misperception error an error in reasoning in which a person relies on inaccurate beliefs or attitudes.

mitochondrial DNA (mtDNA) DNA found in the cell mitochondria, likely to remain present if nuclear DNA has degraded to a point where SGM+ is no longer viable.

modus operandi (MO) the method by which an offender executes their crime.

muzzle the end of a firearm from which the bullet is ejected.

Mylar a polyester film made from stretched polyethylene terephthalate (PET), used for the electrostatic lifting of footwear impressions (*see also* ESLA).

NABIS National Ballistics Intelligence Service (UK).

NAFIS National Automated Fingerprint Identification System, the first-generation UK fingerprint computer system.

NAS National Academy of Sciences (USA).

NCIDD National Criminal Investigation DNA Database (Australia).

NDDB National DNA Data Bank, set up by the Royal Canadian Mounted Police in 1990.

NDIS National DNA Index System, part of the US CODIS system.

NDNAD National DNA Database (UK), set up in 1995.

negative evidence witness a forensic expert called to court to testify about a lack of forensic evidence recovered from the crime scene.

negative impression an impression, such as with footwear, when the underside of a shoe comes into contact with a hard flat surface, and removes material (such as blood, dust or mud) that was adhering to the surface.

NFRC National Footwear Reference Collection (UK).

NGS next-generation Sequencing of DNA, which offers a considerably higher throughput coupled with a lower cost of processing.

NIBIN National Integrated Ballistic Information System (USA).

ninhydrin a chemical commonly used to enhance fingerprint sweat on porous surfaces, which reacts with amino acids and changes colour.

non-intimate sample a sample (such as for DNA) that can be taken without the consent of the donor, e.g. a mouth swab.

non-invasive fingerprints fingerprint enhancement in which there is no physical contact between the enhancing technique and the subject.

non-porous a substance such as polythene or metal that does not easily absorb a solution such as water.

nuclear DNA DNA located in the nucleus, containing the standard 46 chromosomes.

nucleotide a molecule found in DNA that is composed of a base, a sugar and a phosphate.

odontologist a person skilled in dentistry.

outer cordon a large area marked out and protected, usually encompassing the scene of a major incident.

PACE Police and Criminal Evidence Act 1984, the Act of Parliament that governs how the police exercise their powers in the UK.

PCR polymerase chain reaction, the current method of DNA replication, invented by Kary Mullis.

PD physical developer, a fingerprint enhancement technique, particularly useful on porous surfaces that have been wetted.

phosphorescence the emission of light by a substance that is more persistent than fluorescence.

physical fit proving an association between two items by showing that, at one time, they were joined together as one item (*see also* mechanical fit).

Pitchfork syndrome refers to the fact that when police obtain forensic samples from suspects (e.g. DNA, fingerprints), the identity of the suspect must be independently verified.

plastic fingerprint a fingerprint created when a finger is placed in, and then withdrawn from, a soft substance (such as wet paint), leaving a negative impression of the fingerprint ridges.

plea bargain the process of a defendant pleading guilty to a different (usually lesser) offence in exchange for a more favourable sentence.

PNC Police National Computer database containing arrestee and offender data (UK).

point of entry the point at which an offender entered a crime scene.

point of exit the point at which an offender exited a crime scene.

polarised light microscopy a microscope in which the orientation of light waves striking fibre is restricted, used to identify the type of fibre.

porous a substance, such as paper or cardboard, that readily absorbs a solution such as water.

positive impression an impression, such as with footwear, when the underside of a shoe comes into contact with a hard flat surface, and deposits material (such as blood, dust or mud) that was adhering to the underside of the shoe.

primer the chemical compound that ignites the propellant in a firearm cartridge (*see also* firing pin/primer cup).

primer cup the primer cup of a firearm contains the primer, which ignited when struck by the firing pin (*see also* firing pin/primer).

probative value a characteristic of evidence that describes to what extent the evidence is able to prove the guilt of a defendant.

product rule mathematical rule of probability that allows a calculation of the probability of multiple, independent outcomes occurring.

propellant the chemical compound that combusts during the firing process in a firearm, resulting in the rapid production of gaseous products that force the bullet out of the cartridge case.

prosecutor's fallacy an error in reasoning, in which the random match probability is misinterpreted as being the probability that the defendant is innocent.

random match probability (RMP) the probability that a DNA sample matches a suspect, but was actually left by someone else.

randomly amplified polymorphic DNA (RAPD) a type of PCR technique, in which the segments of DNA that are amplified are random.

range for a firearm, the distance from the end of the barrel to the target. For a shotgun, this can be calculated from the spread of pellets or shot.

recordable offence any punishable offence in the UK.

rhodamine a dye used in conjunction with cyanoacrylate to enhance fingerprint sweat on non-porous surfaces (*see also* basic yellow 40).

RI a measure of the bending of light as it passes from one medium to another, always > 1.

rifling helical grooves that are cut into the inside wall of the barrel of a firearm, intended to impart spin to the bullet projectile and to improve the accuracy of the bullet in reaching its intended target (*see also* striation marks).

rim fire a firearm in which the firing pin strikes the rim of the cartridge case (*see also* centre fire).

RTX ruthenium tetroxide, which has been used to enhance sweat fingerprints on cadavers.

Ruhemann's purple the colour change undergone by ninhydrin when reacting with an amino acid. Usually refers to the enhancement of fingerprint sweat on porous surfaces.

scanning electron microscope an instrument that produces a greatly magnified image of a sample by scanning it with a focused beam of electrons. Used e.g. with GSR or glass to determine its elemental composition.

scene examination report a document completed by a CSI during, or immediately after, their examination of a crime scene or of an exhibit away from a crime scene (such as photographing an exhibit in a laboratory prior to its examination).

Schengen Agreement an agreement signed by some EU member states allowing free movement of citizens across member-country borders.

sebaceous sweat glands localised to regions of the body containing hair follicles, the face and the scalp.

self-loading a firearm that automatically uses some of the energy of the firing process to eject the just fired cartridge case and to reload a live cartridge, ready for the next discharge.

SGM Second Generation Multiplex, a sample of 7 areas of DNA that was introduced in 1995 and had a discriminating power of 1 in 50 000 000.

SGM+ Second Generation Multiplex plus, a sample of 11 areas of DNA that was introduced in 1999 and had a discriminating power of 1 in 1 000 000 000.

shaft part of the hair (*see also* cuticle, cortex, medulla).

SKP scanning Kelvin microprobe, a technique used to enhance fingerprints on metal non-invasively.

smooth bore the name given to a shotgun that lacks rifling.

SOCO scenes of crime officer, more commonly known as CSI.

specimen type the type of DNA material, e.g. saliva, blood, semen.

spectrophotometry a device to determine the absorption at a particular wavelength of light. Used to determine the type of a fibre.

SPR small particle reagent, a powder suspension used to enhance fingerprint sweat on non-porous surfaces.

stopping power the behaviour of a bullet passing through a living subject.

Story Model a theory that describes juror decision making, an important element of which is the organisation of the trial evidence into a narrative format.

STR short tandem repeat, a short repeating sequence of between 1 and 14 base pairs.

striation marks the action of rifling along the side of a bullet (*see also* rifling).

surface science analytical technology the collection of material removed from the surface of a specimen to enable identification of both exogenous and endogenous material, such as might be deposited as a fingerprint.

tamper-evident bag a (polythene) bag designed to hold forensic evidence that displays a warning if the seal is tampered with.

telogen phase the third (final) stage of hair growth when it is shed (*see also* anagen phase, catagen phase).

tempering a heat or chemical treatment applied to glass to improve its mechanical strength.

terminal ballistics the behaviour of a bullet after it has hit a target (*see also* external ballistics, internal ballistics).

test cut a series of cuts made on a similar piece of material to that recovered from the crime scene so that both can be compared.

thermal analysis a process in which the energy required to maintain a zero temperature difference between two samples of soil as they are heated is monitored. Used to compare soil samples.

thin layer chromatography a technique in which liquid samples of a dye separate into different colours when placed on a sheet. Employed to determine information about the dye used to colour a fibre.

thymine a nucleotide base found in DNA, often abbreviated to T.

trace evidence small amounts of material transferred during contact, which might then be used to associate the two items that contacted.

trier of fact the person(s) responsible for deciding on the verdict in a trial.

TSB Technology Strategy Board (UK; *see also* ForSIG).

UKAS UK Accreditation Service, oversees ISO 17025 implementation in the UK (*see also* ISO 17025).

vibrational spectroscopy spectroscopic techniques such as infrared and Raman that exploit the energy exchange between molecules and incident radiation through vibration of the molecules, typically used to analyse the composition of paint.

visible fingerprint a fingerprint deposited in a contaminant such as oil, grease or blood and visible to the naked eye.

VMD vacuum metal deposition, a technique to enhance fingerprints on non-porous surfaces such as polythene bags.

VNTR variable number tandem repeats, the repeating sequence used by Alec Jeffreys in his pioneering work.

voir dire often referred to as a 'trial within a trial', in which issues such as admissibility of evidence, witnesses or jurors are determined.

volume crime crimes that occur frequently, such as burglary and vehicle offences.

wadding material ejected from a shotgun during firing that forms a physical barrier between the propellant and the shot. Usually made of plastic, but other materials (such as felt) are also used.

whorls a fingerprint pattern found in approximately 35% of fingerprints.

work function the energy (usually measured in electron volts) required to remove an electron from a solid, a quantity used in a scanning Kelvin probe.

XRD x-ray powder diffraction. Used to compare samples of paint.

INDEX

Note: Page numbers in **bold type** refer to Figures; those in ***bold italic*** indicate additional text on the page.